THE FEAST OF KINGSHIP

A *Monumenta Nipponica*
Monograph

The Feast of Kingship

ACCESSION CEREMONIES
IN
ANCIENT JAPAN

by

ROBERT S. ELLWOOD

PUBLISHED BY

SOPHIA UNIVERSITY, TOKYO

The publication of this volume was made possible in part
by a subsidy from the Commemorative Association
for the Japan World Exposition (1970)

PUBLISHED BY
SOPHIA UNIVERSITY
7 KIOI-CHŌ, CHIYODA-KU
TOKYO, 102

Library of Congress Catalog Card No. 72–92938

PRINTED IN JAPAN
THE KAWATA PRESS, TOKYO

CONTENTS

PREFACE

THE purpose of this study is to make a contribution to the understanding of the *Daijō-sai*, or Harvest Festival as celebrated by the emperor upon his accession, in Heian Japan. Through reflection on the meaning and structure of this rite, I believe very valuable insights can be gained into the history of Shinto, and into both its archaic and Heian religious meaning. It is hoped that some light may be shed thereby on the general meaning of sacred kingship, one of the major areas of discussion in the history of religions.

The *Daijō-sai* is clearly a variant of the *Niiname-sai* (*Shinjō-sai*, 'New Food Tasting', as *Daijō-sai* is 'Great Food Tasting'), or Harvest Festival. The Harvest Festival is the most pivotal celebration of Shinto. The major problem in its history is the matter of its separation in meaning from the ordinary *Niiname* of the Court and of the populace. This history will be explored as far as possible, with major emphasis on mythological material. On the other hand, although the *Daijō-sai* is still performed at accessions in roughly its ancient form, no attempt is made to carry its history past the Heian period.

The major ritual text employed is the *Engi-shiki* of A.D. 927. The Japanese text can be found in *Shinten*, published by the Ōkura Seishin Bunka Kenkyūjo, Yokohama, 1936, with six reprintings since then; in the *Kokushi taikei*, published by Yoshikawa Kōbunkan, Tokyo, latest edition, 1955; and elsewhere. The English translation used is F. G. Bock's *Engi-shiki: Procedures of the Engi Era, Books VI-X*, Sophia University, 1972. Numbers in parentheses in connection with English translations of the *Engi-shiki* refer to this Bock translation; numbers in italics refer to page numbers in the *Shinten*.

Works cited are listed in Western-language and Japanese bibliographies. Japanese personal names are written in Japanese order, with surname first.

Japanese names and words, ancient and modern, are always transliterated according to the modified Hepburn system of romanization. But in the case of very common proper names, such as Kyoto, Osaka, Shinto, etc., the macron is not used over long vowels to avoid the appearance of excessive pedantry.

This study is a revised and expanded version of a section of a dissertation accepted by the faculty of the University of Chicago Divinity School in 1967. I am deeply grateful to the History of Religions department of that faculty, particularly Professors Mircea Eliade, Chairman, and Joseph M. Kitagawa, my advisor, for assistance and encouragement. The major part of the research and writing was done in Japan during the eleven months of July 1966 to June 1967, with the support of a Fulbright-Hays Fellowship provided by the United States Office of Education. The Institute for Japanese Culture and Classics (Nihon Bunka Kenkyūjo) of Kokugakuin University, Shibuya, Tokyo, provided me with full library privileges and generous assistance. In particular, I would like to acknowledge the help of Prof. Ueda Kenji, Director of the Institute, and of Prof. Hirai Naofusa and Ono Sokyō, distinguished members of the faculty of Kokugakuin University. I also received very valuable help from Professor Hori Ichirō, of Tokyo University and Kokugakuin University, and from Prof. Tanaka Hatsuo, of Kaseigakuin College, Tokyo. Prof. Tanaka is a peerless authority on the *Daijō-sai,* and I found a series of conferences with him of inestimable value for this study.

The material in this book on the *Nakatomi no yogoto,* pp. 49-65, has previously appeared in an article, 'The *Nakatomi no Yogoto*', in Harry J. Lamley, ed., *East Asian Occasional Papers (II)*, University of Hawaii, Honolulu, 1970.

Finally, I would like to express gratitude to my wife, Gracia Fay, whose companionship made living in Japan especially pleasant, and who assisted in this project with many helpful comments and suggestions.

CHAPTER I

The Feast of Kingship

THE *Daijō-sai*, the Harvest Festival celebrated by the emperor of Japan to seal his accession, reaches its climax in the darkness of a crisp November night. Then, in the heart of autumn and of nocturnal darkness, has kingship been completed from time immemorial down to the rite of the present sovereign in 1928. On the vast parklike grounds of the ancient palace in Kyoto a wooden palisade is put up. Within it are made many buildings of archaic construction, joined together of rough timber and thatch, innocent of even a nail. The whole edifice is built just before the great ritual, and taken down the day after, before even the fresh grass has acquired the touch of age in this world. The buildings vanish as though they had been but ephemeral glimpses into another age. It is of the nature of the *Daijō-sai* that its appointments be at once extremely ancient and yet always new, used for the first time, and then disappear.

The central structures are two identical rectangular lodges, side by side, called the Yuki-den and the Suki-den. These each contain two rooms. The outer is for preparations, the inner is for the crux of the rite. In the course of the ceremony two mats will be laid in the inner room, one on the floor for the emperor, one on a low table for the food offerings presented the deity.

Toward the back of this inner chamber rests a couch made of several straw *tatami* mats. A number of interesting accoutrements are associated with it. The couch itself bears a coverlet, a pillow of wood, a folded piece of silk, and a fan. At its foot is a neatly set pair of slippers. Beside the head are two lamps, one white and one black, and two baskets of cloth, one of 'rough' fabric and one of 'smooth'.

The emperor himself arrives on the grounds at about six in the evening. As he waits in an outer hall, curious processions move from cooking huts into the ante-chambers of the two lodges. Servants are bearing food offerings on peculiar high-stemmed trays. The major entrees are cooked rice and sake, although there is also seafood and salt. The cooked rice, and the rice out of which the sake was made, had been grown especially for this high feast in two widely separated fields chosen by divination. Its planting and harvesting had been accompanied by ritual action. It had been brought in festal procession to the *Daijō-sai* grounds. There, until the solemn day, it had received divine honors, for this rice was the first-fruits supreme.

Inside the ante-chamber of the Yuki and Suki halls maidens place the food offerings in plates fabricated of leaves in the ancient manner. These are to be presented to the emperor and the gods together with archaic-style chopsticks and toothbrush.

At about nine in the evening the sovereign enters a building near the two halls called the Kairyū-den, or Eternal Flow Hall. Here he bathes, alone, for purification, pouring hot water over himself from a boat-shaped vessel. He then puts on a single white garment, called the *hagoromo*, or feather-robe. In folklore, a garment of the same name is often worn by heavenly beings.

The emperor next approaches the Yuki-den. The impressiveness of this progress, moving with the slowness of ancient ritual and lighted by softly flaring torches, can be imagined. As he moves toward the divine lodge, an umbrella is held over his head. A long white mat is unrolled before him and rolled up behind him. The sovereign's bare feet may not touch the ground, nor may anyone else step onto this mat.

With reverence he enters the inner room of the Yuki-den, accompanied only by two serving maidens. These girls lay the mats; he seats himself on his mat, and they pour a final ablution over his hands. They then bring in the food offerings, ten dishes in all. The emperor arranges nine for the gods on the low table, presumably putting the last on his own mat, and pours sake. While the deities are partaking, he does not move. Then three times he raises rice to his lips, though without eating, and three times raises a cup of white sake. The third time he actually sips of the wine, in solemn communion; he then repeats this action with black sake.

The emperor then withdraws to the Kairyū-den. Once again he bathes. At two in the morning he performs exactly the same rite in the Suki-den, the other of the two lodges.

At six the next morning the monarch receives the imperial regalia, the mirror and sword, and a solemn blessing, from the priestly houses. The festival is completed over the next two days, while the sacred buildings are taken down, with rich banquets and sacred dances presented by the two provinces which supplied the first-fruit offerings. The heroic moments of the divine age and of great kings of legend are relived; provincial dances of planting and harvest are enjoyed by the Court.

I

WE SHALL examine this ritual and all its traditions in detail. But first I should like to present some material which may enable us to set a rite like this against its general background. Rites of kingly accession have long played a pivotal role in spiritual life. For archaic man everywhere, especially archaic agricultural man, the renewal of kingship has often been the supreme sacrament. The renewal of kingship united the renewal of nature, as in planting or harvest, with the renewal of society. The accession of the king, when celebrated as a great festival of renewal, bridged two ways in which man experienced time. It brought the cyclical eternal-return time of nature and its seasons together with time as history, the time of society which could only approximate repeating itself in the line of kings.

Fundamentally, then, the rite of accession is an act of civilization. However primitive the society, it catches up the temporal paradox which underwrites civilization. The rite seeks to impose upon human society a continuity with nature. It assimilates to its renewal the stability of the cosmic cycle. On the other hand, accession shows the discontinuity, for it affirms human continuation through society and culture even in the face of death. It defies any human reversal to mere identity with nature or with biological finitude. Hence it is not strange that accession and kingship were of the greatest importance in emerging ancient civilization, and called forth the greatest display of the myths and symbols, the arts and skills, of the culture.

The theory of kingship has attracted the attention of many scholars. The seminal modern work was that of Sir James Frazer. In his 1905 lectures,[1] Frazer based the emergence of kingship on his general theory that magic—a primitive misapprehension of natural law—is the primal ground out of which religion and culture grew. The art of the magician attracted the most capable minds. Magicians, because of their dreadful power and their native superiority, became the first kings. Hence the unity of the office of king and magician in archaic societies. Moreover, Frazer

---

[1] Sir James Frazer, *Lectures on the Early History of Kingship,* London, 1905. Reissued in 1920 as *The Magical Origin of Kings.*

pointed out that strong kingship is necessary to emergent civilization.

This theory, while based on the incomparably wide learning
of its author, reflects the positivistic confidence and evolutionary
world-view of its age. One sees the inevitable tendency to assume
that religion had to begin with something 'lower'. The focus of
interest, with typical passion to trace back all roots and know all
beginnings, soon enough falls upon the 'problem of origins', and
it is presumed that when we know the beginning, we will know
the meaning.

A second most influential book, and one representative of a
second stage of reflection, was A. M. Hocart's *Kingship*.[2] Concerning origins, Hocart was content to observe:

> The earliest known religion is a belief in the divinity of kings. I do
> not say that it is necessarily the most primitive; but in the earliest
> records known, man appears to us worshipping gods and their earthly
> representatives, namely kings.
>   We have no right, in the present state of our knowledge, to assert
> that the worship of gods preceded that of kings; we do not know.
> Perhaps there never were any gods without kings, or kings without
> gods. When we have discovered the origin of divine kingship we
> shall know, but at present we only know that when history begins
> there are kings, the representatives of gods.[3]

So far as the first paragraph is concerned, Hocart's qualifications
need to be very carefully marked. The 'question of origins' in the
history of religions, which so exercised certain nineteenth and
early twentieth century savants, is now held pretty much in pheno-
menological suspension for the simple reason that there is no access through empirical research to any meaningful data. In the
nature of the case there can probably never be any access, short
of the invention of a time machine.

We are far more aware of the obvious fact that extant 'primitive'
cultures have actually as long a history of maturation or decline,
and cultural exchange, as the 'higher'. It is quite unsafe to assume
that even a gathering culture like that of Tierra de Fuega can be
taken as a model of the primal man of over a hundred millenia
before. On the other hand, what contemporary field work does

---

[2] A. M. Hocart, *Kingship*, London, 1927. Hocart's schema of the coronation drama was
influenced by the pattern of the cult-drama developed by Mannhardt. See Carl-Martin
Edsman, 'Zum Sakralen Königtum in der Forschung der letzten hundert Jahre', *The Sacral
Kingship/La Regalità Sacra*, p. 15. See this entire article for further study of the history of
this area of scholarship.
[3] Hocart, p. 3.

teach us is that the 'hard' material and physiological remains which alone are accessible to paleoanthropology, while invaluable, could convey very little of spiritual culture in its totality.

The Australian aborigines would have left little more of their humanity than skeletons, and perhaps some enigmatic crystals and rock paintings, not even an arrowhead. What would we have known, if their culture had disappeared in prehistoric times, of the intricate kinship system, involving a number system which Claude Lévi-Strauss has compared to binary calculus, or the odd mythological narratives in which Eliade has seen a Proustian concept of time? It may be only prejudice which speaks of such prelithic and paleolithic culture as 'less developed' than the technological; it is just as old, and may be rather a different than a 'cruder' society; a divergent line of movement, and one more mental.

However, it is not to such peoples that one looks for a model of the sacred king. In some cases kingship is found among tuber agriculturalists, such as those of Polynesia. But most gathering, hunting, and nomadic societies and even some primitive agriculturalists manage to find symbol systems adequate to the meaning of their society without making kingship rites central.[4] Hocart perhaps correctly, though misleadingly, speaks of kingship as a central feature of the earliest known records, for these 'records' of course derive from the ancient agrarian empires in which literacy also emerged. But many of these documents, whether in Mesopotamia, India, or China, actually hint strongly at the relatively late emergence of kingship out of leadership by tribal elders, like the 'Judges' of Israel, or a loose confederation of clannish villages, as in China. Its spiritual roots may go deep—one would be equally misled to think that prehistoric man had any secular view of society. But in any case, agricultural man tends to weave into his sedentary communal life a kingship which reconciles the powers of heaven with earth, and of the ancestral past with the present. And as Frazer very rightly pointed out, at the time of the origin of the great civilizations a strong kingship seems to be an almost indispensable condition.

An important distinction may lie in Hocart's words, 'the divinity of kings' and his 'kings, the representatives of the gods'. As

---

[4] See J. Middleton and D. Tait, eds., *Tribes without Rulers,* London, 1960. Concerning the way in which a non-monarchical symbol-system like totemism can serve the same function of integrating human society with nature and the present with the past, Claude Lévi-Strauss says, 'Totemism postulates a logical equivalence between a society of natural species and a world of social groups'. *The Savage Mind,* p. 104.

we shall see, there may be two kinds of divine kingship, suggested respectively by these two phrases.

But Hocart's work served to direct attention to the phenomenon itself and its forms of appearance. He pointed out, as did Frazer in his famous picture of the King of the Wood at Nemi, the precariousness of the holder of the crown. He analyzed the meaning of the regalia and the attributes of kingship. However, undoubtedly his greatest contribution was his discussion of the coronation ceremony. He showed the frequency in diverse cultures of a certain overall structure for this rite, with such basic themes as washing or anointing, ritual combat, and assimilation of coronation to the creation of the world. He indicated that the coronation rite which follows this typology is actually a kind of initiation, amounting to the death and rebirth of the candidate.

Inevitably some of Hocart's material was only suggestive. Certain of his pioneering comparisons are farfetched. It could be argued that he selected only examples which favored his general pattern. But in his defense one may say that he never claimd a universal pattern, but only to have isolated a widespread typology which may have had its ultimate source in diffusion. None the less, his was the kind of approach which could stimulate a generation of scholarship. Hocart, together with other students such as Canney, Rowley, Mowinckel, and A. R. Johnson, laid a foundation for the work of the so-called 'Myth and Ritual School' of the mid-century.

That style of interpretation was mostly the work of Biblical or Near Eastern scholars. Its focus was on Old Testament problems. Naturally, it began as an assimilation of new archaeological work in the ancient Near East to the thought of Frazer and the extreme diffusionist theories of the 'pan-Egyptianists', Smith and Perry. Originally it was heavily inspired by Frazer's assertion, developed by Gilbert Murray and Jane Harrison, that ritual ('magic') precedes religion. But soon important deviations from Frazer's universalism appeared. The diffusionist ideas were rejected in their extreme forms. But diffusionism had called attention to the importance of specific cultures and, above all, 'culture-patterns' informing wide regions such as the Near East. 'Myth and Ritual' was presented to English readers in the three fundamental collections of essays edited by S. H. Hooke,[5] and in the books of Scan-

---

[5] S. H. Hooke, ed., *Myth and Ritual*, London, 1933; *The Labyrinth*, London, 1935; *Myth, Ritual, and Kingship*, London, 1959. See the discussion of the history of the movement in S. H. Hooke, 'Myth and Ritual: Past and Present', and S. G. F. Brandon, 'The Myth and Ritual Position Critically Considered', in *Myth, Ritual, and Kingship*.

dinavians such as Ivan Engnell and S. Mowinckel.

Essential to this pattern was the dramatic expression of its mythology in an annual festival in which the king played a central role. The elements of the ritual were representation of the death and resurrection of the god, recitation of the creation epic, ritual combat in which the god (or king) triumphed over his enemies, triumphal procession, and the sacred marriage.[6]

Something very comparable to the pattern postulated for a vast area, extending from Europe to the islands of the Pacific, by Hocart, was restricted for the purposes of this discussion to a few Near Eastern lands. Even that was not sufficient for some critics. Thought moved to an opposite pole from universal theorizing. In particular, Egyptologists like Henri Frankfort have taken exception to the general inclusion of Egypt in the 'culture-pattern'.

Frankfort, in his *Kingship and the Gods*,[7] argued that the theory of kingship differed betwixt Egypt and the Valley of the Two Rivers. In Egypt the king is the god, in Mesopotamia he is only the human representative or vicar of the god. This distinction reminds us of Hocart's ambiguity on the point.

The question is: Which is more significant for the meaning—similarities in overall form of ritual, or differences in some particulars of rite and art and history which point toward an ideological divide? This perhaps unanswerable query leads to knotty problems concerning the meaning of the diffusion of symbols, and the spontaneous origination of comparable patterns. Frazerians, or believers in the collective unconscious, holding that ritual or archetypes precede the intellectual expression of religion, may find no difficulty in the situation. Probably, adherents of the 'Myth and Ritual School', when they are not diffusionists, fall back upon some such doctrine as the collective unconscious.

Frankfort and the anti-'Myth and Ritual' party apparently hold to a cultural nominalism. They presume that each culture can only be understood in its own terms. 'Universals', or even regional cultural similarities, have little meaning as such. Forms have no more meaning, in other words, within a given culture than that of their function in that culture. Cultural parallels are to be reckoned incidental, either parallel responses to similar situations or occasional borrowings. They are of secondary importance for the understanding of a major integral culture such as Egypt's. Thus, to press the point of ritual similarities between Egyptian

---

[6] Brandon, op. cit.
[7] H. Frankfort, *Kingship and the Gods,* Chicago, 1948.

and Babylonian kingship is only to confuse understanding, since the meaning of kingship for the two cultures was in fact different, as one would easily see through a separate and unpresuppositioned study of each.[8]

The other side would argue that similarities none the less must have *some* meaning as such. One may not go to the extreme of holding that only similar features are the clue to the meaning, that they should be taken as pointing to generic substance, while differences are only specific accidents. But one could assert that they must be considered no less clues to meaning than the cultural elements constellated to form unique patterns. A study of similarities might lead one toward diffusionist or archetypal conclusions. But the parallels cannot be regarded *a priori* as of less value for understanding than the differences or even than the stable and integral pattern of an emerged civilization seen as its own center of gravity. So the 'Myth and Ritual School' might argue, with the Platonists and Jungians perhaps also closely ranked behind them.

It is certainly not the task of the present study to tackle these problems head-on. They are mentioned in passing to suggest the kind of larger issues which have clustered about the study of archaic kingship. It seems apparent, however, that they cannot really be brought near solution until a world-wide, rather than a merely regional or national, study of kingship ritual is available. To the best of my knowledge, this has not been seriously attempted since Hocart's work. Since then, a large amount of new field data and much new theoretical work in the meaning of culture and the history of religions have appeared. Only a world-wide perspective could adequately handle the matter of diffusion—and here much information is probably lost forever—or legitimately point to what can be explained only in terms of man's inherent nature.

For example, S. G. F. Brandon argued that the myth and ritual pattern, held by that school to make central the 'dying-rising god', ritual combat, and the sacred marriage, cannot be regarded as a natural development at a particular cultural level, but is apparently a product of the Near Eastern environment. He cites the case of ancient China which, he says, possessed a roughly similar agricultural base and a king who had an essential ritual role in securing the prosperity of the land, but where there is 'no trace of those elements which are fundamental to the Near Eastern "ritual pattern" '.[9]

---

[8] For an excellent example of this type of critique, see 'Excursus: Tammuz, Adonis, Osiris', in Frankfort, op. cit. pp. 285–94.

[9] Brandon, op. cit. p. 273.

Statements like the above inevitably present a challenge to the student of another non-Near-Eastern kingship rite such as the Japanese *Daijō-sai*. It is hoped that indirectly this study may shed some further light on the problem.

To bring the *Daijō-sai* more concretely into focus, I would like now to present material, in very general outline, from five other cultures. The rites of accession are used, primarily, since that is what is under consideration in Japan. With Hocart, I believe, moreover, the accession rite is particularly instructive. Here the problems with which kingship must deal, continuity of society and the integration of history, society, and nature, are perforce most intently faced. The cultures are the Egyptian, Mesopotamian, Chinese, Polynesian, and Altaic. The first two had no evident connection with Japan, unless one accept the most speculative sort of diffusionism. The latter three—the Polynesian and Altaic in prehistoric times, the Chinese also later—indeed have.

II

THE thought of kingship in Egypt evokes an image of almost countless centuries—twice the number thus far allotted Christendom—throughout which the Nile ceaselessly rose and fell with the equinoxes, watched by the immemorial rites of a proud, mystic priesthood, and the serene gaze of an iconic Pharaoh, secure in divine lineage and the hope of a transcendent immortality. If history, as usual, did not quite equate with this ideal, and dynasties did rise and fall in slower cycles than the Nilotic, yet also as usual there was reason behind the image. The extraordinary stability of kingship in Egypt reflects a high doctrine of royal divinity. Revolutions and conspiracies for the throne were relatively unknown.[10]

Two ideological strains served to undergird the monarchy: the belief that Pharaoh was the son of Re, and the Osiris-Horus pattern.[11] Possibly these represent respectively solar and lunar systems. Re is the supreme solar deity and makes the king the image of the sun on earth. In the other, more dynamic, system, the living Pharaoh was Horus, both sun and moon, the successor and avenger of the dead Osiris. Osiris is the preceding sovereign, now resurrected by Isis and Thoth to reign in the kingdom of the dead. The resurrection pattern suggests both lunar and agricultural symbology.

[10] H. W. Fairman, 'The Kingship Rituals in Egypt', in Hooke, *Myth, Ritual, and Kingship*, p. 75.
[11] I. Engnell, *Studies in Divine Kingship in the Ancient Near East*, pp. 6–7.

On a more practical level, the institution of 'coregency', by which the heir was named and prepared during the reign of his predecessor, aided greatly in making the Pharaoh the supreme symbol of a static social order.

The oldest and most important royal festival of Osiris was the Sed. It was held every three or four years or less, often chiefly as a 'renewal of kingship'. A 'renewal' like this is a very important observance amongst many archaic peoples, often overshadowing the accession itself in ceremonial splendor. In the first month of winter (the time of planting), just after a 'burial of Osiris' the previous month, the Pharaoh would erect a *ded* pillar by the River. A new festival hall would be raised for the king, and a robing lodge. The monarch would then dedicate a field by crossing it to the four directions in a peculiar sort of dance or fast walking. The field clearly represented Egypt. He did this twice, first as king of Lower Egypt, then again as king of Upper Egypt.[12]

The coronation also—like the *Daijō-sai*—displayed duplication. One of its basic motifs was repetition of the union of the Two Lands. On the dawn of the day after the old king's death, again as in Japan, the heir was formally installed. But the coronation, its ritual consummation, did not take place until the beginning of one of the three seasons, the most favored being the first month of winter to harmonize with planting.[13]

During the time between accession and coronation, rites of singular interest were observed. The Pharaoh would travel with a party of retainers to a number of major cities. At each he would visit shrines. He would also, on the barge, participate in the performance of a mystery play. While this was going on, the body of the dead monarch would be prepared for burial.

The play, enacted identically in each place, illustrated the meaning of this critical time. It revealed its mythical analogue: Seth had murdered Osiris, the former king, and the new king is Horus, who is battling with Seth and avenging his father. In the battle Horus loses his eye, but it is restored to him and with it he gathers to himself the fulness of his power. This makes him equal to any god.[14]

The extant text of this mystery play is from about 2000 B.C. Frankfort comments: 'Throughout the play we can observe a de-

---

[12] Fairman, op. cit. p. 273.

[13] Frankfort, p. 102.

[14] The play reveals a distinctive Near Eastern pattern. The dying god is typical of the ancient Near East, but is unknown in India except for Krishna, and is not found in Buddhism nor in China except in the sense that ancestors and saints may be deified after death. But on the other hand Shinto *kami* like Ōkuninushi may, in their myths, pass through a death and resurrection remarkably similar to the Near Eastern pattern.

liberate attempt to fuse the historical event, the coronation of one particular Pharaoh, with the perennial truth that Horus succeeds Osiris.'[15] This is indeed the message. The dying god, rising in his son and successor, the next Osiris, is the fundamental vehicle for unifying nature, history, human finitude, and eternity.

The opening scenes, 1-7, are concerned with the preparation of accessories, and sacrifices are made as at the beginning of many royal rites.

In the important scene 8, regalia such as the scepter and mace are brought out of a 'Hall of Eating and Standing'. Words are addressed by Thoth to Osiris, 'Horus has grown up and takes possession of his Eye.' This is the Eye which when recovered enables Horus (the Pharaoh) to avenge Osiris and also to revive him. The Uraeus on the Crown is called the Eye of Horus.

In scenes 9-18, grain is threshed by bulls and male asses. Later bread made of this grain will be sacramentally eaten. But now the king forbids the animals to trample this grain, for it represents his father Osiris—also an agricultural deity. The king beats the beasts as though they were Seth, and puts spells on the barley to protect it. Then trees and branches are brought on board. A libation is made and a *ded* pillar erected. The last symbolizes the resurrection of the predecessor in the other world. After it is taken down, bread and beer, the staple foods, are offered. A mock battle is fought by retainers, apparently to symbolize the disharmony which is brought to an end by the new accession. The combat is between the 'Children of Seth' and the 'Children of Horus', the latter played by members of the Pharaoh's family.

Scenes 19-25 reveal produce of the land brought to the king for the sacral *hetep* meal. As in the later 'real' coronation, it is taken by the sovereign just before he is crowned. The food, ceremonially brought by such categories of persons as 'milkmaids' and 'butchers', is called the Eye of Horus. The assemblage of food was considered the Eye being restored.

Scenes 26-32 cover the actual coronation itself. Persons with archaic titles approach bearing gifts, two crowns, two feathers, a gold headband. Incense is offered. After the act of crowning, 'half-loaves' of bread are distributed to leading persons.[16]

The last scenes, 33-46, concern the transfiguration of the new king's predecessor. He is shown to become Lord of the Dead. In a pageant of shamanistic overtones, perhaps, the 'spirit seekers', a

---

[15] Frankfort, p. 124.
[16] The description of the mystery play above is based on Frankfort, pp. 126-30.

very old category of priests not otherwise heard of since the First Dynasty, impersonate Thoth and the Children of Horus. The latter are bidden by Thoth to seek Horus' father, and 'make pretence with sticks to set up the ladder for the ascent of Osiris into heaven'.[17] Then two women impersonating Isis and Nephthys sing laments for Osiris. Cloths are presented for wrapping the corpse of the dead king and accessories for the Opening of the Mouth mortuary ceremony.[18]

This mystery play was clearly a very sacred device, and doubtless was held to be more than mere drama. It must have conveyed real power to the Pharaoh. But it was not the official coronation. When the season for that had come around, the sovereign was first purified by lustration. He was bathed in water from the gods at the cardinal points.[19]

After the purification, the Pharaoh was led into the Dual Shrines and crowned, nominally by Horus and Seth. In each shrine, signifying respectively Upper and Lower Egypt, he was given the crook, flail, and casket containing a testament of that realm. He made the following recitation:

O Red Crown, O Inu, O Great One,
O Magician, O Fiery Snake!
Let there be terror of me like the terror of thee.
Let there be fear of me like the fear of thee.
Let there be awe of me like the awe of thee.

---

[17] A. M. Blackman, 'Myth and Ritual in Ancient Egypt', in Hooke, *Myth and Ritual*, p. 31.

[18] ibid.

[19] Hocart has shown that the lustration, like the bath in the Kairyū-den of the *Daijō-sai*, is a very widespread part of the enthronement pattern. It is, for example, integral to the death and rebirth action of the ancient Hindu king. He was bathed in two streams of water, and afterward was clothed in a threefold robe representing the womb. This rite became the Buddhist *abhiṣeka* baptism of initiation. Hocart, p. 79.

According to J. Gonda, *Ancient Indian Kingship from the Religious Point of View* (reprinted from *Numen* III and IV with Addenda and Index), the consecration of the king began with an anointing on the model of the *Mahābhiṣeka*, or great anointing of Indra or Prajāpati, with Indra here the prototype of the Kṣatriya, or ruling caste. The Brahman priests read texts indicating that the king is authorized by the gods to be victorious, with Soma's glory, Agni's brilliance, and the radiance of the sun. The king was addressed as Indra conquering his enemies, reminding us of course of both the Egyptian and Mesopotamian accession. The new king then takes the three Viṣṇu steps in the cardinal directions, reminding us of another Egyptian motif and the idea of world mastery and orientation. Then, in an interesting ceremony, a wheel is placed flat on an axle put upright in the ground and spun to activate vigor. Next follows the *abhiṣeka*, or baptism with water, and the king is said to be reborn as the son of the sages who act as priests. He is embraced by them, and ascends a chariot. Finally, the new king circumambulates the city on an elephant (pp. 82–9). The accession is of course accompanied by Brahmanic offerings; the connection of accession with the well-known horse sacrifice of Vedic times confirms the inevitable association of accession with a sacrifice.

A separate rite for the renewal of kingship might take place later; then the king took on new triumphal attire after anointing. Then follows honoring of priests, granting of amnesty, etc. (p. 95).

Let there be love of me like the love of thee.
Let me rule, a leader of the living.
Let me be powerful, a leader of spirits.
Let my blade be firm against my enemies.

O Inu, thou has come forth from me;
And I have come forth from thee.

Inu is the goddess of the Crown, identified with the Eye of Horus. The identification of the king with the god in combat against the enemy, mythological and actual (also identified), can hardly be plainer. After the crowning, probably taking place during these words, the Pharaoh is worshiped in these sentences:

The Great One has borne thee;
The Exalted One has adorned thee;
For thou art Horus who hast fought
For the protection of thine Eye.[20]

There followed a banquet. Sometime during the rite a circumambulation of the walls was made. This is usually thought to symbolize taking possession of the kingdom, but may also be equated with threshing.[21]

We should also take note of the Egyptian Harvest Festival, the Min, held in the first month of summer, since the *Daijō-sai* was in the harvest context. In Egypt too this occasion concerned not only harvest, but also kingship. The Pharaoh went in procession to pour libations and burn incense at the temple of Min, the Harvest Deity. He then processed with the god, incarnate in the form of a white bull, to a temporary shrine in the harvest field. There were oblations to the king, his *ka* (or spirit), and his ancestors.

The queen was the only female to accompany the king in this procession. Perhaps for this reason she was called the 'stranger'. But she expressed his divine nature by walking around him.[22] In general the Egyptian queen, though often mentioned in texts together with the Pharaoh by a feminine variant of the royal title, received little separate attention. But C. J. Bleeker notes that the picture illustrating the birth of the famous Hatshepsut is a dramatization of her ritual role as 'the vehicle that conveyed the divine substance to the royal child'. Her divine prototypes are Tefnut, the oldest goddess, and Mut, consort of Amon. In the eighteenth dynasty title as queen passed from mother to daughter.

---

[20] Frankfort, p. 108.
[21] Fairman, op. cit. pp. 78–9.
[22] C. J. Bleeker, 'The Position of the Queen in Ancient Egypt', in *The Sacral Kingship/La Regalità Sacra*, pp. 267–8.

In the daily cultus she handled the sistrum and conducted singing in the temple. She had a passive role in the Sed. But Bleeker suggests that in the Min she is superior even to the king, for she seems to be giving him the divine forces he needs. One is reminded that the throne is often equated with Isis.[23]

However, while it has been suggested that ritual intercourse may have taken place at the Min, the allusions to 'sacred marriage' in Egypt adduced by earlier 'Myth and Ritual' scholars seem to be highly controversial.

We see that these Egyptian rituals, centering upon the major foci of the agricultural year, affirm the plenary divine status of the sovereign. This is confirmed by his participation in the death and resurrection drama. But the full process of deification is not completed until the death of a king, when he becomes fully Osiris, and his spirit the *ka* of the living Pharaoh. The divinity of the king then is linked with ancestrism. The totality of the imperial company, deceased and living, held the power, and the living incumbent is only its manifestation. The idea of kingship was united with that of history. Frankfort believes that the statues of previous kings were worshiped as a collectivity, as a 'nebulous spiritual force' supporting the living ruler on the throne of Horus.[24]

But S. G. F. Brandon affirms that the monuments with lists of rulers, autobiographical boasts, citations of battles, and the like, indicate that Egypt rather

> . . . rejoiced in the definitive nature of historical events and was greatly concerned that the memory of what was deemed to be notable achievements should not be lost. . . . Moreover, it is evident that as the Egyptian, at any specific period, looked back over the past, he envisaged the sequence of events as linear extensions backwards. There is no hint of a repetitive cycle of events, an 'éternel retour' to some primeval situation.[25]

While this statement seems scarcely borne out entirely by the mystery play, in any case the accession would have been solemnified not only by the presence of transcendent deity, but spiritually also in the awesome presence of the predeceased monarchs. The new sovereign would have been incipiently entering their fellowship with that of heaven. The numinous would have resided in the

---

[23] ibid. *passim.*
[24] Frankfort, p. 89–90.
[25] S. G. F. Brandon, *History, Time and Deity*, pp. 67–8.

weight of the past as well as in the gods of the land.

III

IN THE Valley of the Two Rivers we have the feel of a different situation. Society is less sublimely divine and ordered; life and history are more dynamic, more uncertain, more prone to chaos. Kingly power seems to be a subject of desperate wrestle between the incumbent, the gods, and pitiless destiny.

Mesopotamian political institutions developed from two directions. On the one side was a certain 'primitive democracy' typical of the first known level of culture. The independent agricultural towns settled their affairs in an assembly of elders. Doubtless, as in Israel at the time of the Judges, the assemblies could easily be dominated by strong men whose words ended debate. Naturally, as society became more and more complex, strong personal administration of that sort became increasingly desirable. Movement to kingship would then not be difficult.

But the sacral character of kingship was supplied from another direction. Even in the early agricultural town, it was held that the land was owned by the regional god. In his stead, the priest of his temple had some authority in the administration of these divine estates. This sacerdotal office somehow merged, in early dynastic times, with the role of the strong man who emerged out of the aldermanic assembly. When the two become one office, we have what may be called the Mesopotamian style of sacral kingship.

This conflation of ethnarch and divine vicar was natural, yet the office never quite overcame the instability suggested by bifurcative origin. Somehow the limitations of both roles were never forgotten; the king was only viceroy of deity, and his title was dependent on the well-being of the people. 'Kingship descended from heaven' and was instituted by the gods for men, according to the theory; yet the king as an individual was more possessed by it on sufferance than personally divine.

He received the throne by divine election, but we do not know just how the choice was revealed. But transition was always an uncertain matter; there was always something *ad hoc* about each accession. The death and mourning-period of a king was a transit of darkness. Even if a prince succeeded his father, the process was never, as in Egypt, psychologically or politically smooth.[26]

An attempt was made to solve the problem by the induction of

[26] Frankfort, p. 243.

the heir in a 'House of Succession' before the death of the predecessor. In this place the crown prince was initiated into his future
task by taking an active part in celebrations and government. After
the royal death and mourning, the prince's accession was accomplished by coronation. Then the transcendent essence of kingship
descended upon the candidate. The regalia given him, scepter,
crown, tiara, and staff, conveyed this power. He received them in
the temple of the city-god upon a throne dais. A Sumerian text
describing a coronation in Erech speaks of a 'Lady of the Scepter'
and a 'Lady of the Crown' on a 'Throne Dais'.[27] Perhaps these
'Ladies' are seats or altars, and one may properly be reminded of
the Egyptian identification of Isis and the throne as support of
sovereignty. It appears that, as in many other places, the ruler's
name was changed during the coronation.

Frankfort thus describes the coronation of the king in Assyrian
times:

> The king went to the temple of the god Assur, where the royal in-
> signia rested upon 'seats'. (It is interesting that the Assyrian kings
> were crowned, not in Calah or Ninevah, the capitals of the empire,
> but in the ancient city of Assur from which the empire took
> its rise.) The king on his portable throne was carried to the
> temple on the shoulders of men, while a priest going in front beat
> a drum and called out: 'Assur is king! Assur is king!' This phrase
> emphasized that the new ruler—as yet uncrowned, and hence not
> 'king' in the fullest sense of the word—was on his way to the god who
> was the depository of kingship in Assyria. The king entered the
> temple, kissed the ground, burned incense, and mounted the high
> platform at the end of the sanctuary where the statue of the god
> stood. There he touched the ground with his forehead and deposited
> his gifts: a gold bowl with costly oil, a *mina* of silver, and an em-
> broidered robe. He then arranged Assur's offering-table while priests
> set those of the other gods. Next followed the last preparations for
> the coronation. The text is damaged here, but it seems likely that the
> king was anointed with the oil brought in the gold bowl. The
> account then continues: 'The crown of Assur and the weapons of
> Ninlil [Assur's spouse] are brought,' and they were put on 'seats' at
> the foot of the platform before the god. However, the central cere-
> mony of the coronation is preserved in one text. The priest carried
> the crown and scepter, still on the felt cushions which supported
> them when lying on their 'seats', and brought them to the king.[28]

The priest then crowned the king, reciting a prayer for favor to
Assur and Ninlil. The other dignitaries also said prayers, then

[27] ibid. p. 245.
[28] ibid. pp. 246–7.

gathered before the throne to do homage, presenting gifts and their insignia of office. Without these emblems, they deliberately took an irregular order, avoiding the usual arrangement of precedence based on rank. But the king said, 'Everyone resume his office,' and they took up their badges and ranking again. Here is a tiny vignette of the return to chaos and creation anew of order which marks the death of one king and the taking of the crown by another. The same pattern also informs the New Year, when the king was ritually humiliated.

For it was no life of festive and serene joy to which the new king had been initiated. Rather it seems to have been a career of considerable anxiety dominated by omens concerning whether or not the monarch had served the gods well in his great commission.

Yet the king had supernatural powers. Both to protect and multiply his numinous presence, substitutes for the king, persons or objects, were often used in rituals. Those items touched by the king, and as well his statues, were oddly enough given more evident divine honors than the uneasy monarch himself, as though they were merely the repositories of the divine power of kingship untouched by the humanity.[29] Such objects found use in the establishment of temples and the performance of seasonal or occasional rituals in various places throughout the realm.

The most famous exercise of kingship in the Valley of the Two Rivers was the New Year's Festival, called in Akkadian *akitu*. This festival is virtually a locus classicus for the 'Myth and Ritual' approach, even though the king's role is more of a symbolic than an actual participation. But it does involve the king in the ritual re-enactment of creation, the defeat of chaos in the form of Tiamat, the rescue of Marduk (as dying-rising seasonal deity) from imprisonment in the mountains by his son Nebo, and the giving of kingship. Unlike Pharaoh, who seems to maintain a divine passivity amid somewhat similar performances, the Assyrian king undergoes a parallel personal crisis, even if it is programmed.

The opening days of the festival saw the making of long preparatory prayers, the manufacture of images, and finally on the fourth day the recital of the Creation Epic. On the fifth day the temple was purified. A scapegoat was sacrificed and the carcass thrown into the river.

On the fifth day also the king entered the temple for the first time, after the setting of a meal before Marduk:

---

[29] See ibid. Ch. 21, 'The Deification of Kings', pp. 295–312.

Escorted in by priests he was immediately left alone before the statue. Soon the high-priest appeared and took away from him his regalia, his sceptre, ring, and crooked weapon, and his crown, which he placed upon a stool before Marduk. Next he struck the king a blow on the cheek, pulled his ears, and forced him to kneel before the god. In this humiliation the king had to recite a sort of 'negative confession'—'I have not sinned, O Lord of the lands, I have not been unregardful for thy godhead. . . .'[30]

The king then received his sovereign bearing and tokens back again, together with words of reassurance. Once more, however, the priest struck him; if tears came to his eyes, it was a sign the god was gracious.

At this point the ritual days had entered their deepest hours. The ordinary had been reversed, the king subjected, the established order ritually overthrown. Chaos had risen to the surface. Crowds surged into the streets mourning Marduk, who was said to have been imprisoned in the mountains.

But the city awaited the arrival next day of Nebo, his avenging son. On that day statues of gods from many cities arrived on barges at the capital, and among them was the hero Nebo. In triumphal procession—and with another extreme shift of emotion—he was led from the quays to the temple. The king may have led the procession himself. In Assur he himself somehow played the role of the divine protagonist, Nebo.

Unfortunately, we do not know just how the enactment of the liberation of Marduk was staged. But after this drama, the visiting gods all met in a solemn assembly called the 'determination of destiny' in which the course of the coming year was believed to be decided. Afterwards a banquet was held.

The sacred marriage, so much remarked, was also held in a number of places in Mesopotamia during this season. The king, or high priest, and a priestess would be the principals. They would share a bedchamber set up in the temple for all or part of the sacred time, clearly enacting the marriage of the gods, of heaven and earth. Again, there is, however, regrettably little precise information about this usage.[31]

Certainly the respective tone of the Egyptian and Mesopotamian rites indicates something of the ideological differences. In one, the king is strictly divine; in the other, he is a viceroy and mediator between the gods and men. But underneath the important ideological level, common themes—the dying-rising god, a ritual return

---

[30] C. J. Gadd, 'Babylonian Myth and Ritual', in Hooke, *Myth and Ritual*, p. 53.
[31] Frankfort, pp. 295–6.

to chaos and renewal after ritual battle, the sacral importance, at least, of royal marriage—are not lacking. If nothing else, this is evidence of the fact that symbols change according to different laws, and usually more slowly, than ideas. There are also deep ideas, or assumptions rather, that link the two fluvial civilizations. Both suppose a cosmic struggle between order and disorder, in which one side must defeat the other continually, perhaps every year, and in which the stakes are nothing short of life against death.

IV

WE HAVE noted above that S. G. F. Brandon felt there was 'no trace' of the main pillars of the Near Eastern 'Myth and Ritual' pattern in China. We shall now have occasion to see in what sense this may be true. Indeed, the institutions of the Flowery Empire seem always oddly twisted in comparison to Western antiquity. The sovereign on the throne is a personified triumph of order over chaos. But it is a quite human and historical chaos. There is a seasonal battle of polar forces, but the king is supposed to assure that victory is alternated rather than always going to one side.

Yet, as in our other examples, Chinese kingship was founded on the unity of nature (the agricultural year) and history (the line of imperial ancestors) in the reigning monarch as unique person, the midpoint which makes contact between heaven and earth, and between past and present. The emperor achieves the unity through his yearly sacrifices. The accession rites are not so much the enactment of the essentials themselves as a juridical assumption of the office in which they can be performed.

The installation of the Chinese emperor meant his receiving of the regalia, particularly the seals of office. The classical writers put relatively little emphasis on the rites of accession, and much more on the annual functions, as though wishing to minimize the fact of transition in favor of eternal stability. Thus the classic ritual books—the *Chou Li*, *Li Chi*, *Tz'u Ling*, etc.—contain no accession rites, unlike their Japanese equivalents.

The accession then shows how society and history are integrated into the continuing pattern which kingship establishes. Stability rests in the office rather than in the dynasty or individual. The 'mandate of heaven' theory assured that the historic, if not ritual, circumstances by which a new line came to the throne were not as important as subsequent signs of heavenly approval.

The function of unifying man with nature and the past was

evident in the oldest key task of the newly acceded monarch. Mo Tzu tells us that:

> Formerly in the time of the sacred kings of the three dynasties, when they first founded their kingdoms and established their capitals, they selected a site for the principal earth altar of the kingdom, erected the ancestral temple, and chose luxuriant trees to make a sacred grove.[32]

Thus there was the unity of soil and ancestors, and the organization of sacred space around the mound and grove. In the Shang period, the mortuary aspect was of no small importance. Kings were buried in a deep pit, with finely decorated walls, and human sacrifice accompanied their obsequies. After death, former kings were worshiped as divine beings, as in Egypt. In fact, at least by the time of the *Li Chi* and the beginning of the Han era, all official worship was broadly ancestral, performed on the pattern of filial piety. Thus every clan and dynasty believed that the Sovereign on High, Shang Ti, had taken part in the birth of its founder. 'The birth of the founder of the dynasty is subject to the influx of heaven,' and so the worship of Shang Ti was actually ancestral, in accordance with the imperial title 'Son of Heaven'.[33]

The tradition given in the *Book of History* concerning the accession of the second of the legendary primal emperors, Shun, is of great interest. While not historical, it surely reflects normative concepts in western Chou. When Yao, the predecessor, asked his ministers for a suitable successor, they rejected Yao's own son in favor of the relatively obscure Shun. Thus kingship was not regarded as necessarily hereditary. Exemplifying the Egyptian and Babylonian pattern, Shun long served as co-emperor with Yao. During this same time Yü, Shun's future successor, did his mighty works of battling a deluge and making the land habitable.

Finally, on the first day of the year, Yao handed over the power to Shun before the tablet of his first ancestor. Then Shun began to perform his proper duties. He checked the movements of the Seven Ruling (astronomical) Bodies. He performed the *lei* sacrifices to Shang Ti, the Heavenly Lord. He worshiped six other ancestral tablets in the ancestral shrine, together with the gods of mountains and rivers.[34]

Then, 'In the second month of the year he journeyed east on

---

[32] Cited in D. H. Smith, 'Divine Kingship in Ancient China', *Numen*, IV, 1957, p. 180.

[33] Kashihi Tanaka, *A Comparison of the Tz'u Ling and the Jingi-ryō*, Thesis, Claremont, 1966, p. 62.

[34] Smith, op. cit. p. 186; J. Legge, *The Chinese Classics*, III, *The Shoo King*, Pt. 1, pp. 23–7.

a tour of inspection and made a visit to Tai-tsung (Mt T'ai). There he made a burnt offering to Heaven and sacrificed from afar to the various mountains and rivers in succession.'[35]

This is the prototype of the great sacrifice on Mt T'ai of certain Ch'in and Han emperors which is an important part of the kingship pattern of those days, and a very revealing part. Before discussing it further, though, let us compare one or two general accounts of later accession.

Ssu-ma Ch'ien, the great historian of the Han dynasty, tells us that when Kao-tsu, the rebel of humble background who defeated the Ch'in tyrants, was victorious, his nobles and generals begged him to take the imperial title. But at first he declined three times. Then, 'seeing that he could do no more, said, "If you, my lords, consider it a good thing, then it must be to the good of the country." On the day *chia-wu* (28 February 202 B.C.) he assumed the position of Supreme Emperor on the north banks of the Ssu River.'[36] He then named the incumbents of feudatory states; for obvious reasons there would be no ancestral offerings.

The fact that Kao-tsu, perhaps perfunctorily like later monarchs, first declined the title at least indicates that divine or hereditary election was not thought absolute, or perhaps worked through humility. None the less myth began creating divine descent for the Han sovereign, as it has for other notables of China. All rulers before Kao-tsu were believed to be of divine origin. Even the Ch'in monarchs were considered descended from Po-ti, the White God, by Han historians. So Kao-tsu was likewise said to have been conceived by a god, a dragon was seen hovering over his birth, and a recognizable cloud always floated above his head. He was a son of the Red God who battled and defeated the son of the White God.[37]

The living emperor was not, however, worshiped; his divinity was putative only, though the august court ceremonies introduced by aid of the Confucianists in 201 B.C. served to distance Kao-tsu

---

[35] From Ssu-ma Ch'ien's version based on the *Shu Ching*, or *Book of History*. Burton Watson, *Records of the Grand Historian of China*, I, p. 14. According to one tradition, Shang Ti had his throne in the Pole Star. He was assisted by two ministers of state, one who was the spirit of Ursa Major and who ruled the heavenly empire, and one who was the spirit of Mt T'ai and who had charge of the earthly realm. A number of shrines to the stars of the Big Dipper are found along the pilgrim path to the summit of Mt T'ai. The Pole Star and the Big Dipper were a heavenly model of the earthly court in much Chinese lore. Gertrude and James Jobes, *Outer Space*, pp. 352–3. According to Chavannes' classic study of Mt T'ai, the mountain was identified with the Great Bear and the Pole Star. E. Chavannes, *Le T'ai Chan*, pp. 433–4. The mountain was also an abode of the gods, of the dead, and a source of fertility (pp. 8, 13).

[36] Watson, I, p. 346.

[37] Wang Yü-ch'üan, 'An Outline of the Central Government of the Former Han Dynasty', *Harvard Journal of Asiatic Studies*, XII, Nos. 1–2 (June 1949), pp. 139–40.

from the earlier companionship of the field. On the intellectual level, this divinization represented a mythological and ceremonial rationalization of historical events, for the Red and White Gods are entities in the directional and five-element scheme. The White God is of metal, the basest element, and of autumn and the west; the Red is of the more auspicious summer, south, and fire. Needless to say, the imperial court ceremonial was based on the same schema; the whole integrated history and nature in a rationalized pattern around the sovereign. Moreover, the Han sovereign had his ancestral temples erected in many places; by 72 B.C. there were 168 such fanes in the empire.

But the basic formula of accession was only somewhat changed in the case of a later Han emperor, Wen. When as the eldest surviving son of Kao-tsu he was begged to take the throne upon the death of the infamous dowager empress L^u, he replied, 'It is a grave task to undertake the service of the ancestral temple of Emperor Kao-tsu. I am a man of no ability and am not worthy to be appointed to such a charge. I beg you consult with the king of Ch'u and select someone who is suitable. I dare not undertake the task.' But after declining the officials' importunities five times, he finally acceded. Then, 'On the following day, the day *hsin-hai*, the emperor officially ascended the throne and paid his respects at the ancestral temple of Emperor Kao-tsu.'[38] Several further passages indicate that the position of emperor was above all defined by 'care of the ancestral temples' and 'the sacred altars'.

But what of the sacrifices to mountains and rivers and Mt T'ai reported of Shun? These are not mentioned in connection with the accession, but Ssu-ma Ch'ien adds the following note at the end of the chapter on Wen:

> Emperor Wen reigned some forty years after the founding of the Han, and his virtue was of the highest order. The time had drawn near when he might appropriately have changed the beginning of the year, altered the court vestments, and performed the Feng and Shan sacrifices. But the emperor modestly declined within his reign to take such steps. Ah, was he not benevolent indeed?[39]

The Feng and Shan sacrifices, those performed on Mt T'ai, were, however, offered by the fifth Han sovereign, the Emperor Wu. It was in his day that Ssu-ma Ch'ien wrote, and in the great historian's opinion he was much less 'virtuous' than Wen. But rather than discuss the events of Wu's time he apparently was moved instead

---

[38] Watson, ibid. p. 346.
[39] ibid. p. 366.

to compose a treatise on the Feng and Shan sacrifices which Wu performed. This study is preserved in the history.

Ssu-ma Ch'ien begins by asking the question, 'Among the emperors and kings who from ancient times have received the mandate of heaven, why are there some who did not perform the Feng and Shan sacrifices?' He points out that an emperor must receive favorable omens before offering them. But a few emperors who did not receive such omens took it upon themselves, and others, virtuous sovereigns who did, declined, largely out of a commendable modesty.

Fortunately, the historian gives us a fine picture of the history and performance of this ceremony from the time of the Ch'in on. Despite the reference in the *Book of History*, it does not seem to be of great antiquity. Although the Mt T'ai sacrifices may not have been offered until many years after the accession, they had some connection with it—like the Sed in Egypt—in the sense that they were a culmination of kingship. They were a report of a successful carrying out of the mandate of heaven given the sovereign, yet also a time of crisis and omen.

When the first Ch'in emperor, of evil memory, presumed to offer these august rites, a violent rainstorm caught him on the way down the mountain, and this was taken as a much-deserved ill sign by the later historians. The offering of Wu, described by Ssu-ma Ch'ien in detail, was heralded by the finding of an ancient cauldron, considered a token of the Great Unity (not explained further), which was appropriately worshiped. Successfully performing this ultimate act of royal worship seems also to betoken a supreme 'breakthrough' in the personal spiritual life of the monarch. After the great event, Ssu-ma Ch'ien tells us, the Emperor Wu was given the congratulations of the court, and assurance from the magicians that he would soon be ready to see P'eng Lai, the Islands of Immortality, from the coast, and that good signs would burst forth in the heavens. It was then Wu's intention to offer the sacrifices in connection with a tour of inspection every five years or so, indicating that like the Sed they might be repeated at long intervals.

When Wu performed the Feng and Shan, first a stone was set up on the mountain. The erecting of a monumental pillar—a megalith—as a token of the completion of a successful term and the marking of a renewal rite also remind us of Egypt and elsewhere.

Then at the eastern foot of the mountain an altar mound was made, and beneath it was buried a jade tablet inscribed with a secret message and arrows in the four directions to announce the unity of the Empire. After this ceremony, the emperor, accompanied only by one attendant, ascended Mt T'ai and made the Feng sacrifice entirely in secret.

On the next day he performed the Shan sacrifice in the northeast foothills of T'ai. The sovereign made obeisances and wore yellow. This is the color of the element earth, representing directionally the Center and the universal lord Shang Ti. Rush mats were made for the offerings, which would have been wine and flesh.[40] Then:

> Earth of five colors was heaped on the sacrificial mound. In addition to the offerings all sorts of strange beasts, flying creatures, white pheasants, and other animals brought from distant regions were set free so that the ritual would be complete. Rhinoceroses, elephants, and such creatures, however, were not set free, but were brought to Mount T'ai and then taken away again. While the Feng and Shan were being performed, something like a light appeared in the sky at night, and during the day white clouds rose from the mounds.[41]

The Chinese accession then is marked by common characteristics —the juridical reception of regalia, the primary duty of ancestral piety (which seems somewhat at variance with the 'democratic' forms preceding accession), and the periodic ritual of renewal. In all cases the king unites himself with history by assimilation of the past line of kings. But certain ideas beloved of the 'Myth and Ritual' scholars and prominent in the Near East are not so apparent. The monarch is not a champion of right in cosmic battle directly enacted in the rituals, or so it seems. D. H. Smith comments, evidently having in mind the important royal functions which 'strengthen' the alternating forces of *yin* and *yang* in their season, that 'the duality which arises out of a primal unity is a duality of equally necessary and beneficent forces, which in turn attain ascendency in the seasonal process.'[42]

But it is always a mistake to impose too heavily the perceptions of Chinese philosophy on the totality of Chinese spiritual life. If an observation such as Professor Smith's explains much, one could

---

[40] According to the *Li Chi* interpretation of sacrifice, the spreading of a mat and the placing of it on a stool with servings for two is to make a resting place for the united spirits of husband and wife—J. Legge, *The Li Ki*, II, p. 245. This may be kept in mind in connection with the *Daijō-sai* mats, which were spread on a low table, and which may represent a marriage feast of heaven and earth in the first-fruits. According to Chavannes, the Feng sacrifice was to Heaven, the Shan to Earth, and these consecrated the reign's legitimacy (Chavannes, p. 17).

[41] Watson, II, p. 59.

[42] Smith, op. cit. p. 194.

also remark concerning the accession and all its associated rites, including the Feng and Shan, that they represent a triumph of an absolute good, order, over the ultimate chaos. Chaos is not ritually represented just because ritual itself, pre-eminently the seasonal rituals, deal with a secondary and orderly interplay of forces. Ritual is order itself, made manifest. Perhaps that order is the mysterious Great Unity which came into symbolic prominence as successful kingship progressed to its culmination. The obverse, sheer chaos, may not be spoken of in the ritual, unless sacrifice itself bespeaks it, but it is evident in the ideology of kingship. It is historical and political, enacted in actual rather than ritual combat, in the battles which a dynasty having received the mandate of heaven must wage in order to win security for the throne.[43] As we have seen, the battle may well be mythologized into the combat of scions of deities, as well as into the typologies of the five-element system and so on. If these myths are not precisely dramatized, it is because history itself is the ritual enactment of the scenario—though they have been made the subject of innumerable of the quasi-liturgical Chinese dramas and operas.

When a king triumphs in this arena and takes the throne, he worships—in effect deifies as a token of the legitimacy of the dynasty—his ancestors, as Pharaoh made his predecessor Osiris. If one feels there is no hint of a death and resurrection pattern in Chinese monarchy—and there may be none in the 'dynamic' sense —one may still look again at the implications of this ancestrism, and at the promises of immortality which followed upon Wu's Feng and Shan offerings, with their atmosphere of a time of crisis and testing. A possible movement toward a full-blown sacral kingship with no small attention to royal immortality, perhaps on the Egyptian pattern, aborted with the collapse of the Ch'in. But spokesmen for at least bits and fragments of this approach continued to be found in the Taoist 'magicians' always present at Court if always despised by the Mandarins. Indeed, Confucianism itself could be read as a 'triumphalist' rationalization of the cosmic

---

[43] This seems to be reflected in the story of the legendary third emperor, Yü, as told in the *Shu Ching* and in Mencius. Yü, long before his accession, battled the waters of a great primordial deluge, made channels, established agriculture, and divided the empire into provinces. Later, after defeating certain enemies on the field of battle, Yü took the throne but, exhausted from his heroic labors, sought to retire. He was persuaded by the people to stay, but he finally died away from the capital in remote mountains. One sees in this sort of story many of the features of a myth and cultus like that of Marduk—the defeat of chaos, the culture hero as it were lost and called back, and final mountain-hiding. But in China the story is told in the idiom of secular history. The order which Yü finally established makes ritual one with political justice and tranquility. But on the other side of this order is the deluge and the battles with barbarians.

battle. One need not look far to see remythologization of it in modern China.

Similarly, there is no explicit role given sacred marriage and no ritual function given the queen. Some evidence of the concept behind it may be located in the vernal exchange of odes in the fields which led to marriage in archaic China. During the former Han, a dowager empress like **Lü** was able to exercise great power, but without ritual base comparable to that of Hatshepsut in Egypt.

In Chinese kingship we see a supremacy of ideal order over any sense of the profoundly dynamic activity of the sacred. The latter is left to history itself—the crises and renewals worked by the mandate of heaven in the rise and fall of dynasties—and to secondary religious acts. History itself, and the operations of omens and the quest for immortality, may press upon the king. But the king in his official capacity is to establish a continuity and unity of heaven and earth which works in the opposite direction, toward the stability of society, rather than to give the dynamic and irregular ritual expression. The king is not absolutely divine just because heaven itself is less rational—unless in the largest perspective—than the properly constituted human order. Thus the Chinese emperor more resembled the Babylonian in ideology, being a representative of the gods placed in ritual and administrative charge of earth, and concurrently the representative of man before heaven. He is under responsibility. But the rites of accession, being more juridical or triumphant than dynamic, are rather more Egyptian. The accession crisis of death, chaos, and renewal remains a historical myth, under heaven, rather than being entirely assimilated to death and resurrection like that of Osiris or Marduk.

V

IN POLYNESIA kings were also deified, partially in life, definitively after death. On Paumotu, kings were buried in a certain cave, and after this burial were afforded divine worship and took their place among the gods. The prayers recited at cutting the navel cord of a royal child were simply invocations of departed rulers.[44] On Urea, the fear of the departed chief was more emphasized. His spirit was expected to return and possess relatives. Often through these mediumistic communications kings told of their great honors in the kingdom of the dead.[45] We are reminded of Osiris.

---

[44] R. W. Williamson, *Religion and Social Organization in Central Polynesia,* p. 26.
[45] ibid. p. 30.

The king or chief is always chosen from out of a ruling caste. The actual candidate was not always predetermined, and often was selected by divination from among several possibilities. On Easter Island it was by means of an annual egg-gathering competition. But great sacred power, *mana*, surrounded all members of the caste. They were believed to possess ability to produce marvelous crops and catches, and could not even be touched by commoners without magical precautions to dispel the danger of the concentrated power.

As elsewhere, the chieftainate was marked by the possession of certain regalia. He who held and wore them was king. In Fiji it was a sacred whale tooth.[46] Elsewhere, objects made of coconut leaves were common. The coconut plant had ritual use in other contexts too, indicating an association of sacred power including kingship with a major economic plant. A coconut frond may be used as a scepter, or a sacred headdress made of it.[47]

The most striking regalia, though, are made from red feathers. These may become headdresses or belts. The belt, when used, is the most significant symbol of all. In the Society Islands head chiefs are called *ari'i maro ura*, 'The chief who wears the *maro ura*', or red belt. Perhaps the word *maro* can be compared to the Japanese *maro*, which means circle and is also an ancient title of nobility. Captain Cook described the *maro* as a girdle about five yards long and fifteen inches broad, ornamented with red and yellow feathers. Upon ceremonial occasions additions were made to it. When peace was declared, or a new monarch enthroned in the belt, new lappets were added. These contained ornamental symbols of the respective kings. The belt was thus almost a written history. The sacrality of the belt was such that human sacrificial victims were required during its making and subsequent lengthenings. Its fabric retained the holy power of these grim rites and of all the important events associated with it, and it in turn invested the monarch who wore it with divinity; the belt was more sacred than images of the gods.[48]

Upon the birth of an heir, a proclamation of restrictive taboo was issued, and the mother retired to a parturition lodge built at the back of the chief's ancestral lodge. Those in attendance chanted prayers. When the child was born, the cord was cut and wrapped about his neck. His body was anointed with sandalwood oil. Several days later the umbilical cord was placed in a recess of the

[46] B. Quain, *Fijian Village*, pp. 208 ff.
[47] Williamson, pp. 180–1.
[48] ibid. pp. 181–2.

hut. Everything else associated with the birth was buried. The infant was bathed, with incantation on behalf of his future as a warrior. Then the father received the child and conferred upon him a name, embracing his feet. He was next received by the high priest at the national shrine. The priest laid the infant prince upon a carpet of mats in the same manner as the image of a tutelary god in a high ceremony.[49]

When the time came for the accession of a new king, as elsewhere months of preparation went into the feast and accessories. The most important labor was the making of a new lappet for the *maro ura*. It was woven with exquisite care with a needle of human bone. This needle, expressing the continuity of the sacred work, was never taken out of the fabric.

Preliminary to the ceremony was a solemn festival of prayer in the national shrine. On the day of accession itself the chief was led to the sea, where he was bathed to the accompaniment of an invocation concerning him and his *maro ura*. Tradition had it that while the king was in the water two sharks approached which rubbed their bodies against his if he was the legitimate heir, but kept away if he was a usurper.

After this he is enthroned on the seashore and invested with the regalia, a feather headdress, a spear, a walking stick, and finally the sacred girdle, and is publicly acclaimed king. Then the new sovereign is taken to the national shrine and enthroned. In a rite reminiscent of the Eye of Horus, he is presented with the eye of a human sacrificial victim, and he pretends to eat it.[50] In some rites, as on Oro, he is struck on the back with a branch of a sacred tree; we are reminded of Mesopotamia.[51] The king then receives homage from his subjects, and feasting and carnival follow.

The role of the Polynesian king is above all ceremonial. In many places first-fruits, and the first heads of enemies, are presented to him. His marriage is celebrated before the skulls of his ancestors. Before war, the chief conducts solemn rites of prayer and sacrifice in the temple; there is a human victim, and again the eye is presented to the chief.[52]

The Polynesian temples are built in a manner reminiscent of the *Daijō* structures; there is a large enclosed space containing a number of separate thatched buildings for diverse functions. We are also reminded of the Yuki and Suki halls in the chief's lodge;

---

[49] ibid. p. 260.
[50] ibid. p. 261.
[51] ibid. p. 48.
[52] ibid. p. 265.

the throne is a couch of mats, and the chief's couch will be higher than anyone else's. The chief and his family will have separate fire and food which may not be touched by any person not of the blood. In some places his feet may not touch the ground but are always shielded by mats. Often the sacred chief is so inhibited by ritual and taboo that he may not conduct ordinary political affairs; these are handled by a sort of prime minister called the 'talking chief'.

The death of a chief signaled a temporary return to chaos. A priest would garb himself in fantastic raiment, and lead a band of young men—these would run amok for weeks, wounding or killing anyone they met. Finally the terror would be terminated with hand-to-hand combat between the band and a nearby village, the priest would shed his harlequin garb, and normality would return. But the body of the chief would lie in state in the shrine for as long as a year, and be brought divine offerings, and perhaps be taken on a tour of the realm. Only after it had decayed would the successor be enthroned.[53]

In the areas of kava culture, the preparation and drinking of this sacred beverage made of the root of the kava plant is an important part of the accession. One is reminded of the solemn rice-pounding before the *Daijō-sai*. On Fiji the kava is made during a time of sacred caution before the bathing and enthronement. Women and strangers are excluded from the area around the royal lodge, and a guard is kept. A champion offers his service to the chief. Silence is maintained, as at a death. For a period of four days, kava is pounded in the morning and early evening. Bystanders keep time with the beaters by clapping their hands. The chief drinks on each occasion. Only after this period is celebration released as the chief undergoes the bathing, enthronement, and robing ceremonies as described above on the evening of the fourth day. Later, as he makes his post-accession tour of the land, he is received with ceremonial kava at each village. Kava is always a ceremonial drink, an ambrosia, prepared with ritual on sacred occasions.[54]

VI

LASTLY we shall consider the Altaic kingship pattern. The group of Turkish, Mongol, and Tatar peoples based in Mongolia and southern Siberia who are collectively called Altaic had, presumably

---

[53] ibid. p. 264.
[54] Hocart, pp. 76–7.

through prehistoric immigration, at least as much impact on Japanese culture as southeast Asian societies. According to Ono Susumu, in pre-agricultural Jōmon times (*c.* 4000-250 B.C.) a southern language of Polynesian affinities was widespread in western Japan. About 300 B.C. a new northern language of Altaic character entered Japan along with rice culture, metals, weaving, tumuli, and other marks of Yayoi culture (250 B.C.—A.D. 250) and spread south and east from northern Kyushu. Probably this mixture of northern language and such south-Asian traits as rice cultivation had previously developed in Korea, and came to Japan from there. The northern wave extended from Kyushu as far as Azuma (the region about modern Osaka where a cultural and linguistic barrier long lay) and also to the Ryukyus.[55]

The sorting out of the various constituents of Japanese culture according to extrinsic origin, although attempted by such scholars as Oka Masao,[56] is fraught with technical controversy and is frequently thankless. Above all this might be true in the case of the components of a single rite like the *Daijō-sai*, or a single institution such as kingship. It will suffice now to point out that while the physical organization of the rite—the enclosure, the royal couch, the purificatory bath—reminds one of the South Seas, the food elements—rice and sake—certainly derive from the later cultural invasion, being part of the Yayoi economy.

Oka associated the southern influence with a 'horizontal' mythological cosmology, the northern with a 'vertical'. In the former, gods come in from over the sea, in the latter they descend on mountains and trees from high heaven. The generalization is not entirely valid, for in most of Polynesia the chief god is a variant of Tangaloa, who lives in the skies, and from whom kingship and often the chiefly families are descended. According to a tradition in Samoa, the Tangaloa family of gods came down from heaven to bestow the chiefdom on a newly born boy, and dwelt for a time in a house on earth built especially for their reception.[57] But Altaic religion is more intensely celestial than Polynesian. Usually it centered upon a high god, more than a *deus otiosus*, whose name often means 'Sky' or 'Heaven', like Num of the Samoyed, Tengri of the Mongols, Tangare of the Tatars, Tingir of the Beltir, Tan-

[55] Susumu Ono, 'The Japanese Language: Its Origin and Its Sources', in R. J. Smith and R. I. Beardsley, eds., *Japanese Culture*, pp. 20–1.

[56] His position is summarized in J. M. Kitagawa, 'The Prehistoric Background of Japanese Religion', *History of Religions*, I, No. 1 (Winter 1963).

[57] Williamson, p. 40.

gara of the Yakut, etc.[58] This god has 'sons' or messengers who are
subordinate to him and watch over human beings. The Japanese
myth of the descent of the Imperial Grandson of the High God
appears to derive from this tradition, for it has been traced to
Korea.[59]

It is shamanism, meaning especially the dynamic and ecstatic
ascent and descent of the adept between earth and the heavenly
regions, for which the Siberian peoples are best known among historians of religion. In north Asia this very widespread phenomenon
has been developed to its 'classic' shape. The Siberian shaman,
going into trance with the help of a drum, ascends to heaven to
converse with the high gods, or perhaps descends to the underworld to plead with the lord of the nether regions on behalf of
his people.

The process by which one becomes a shaman varies in detail
from one tribe to another, but will mean a stringent initiation.
Whether his vocation is hereditary or spontaneous, the future
shaman will receive dreams and visions from the supreme god or
the archetypal shaman. He will pass through an ordeal, involving
a mystical death and rebirth experience, and perhaps a magical
flight to the home of the original shaman or the god. Eliade comments that this indicates passage through a psychopathology. Often
during the initiatory sickness the novice is said to be cut in pieces,
dismembered, his bones counted, by the attending gods. But the
candidate who has passed through this ordeal frequently attains
remarkable strength and psychic powers, while his general health
and mental stability and intelligence revert to full normality, if not
superiority, within the terms of the culture.

What is of great significance are parallels between the structure
of shamanism and that of kingship. Jean-Paul Roux, in a recent
article,[60] has provided striking material in support of such a comparison. This is in the form of a series of inscriptions from the
Turuk Empire (A.D. 551-754), found in Outer Mongolia near the
Orkhon River and dated 732 and 735.

In more recent times, with the general decline of Siberian-
Mongolian society into nomadic fragments, political leadership

---

[58] M. Eliade, *Shamanism: Archaic Techniques of Ecstasy*, p. 9. Note that these names are
clearly related linguistically to the name of the Polynesian high god who gives kingship,
Tangaloa. This is discussed by Ōbayashi Taryō, *Nihon shinwa no kigen*, pp. 42–3.
Ōbayashi also connects this root with the Chinese *t'ien* (Heaven) and the name of the
great Polynesian deity Kane with the Altaic word for king, *khan*.
[59] Ōbayashi, p. 216.
[60] Jean-Paul Roux, 'L'Origine céleste de la souveraineté dans les inscriptions paléo-
turques de Mongolie et de Sibérie', *The Sacred Kingship/La Regalità Sacra*, pp. 231–41.

has lost its ideological and ceremonial undergirding. It has apparently been only a more or less informal hegemony of important laymen in a society whose capacity for the sacred, for meaning and power, was largely exhausted by the marvels of shamanism. But the shaman was an agent of healing and revelation, not a political leader *de jure*. Of course this situation was accelerated by the eventual failure of these cultures before Lamaist, Chinese, or Russian dominance.

But in the grand days of Mongolian and Altaic civilization, the days of the Turuk Empire and after it the far greater sway of Genghiz Khan, the structures of kingship and shamanism were not dissimilar. Undoubtedly this background had some part in the development of sacral kingship in Russia, the Ottoman Empire, and China, as well as in Japan. But unfortunately we have very little information, at least in published form, about the myths and rituals of accession and kingship in either classic or more recent stages of Altaic culture. Such scholarly attention as has been devoted to the religion of these people has concentrated on shamanism, cosmology, spiritism, or folklore. Lack of material will prevent us from outlining the kingship myths and scenarios as has been done for the four preceding cultures.

However, Roux lists several conclusions concerning kingship based on the Turuk inscriptions which he studied. These are:

1   The *kagan* or king came from heaven.[61] Genghiz Khan was born of a luminous being who entered the womb of his mother, or of a celestial wolf. We may compare the similar stories of Chinese kings and sages.
2   The king possessed a heavenly mandate given by Tengri, the high god.
3   The king executed the divine will.
4   The cosmic order corresponded to the political order.

One passage is especially significant. The inscription writer refers to the defeat and enslavement of Turuk folk by the Chinese, and says that the Chinese emperor resolved to annihilate them. Roux translates:

Mais en haut le Tängri des türük (*üzä türük tangrisi*) en bas la terre et l'eau sacrée des türük (*asra türük yer sub*) dirent ainsi. Ils dirent: que le peuple türük ne devienne pas rien; qu'il devienne et soit un peuple; et, du haut du ciel, ayant saisi le kagan El Terish,

[61] On this see also Uno Harva, *Les représentations religieuses des peuples altaïques*, pp. 101–2.

mon père, et la katun El Bilgä, ma mère, ils les éleverènt en l'air.

Roux continues to comment:

> Dans ce récit, dont la dernière phrase peu claire ce réfère peut-être au voyage extatique du chaman, il est impossible de décider quel est le rôle de Tängri et quel est celui de la terre et de l'eau. Si nous pensons que le role du Ciel est prépondérant, c'est que nous nous référons à d'autre textes. L'un d'eux particulierement insistant: nous l'ayons tout a l'heure soustrait a l'une de nos citations pour le presenter seul avec son relief: *el berigmä Tängri*='Tängri qui donne l'empire'.[62]

But whatever the exact meaning, it is evident that the sovereignty of El Terish and El Bilga depended in some sense on their possession and elevation into the air by the high god, a phenomenon like the ecstatic voyage of the shaman.[63]

If kingship is given from on high, by celestial messengers, it is not surprising that the commerce should be reaffirmed in this way. As we shall see, the heavenly descent of the first king on clouds and oracles from underground and from sacred water have important echoes in Japan. The Altaic word for shaman, *kam*, probably has affinities with the Japanese word for deity, *kami*.

VII

WE HAVE given five representative patterns of kingship. What general conclusions can be drawn from this very brief and partial survey?

The first is that kingship is given by the gods. Usually the presumptive candidate for kingship is a son of the previous ruler, or at least of a royal house. The essence of kingship, originally

---

[62] Roux, op. cit. p. 236. Talât Tekin, in *A Grammar of Orkhon Turkic* (Bloomington, Indiana University Publications, Uralic and Altaic Series, vol. 69, 1968), p. 265, translates the Orkhon inscription as follows:

> But, the Turkish god above and the Turkish holy earth and water (spirits below) acted in the following way: in order that the Turkish people would not go to ruin and in order that it would be an (independent) nation again, they (i.e., the Turkish god and the holy spirits) held my father, İlteriš Kagan, and my mother, İlbilgä Katun, at the top of heaven and raised them upwards.

We then read that because heaven had granted strength in this way, İlteriš Kagan and his armies were for a time successful.

[63] The first king of Tibet was said to have descended on a rope from heaven, and such access between heaven and earth continued in mythical times. Kings returned to heaven by means of the rope after death, and this rope was represented on their tombs. Eliade, *Shamanism*, pp. 430–1. This relation of kingship and shamanism was doubtless characteristic of much central Asian culture before the weakening of the old shamanism by the rise of the great religions. We may note also that the Ainu of archaic northern Japan, now restricted to Hokkaido, have had chiefs whose wife or sister was a shamaness and who gave oracles in trance on matters of state. The same seems to have been the case in pre-Buddhist Japan, and until much later in Okinawa.

descended from heaven, normally flows through the procreative
process; it is too precious to be given at random. Moreover, the
king would require a special relationship to the royal ancestors,
whose power he must conserve and whom he must worship, Yet,
even in Egypt, primogeniture alone is not the mark of a king. Even
if circumstances modify this qualification, the king will still be a
king if he possess other marks of sure election, such as selection by
the previous monarch. Or other signs may appear in times of dynastic upheaval. It is generally recognized that kingship is under the
power of the gods and subject to their power to dispose of as seems
best to their wisdom. Even if the king serves as vicar of the gods
during his reign, the time between kings is seen as a critical time
when, there being no king, the gods may intervene directly into
the matter at hand, the appearance of a new sovereign. But man,
fearing these interventions, endeavors to make the transition as
smooth and ritualized as possible, hence primogeniture.

This leads to a second observation, that the death of a king puts
society into chaos, if only a ritual chaos. But it is an *occasional*
rather than an annual return to chaos which the institution of
kingship at once creates and seeks to alleviate. Thus, as we have
seen, the institution of kingship creates a sense of history even as
it tries to defy it. Kingship tends to emerge coevally with sedentary
agricultural or island culture. Hunting or nomadic man makes
history by movement; agricultural man, who above all desires the
absence of history and only the seasonal cycle, seeks to stabilize
time through kingship. But this effort leads only to the discovery
of a more radical betrayal by time, a betrayal rooted in human and
societal finitude rather than the vicissitudes of nature. The king
may counteract ritually the infelicities of nature, or reassure man
by trying to; but the king dies, or wars erupt, even when nature
smiles.

Then a larger circle of stability is needed. A third observation
is produced: the king is not dissociated from his ancestors, but his
power is one with theirs. Usually the king assumes office before
the monuments, or the bones, of his royal ancestors. Sometimes
this is connected by religious logic with a death and resurrection
scenario; the process amounts to a deification of the previous king
or, by extension, of the incumbent.

The larger circle of stability is also expressed in a fourth characteristic. There are always solid objects, regalia, in which the
kingly power is concentrated, and which are always held by the
true king. Possession of the regalia, in fact, may be deemed the

decisive mark of the rightful sovereign. Once it has been conferred, by more or less proper means, the man is king; this test supersedes even heredity. In medieval Japan Kitabatake Chikafusa was not amiss in putting the holding of the regalia above ceremonial or political function as the indicator of the true imperial incumbent.

A fifth virtually universal mark of kingly rites is that sacrificial offerings accompany the accession, as though they were sources or conveyors of royal power. Even when self-validating mysticism emerges within certain circles of the spiritual tradition, so long as any connection between king, cultus, and society is upheld, the kingly usages will maintain the older and more exoteric forms, including sacrifice.

Following the accession, one finds always festivity and banqueting, the opening of a new cycle of joy.

Other parts of the accession drama, as Hocart outlined it, seem to be more occasional. Among these is purification. Of the patterns we have examined, it is found in all except China and the Altaic. In China, while lustration is not specifically related to accession rites, it is a normal prerequisite of any sacrifice.[64] Hocart believed lustration, as in India, to be a ritual death and divine rebirth. Always the king enters danger, ritual or actual, in connection with accession. But whether the rebirth is of the king, or of the previous king, or of kingship as an institution, is not clear.

Except in the case of the nomadic Altaic, we see kingship in conjunction with a sedentary and/or agricultural society. The duty of the king is to produce victory and fecundity. This is obvious in the classic examples, the Akitu, the Min, and on Mt T'ai, where the release of animals is evidently a gesture in this direction.

But these rituals are not necessarily part of the accession itself, as they are in the *Daijō-sai*. Hence it is not the ritual of accession alone which makes the king. Rather, that ritual prepares him for even greater and perhaps more precarious responsibilities. Kingship is not completed until the great annual rituals have been performed. And then there will typically be a great ceremony, a peak rite, which comes several years after the accession. The years leading up to it will be years of the testing of the virtue and stability of the king.

It is therefore not the accession rite alone which makes the king. Often, in fact, that rite pales to a rather juridical point. Its very juridical nature—the passing of the regalia—affirms the human,

---

[64] Legge, *Li Ki*, I, p. 214.

societal, historical nature of formal succession. The plenary scope
of kingship is as yet only foreshadowed. Yet its importance as the
point of meeting between cyclical nature and history must not be
minimized. For with the increase of historical awareness it is just
this point, often augmented by the assimilation of an especially
grand form of a regular rite, which in time develops to become
almost the full statement of kingship. So the great coronation rites
of Europe, set into the Mass; so the *Daijō-sai* of Japan, a special
form of the Harvest First-fruits. The *Daijō-sai*, coming perhaps a
year or two after the first juridical passing of the regalia, has had
something of the character of both accession and culminative rite;
but as with the Western coronations and all civilized rites, the
meaning and power have tended more and more to be conflated
into accession. As this happens, monarchy achieves a new stability;
it becomes increasingly unlikely that vicissitudes of nature, or even
of politics, will subsequently unseat the king.

We must now move on to a fuller study of the Japanese *Daijō-sai*
rite, beginning with its mythological and archaic background. We
may have noticed that all the rites presented above have their own
atmosphere, yet all have features reminiscent of each other. Frankfort's distinction between the king as god, and the king as mediatorial representative of the god, in the cases of Egypt and Babylon,
is well taken. A similar comparison could be made between China
and Japan. In both the Near and Far East this distinction has been
historically consequential.[65] Yet one may also note that the ritual
pattern, both juridical and religious, does not always vary markedly
between the two ideologies on any predictable lines. Other pheno-
menological classifications could be made among kingship rites
which would cut across this ideological distinction; e.g. concerning
the role of the queen, of purification, of shamanistic elements.
Rather, all the rites, as rites, are like a circle of mirrors, each
reflecting the others in part. So the *Daijō-sai* offers elements common to one or more, and as well its own unique flavor.

---

[65] Kingship in India suggests still a third way of rationalizing the way in which the king
is believed to be divine. The Hindu king was not himself one with the great god, as in
Egypt, nor a Son of Heaven or vicarial agent of the gods, but a *deva*—one of a class of
powerful beings controlling departments of nature or of human affairs. He was Indra,
Prajāpati, or Kṣatriya, but not one of the soteriological deities in their aspect of giving
mokṣa, or liberation (Gonda, p. 24). Thus the king is divine, but on the level of *dharma*,
or the order of this world. He is the upholder of *dharma*. On this plane he is responsible
for everything that happens in his realm. The *Mahābhārata* says, 'As is the king so is his
people.' If he is good, it is a general blessing; if bad, a disaster. An evil king will bring
drought, hunger, disease, famine. Above all he is responsible for rainfall. Under a bad
king, cows will not give milk (ibid. p. 7). The king's throne is treated as an altar or seat
of the gods, and his palace a temple. With the effusion typical of India, the king is given
honors typical of divinity. He is accompanied by music and banners, and for him, as for a
deity in procession, triumphal arches are built (ibid. pp. 45, 56).

CHAPTER II

Myths and Early Shinto

I INFORMATION ABOUT EARLY SHINTO

WE SHALL now endeavor in the next two chapters to trace the development of Shinto religious life—its shrines, structural organization, forms of worship, mythology and practice—from the earliest times to the situation reflected in our primary document, the *Engi-shiki*, with a view to determining against what background the *Daijō-sai* emerged. Because the *Engi-shiki* presents a religious world centered around two poles, the Imperial Court and the Grand Shrine of Ise, we will give special attention to the emergence of these two institutions.

Shinto, for all its apparent simplicity, is a religious system to which an extremely complex mixture of influences has contributed. In the Shinto of today may be found traces of virtually every culture area contingent to Japan, and some further away, as well as the crystallized essences of virtually every century of Japanese history. In the richness and variety of its origins, and the uniqueness of the religious vision it has finally come to present, Shinto excellently reflects the genius of the Japanese people for combining assimilation with preservation of the past and conservation of the special spirit of the culture.

This process begins in the remotest antiquity, for in Japan as elsewhere there has been no known culture entirely indigenous and isolated. The Japanese mind, despite periods of nationalist reaction, has been capable of giving recognition to the significance of this fact, both in ancient and modern times. The national mythology, for example, in contrast to that of China, does not presuppose continuous and isolated habitation of the same land by the same people from the time of creation. It is instead full of explicit and implicit references to immigration, contact between various cultural traditions, and conquest. In fact, over against the definitive writings of other Oriental religions, whether Buddhism, Confucianism, Taoism, or Hinduism, the *Kojiki* and *Nihon-shoki* possess a sense of historical teleology, of myth as expression of the divine will working in history and in a time continuous with the present, which is almost Biblical. The two major chronicles, especially in that their pivotal recitation is the quite human conquest of the land under divine mandate by the first emperor, Jimmu, but also in the whole concept of articulating the religious world-view through the medium of historical chronicle, represent cosmos and society to be *emerging* rather than static entities. The *Kojiki*, *Nihon-shoki*, and *Kogoshūi* all recognize this historical-situation point of view. The *Engi-shiki*, by assuming the intimate relation of the Shinto religion to the Court and dynasty which has derived from such a history, implies history, although like the Law Of Moses it presupposes no future change. Historicism, of course, would be most insistent at times of radical cultural confrontation and social change and national formation, such as seventh- and eighth-century Japan, but none the less other cultures have undergone similar experiences without achieving quite such a historical mode of self-interpretation. In Japan, under Buddhist and Confucian influence, it was soon enough diminished.

But, therefore, although from *our* point of view it would be necessary to deal with the 'historical background' of the *Engi-shiki* in order to exegete its contents, since the importance of such historical background is assumed by the world-view upon which modern scholarship depends, we may bear in mind that for the lettered Shintoist of our period it was also crucial. It was important for those of predisposition toward official Shinto matters in a way it was not for the Buddhists, for the former were naturally concerned for the conserving of the past over against Buddhism. Moreover, the Buddhists in any case adhered to an anti-historical cosmic view. To them, although social order may be of no small temporal consequence to the advancement of the Three Treasures, ultimately, seen in the light of eternity, courts and dynasties and nations were of transitory significance, and salvation is *out* of a world of such concerns. That world is cyclical, a mode of karmic action and reaction, passing away like morning dew.

Against this view the *Kojiki* and *Nihon-shoki* are in conscious protest. They affirm that instead history is a linear working out of divine will; that discrete, irreversible events of history such as the foundation of the Empire at Kashiwahara or the conquest of Korea are important for all times because they reveal the source of cosmic and social authority and the end for which man was created, the service of the *kami* and the pacification of the land under an authorized sovereign. The implications of the expression of this thesis by means of writing history are much greater than mere dynastic apology.

Concerning the life of Japan before the historical period, three very different sources of information exist. One is the archaeo-# / logical remains, relics of houses and tombs with their works of art, which give us insight into the material culture and the externalization of the spiritual culture. The second is the writings of the #2 Chinese who visited Japan in the early centuries of our era and left brief but provocative descriptions of the land and its customs. The third is the earliest writings of Japanese which purport to # 3 record the histories of the divine land, dating from the eighth century but clearly containing much old material, material deriving from the same world as the tombs and Chinese visitors. These writings ought to provide an interior view of the spiritual history of the period.

The interpretation of all three sources is laden with many problems. It is not always easy to reconcile the indications of each to the others. Archaeology presents us with an overwhelming impression of vast tombs full of clay retainers and grave goods of the great, as though this were a land as dedicated to the departed as Egypt; but the mythologies give often only the most perfunctory reference to burials, and suggest that dynamic functions of deity toward the living, in mediumship, war, harvest, and succession, were far more important. In any case, in studying Shinto worship, one must give first attention to the mythological-historical sources, or to the living traditions of shrines, since early worship did not depend on monumental sites; and virtually nothing in the way of cult places and objects has survived the moist and fickle climate of Japan. The tombs give their testimony to the world-view; the spears, bells, mirrors, and swords tell their often enigmatic stories; but these do not refer to worship in the strictest sense, as far as we know, but to general spiritual or magical beliefs. Nor do they give much of a clue as to mythical or theological beliefs.

For all this we must turn to the early writings. The most important of these are the *Kojiki, Nihon-shoki, Kogoshūi,* and the several *fudoki*. The *Kojiki*, the preeminent classic among this kind of writing, was written at the order of the Emperor Temmu and completed, after considerable revision, in 708. It is said to depend on an oral tradition. Although no doubt unadulterated antiquity has been sacrificed to conflation of sources, charm of verse, and above all the univocal exaltation of the Yamato imperial house, some of the most fundamentally important ancient material also appears here.

The *Nihon-shoki* is the second major historical source, completed in 720. It is much longer than the *Kojiki*, presenting much the same material (with the significant exception of the Ōkuninushi cycle and certain other regional myths). But the *Nihon-shoki* also presents many valuable variants of a number of the myths, and is far fuller in the 'historical' (i.e. post-Jimmu) sections. The earlier history is mostly fabricated out of Chinese precedents, or from Japanese myths and stories, but of course becomes increasingly reliable as more recent years are approached.

The *Kogoshūi* is a book written in 807 by Imbe no Hironari (an advocate of the Imbe of whom little else is known). It was written to defend ancient prerogatives of the Imbe priestly house which had allegedly fallen into disuse, mainly because of the rise of the Nakatomi to supremacy on the fortunes of the Fujiwara, and also perhaps because changing social institutions had rendered certain of them obsolete. But the author is determined to press his case, hopeless as it was, and in so doing describes many ancient ritual usages, myths, and traditions not preserved elsewhere. Of particular interest is the variant of the Amaterasu myth, the myth of Mitoshi connected with the *Toshigoi*, or Court Spring rite, and the account of the role of the Imbe in the *Daijō-sai* and the Ise Rebuilding Rite.

Finally there are the *fudoki*, a series of collections of regional myths and descriptions authorized in the Nara period. Although these vary from the extremely ancient to the obviously recent and contrived, many are of inestimable value, particularly in presenting variants of *Kojiki* and *Nihon-shoki* themes not turned in their particular ideological direction. The *fudoki* naturally tend to present the truly popular or local rather than the Court account of things. On the other hand, some of the material is difficult to assess, and some is as touched with literary flourishes as any of the Court mythology.

These are the four major sources for early mythology. There are of course other sources too, particularly the traditions and ancient books of shrines and folklore in general. These sources must all be evaluated very carefully. Few produce material which is actually much older than the above, but there is much of value in supporting the patterns which appear. In addition, early literary sources like the *Man'yōshū* are rich in allusions which help in understanding myth and ritual of the Nara period and before. One should also mention liturgical sources themselves, such as the *norito* and *yogoto*, since ritual is necessary to the full understanding of early myth.

The archaeological remains are above all the great burial tumuli of the Kofun period (A.D. 250-550). The grave goods, consisting of combs, swords, knives, bows, beads, mirrors, and clothes are items which show up again in the *Engi-shiki* as typical imperial offerings, or which serve as regalia. But by and large the archaeological remains, including the famous *haniwa* human figures and the interior tomb paintings,[1] indicate little that relates directly to prehistoric worship or the history of the gods, since there are no temples or statues of deities.

This is not surprising, for we learn from the mythologies that the *kami* did not demand such edifices, but only a cleared space in the wood by a stream, or at best a new temporary house for the harvest festival. The *kami* were thought of as essentially active, changing their location or mode of work with the seasons or the fortunes of the tribe. They could not be permanently trapped in a temple made by human hands, but could only be recognized where they were, and in their relation to the lineage of the tribe.

II   THE BASIC CONTENT OF THE MYTHS

A MYTH from the *Ise fudoki* (a work not in the same class as the early *fudoki* mentioned above) regarding the antecedents of the priestly Watarai house admirably displays virtually all the elements of the early myth and cultus. So beautifully is this done, in fact, that one feels this particular version is a rather late and self-conscious literary effort, but none the less, or for this reason, it is very instructive.

According to this story, the name of the town Yamada, near the Grand Shrine, was originally Watarai, which literally means 'crossing-meeting'. This was because, the myth says, Emperor Jimmu sent an envoy named Ame-no-hiwaki (heaven-fire or heaven-sun envoy) to Ise. An Ōkunitama, or land-spirit, made a

---

[1] Concerning the tomb paintings, see Kobayashi Yukio, *Sōshoku kofun*. In some cases, the boats will be long and narrow, high-prowed, and full of stick figures, but with no visible means of propulsion. Often a brilliant and many-rayed sun will loom over the scene. It seems to me there is an oddly Egyptian note about such paintings, although a Japanese scholar to whom I commented this said that, instead, the treatment of the sun reminded him of American Indian art! However, Ōbayashi, *Nihon shinwa no kigen*, pp. 204–5, shows parallels between these paintings and soul-ship representations of Indonesia and Polynesia. He notes that birds are also associated with the figures, and believes the spirits are Sukuna-hikona, the immortal soul. Thus the pictures are related to old Japanese ideas of the *torii* (literally, 'bird-roost', the characteristic gate to the Shinto shrine) and the *hagoromo*, the feather-robe worn by descending heavenly *kami* in several myths and by the emperor in the *Daijō-sai*.

bridge of an *azusa* bow, and Ame-no-hiwaki *crossed* (*wataru*) and *met* (*ai*) the daughter of the Ōkunitama, whom he married. According to the later *Yamatohime-no-mikoto seiki*, their child started the Watarai line of priests at the *gekū*, the outer shrine at Ise.[2]

Thus the fundamental concept of this mythology is that a heavenly male deity, connected with fire or the sun or both (probably fire is seen as a *bunrei* or terrestrial offspring of the sun)[3] comes to earth. There he overcomes a difficulty, marries the daughter of a land *kami*, and produces a sovereign or priestly line. This motif is repeated over and over again, in various guises, both in and out of the *Kojiki* and *Nihon-shoki*. It is, as we shall see, implicit in the *Daijō-sai*. We will give examples later, such as the descent to the undersea world of Hiko-hoho-demi (whose name also suggests fire), the place of fire in the Izumo priestly succession, and the descent and return (after fathering Tamayorihime) of Kamo-no-taketsunumi, the ancestor of the Kamo family.

Myths of this type came to have agricultural application. In the mythology, they are often put in conjunction with the harvest festival. The daughter of the earth *kami* becomes the earth mother or corn-maiden; the child, the new harvest. This is the basic theme of the *Niiname*, the central festival of all Shinto. But when the *Niiname* becomes the *Daijō-sai*, the meaning expands to include succession. Thus it is easy to see that the myth has roots in pre-agricultural society, for its fundamental imagery is non-agricultural. The high god who sends down the descending *kami* is Takami-musubi, the last part of whose name means 'to tie' or, according to one theory, 'to give birth'.[4] Fire is the fundamental symbol of succession, it appears, and is a pre-agricultural symbol. One feels the *Niiname* may have been a New Year's rite of the renewal of tribal succession and spirit pacification with a new fire, as at Izumo, before it was a harvest festival. Such elements in the myths would not be surprising since agriculture was only a few centuries old in Japan at the time the myths were written down.

Thus the fundamental interest of the mythology and rites in family and succession must not be forgotten. Shinto is not basically rites of productivity in the fields, much less the 'nature-worship' of earlier commentators. While such secondary meanings, rightly interpreted, may not be excluded, it is essential to understand that

---

[2] This myth is given and discussed in Ōnishi Gen'ichi, *Sangū no konjaku*, p. 200.

[3] Sasatani Ryōzō, *Kamigami no sekai*, p. 18.

[4] ibid. p. 3. *Musubi* is clearly related to the verb *musubu*, to tie. Sasatani also connects its root with *umu*, to give birth, a relation perhaps preserved in *musume*, daughter.

the fundamental thrust of Shinto, ancient and modern, is sociological. That is, it is concerned with the life of social groups, from hamlet to nation, and their collective symbols and sources of power. If the *kami* bless agricultural or economic activity, it is because it is a part of the life of the people to whom that *kami* is related. Even today, Shinto worshipers are usually disinclined to offer more than perfunctory worship at shrines other than their own, except those recognized as of national significance, and hence 'theirs' in a broader sense. This shows that, despite the fact that many shrines are at places of great natural beauty or before dramatic natural phenomena, Shinto is not at all a generalized worship of the numinous in nature. Rather, while such sites may have been chosen in part because their awesomeness suggested divine activity, they were chosen by groups such as *uji*, the ancient clans, as places for the worship of their patronal *kami*. Most shrines are originally of this character.

The clan *kami* is called the *ujigami*. At the time of the writing of the *Kojiki* and *Nihon-shoki*, the *ujigami* was not thought of as ancestral. Thus the clan *kami* of ancient Yamato was apparently Ōnamuchi of Miwa, although the ruling family was said to have been descended from the heavenly *kami* through the Emperor Jimmu. The principal deity of the Nakatomi clan *kami* shrine, Kasuga, was brought for some reason from Kashima, although they were descended from Ame-no-koyane. The clan *kami* shrine of the Mononobe, Isonokami, was dedicated to Futsu-no-mitama although the clan was descended from Nigihayahi-no-mikoto. However, in the Nara period or after, the ancestral *kami* were also added to these shrines and the ancestral idea became more important.

In the earliest period there were no shrine buildings. Probably the clan *kami* was worshiped at a *shiki* or field spread with white stones set outside the community. It would be across a stream, and the crossing would be an act of purification. It would probably be on high ground, even far up a mountain. Such a *shiki*, still used, can be seen at Munakata Shrine in Kyushu. The *shiki* would be marked off by the emblems of a sacred place, evergreen branches (*sakaki*) or strips of white cloth. In the center of it there might be a sacred tree, *himorogi*, perhaps with branches lopped and bound with rope like the *miare* pillar of upper Kamo. It too would be marked with symbols of purity.

Thus the worship of Shinto was spatial, centering upon a controlled space, like the field of the *Daijō-sai*. There was of course also a temporal orientation, a festival cycle. Apart from the New Year's renewal, it is not easy to ascertain what this was before agricultural times. Historically, it has fallen into a basic cycle of spring planting prayers, summer intercession against disaster, harvest (into which the *Daijō-sai* fits), and a subsidiary cycle based on lunar phases.

The modern Shinto festival, or *matsuri,* has four basic parts: purification with washing and waving the *sakaki,* presentation of offerings, prayer, or *norito,* and participation in the spirit of the present deity with eating and celebration—dancing, procession. The same general pattern obtains in the earliest extant sources and there is no reason to think the prehistoric pattern was much different. Thus probably the ancient *shiki* was first swept and ornamented with branches, the participants wading the stream and bathing to reach it. Then offerings of food and branches (*tamagushi*) were set up within it, prayer was chanted to the awakened *kami,* and feasting and celebration in the sacred area followed.

It has been suggested that the possession of mediums (*miko*) by the *kami* was a part of prehistoric worship, even taking the place now held by the *norito.*[5] Certainly shamanism was a more important part of ancient Shinto than of Shinto today. The worship was officially conducted and the offerings were made by the clan chieftain, but *miko* who were 'married' to the deity seem to have been attached to important places of worship, even those deep in the mountains as well as those in the palaces, and gave oracles. However, it is not clear whether such oracles were a regular part of all worship, or were resorted to mainly outside of the regular festival calendar when required by circumstances, or when special portents were given. One is inclined to feel the shamanistic element of religion is never entirely merged with the liturgical, and probably moved sometimes within but largely outside it in ancient Japan as elsewhere.[6]

There were many variations of the basic myth and pattern of

---

[5] Kaneko Takeo, *Engi-shiki norito-kō.*

[6] Oracles from shamans could still be important in the historical period for determining official religious developments within Shinto, such as the famous oracles of Usa which led to the bringing of Hachiman to the Tōdaiji temple, and to the scandals connected with the empress and the Buddhist priest Dōkyō in the Nara period. In the Heian period the Court propitiation of the spirit of Sugiwara Michizane, a gesture which led to the founding of the Kitano shrine in Kyoto and the Temmangū family of shrines, was begun because of oracular revelations by a medium. See the article by Prof. Hori, 'Hito-tsu-mono'. In the article, Hori asserts that the word *matsuri* is probably derived from *matsu,* 'to wait', that is, waiting upon the descent of the possessing *kami.* This *matsu* sounds the same as the word for pine-tree, which, he believes, may have a connection with the symbolic importance of these trees in the traditions of shrines such as Sumiyoshi in Osaka.

worship. Probably the succession rites and New Year's renewal were held in or near the residence of the sovereign rather than at the *shiki*.

The introduction of agriculture must have required far-reaching modifications of primitive Shinto. It was now not enough that the divine power be only in the pure place in the wood, or dwelling with the sovereign, but it also was seen to dwell in the field, and must be made to dwell there. The *kami* must be brought down from the mountains to the fields in the spring (or else be met as he comes in his own sovereign power) and implanted amid the crops. Hence there are rites, which at least early acquired agricultural meaning, of going to the mountain place in the early spring and in some way bringing its power—perhaps as metal or fire—into the fields. The deity then labors divinely in the fields all summer. At harvest time, what may have been the first shrine, a *yashiro*, or temporary house, was erected in the fields. Here the deity was housed, and it was like a parturition hut in which the harvest-child was brought forth, just as if he were a successor to sovereignty. This house, modeled after the early granary, was the harvest lodge of the deity who otherwise dwelt at his high *shiki* (or else the *shiki* of his mate); he moved to and from it with the grain and with ceremony, the flavor of which is preserved in part of the *Daijō-sai*.

The clan *kami* of the *shiki*, however, did not exhaust the experience of deity. Even in pre-agricultural times, there was doubtless also a high-god idea, personified by one like Takami-musubi, or the Tengare or Tangaloa of Siberia or Polynesia, who might send down envoys and possess powers beyond what adhered to the familiar clan *kami*. Moreover, the clan *kami* might be served by a shamaness or *miko* whose office was half divinized, judging by the frequency of divine names suggesting this position. Even before agriculture, the three basic persons of the myth seem to be represented—the male envoy of high heaven, the spirit of the tribe or land (clan *kami*), and his daughter (*miko*), who marries the first to renew sovereignty and power. In some cases the land deity was herself female and directly mated with the sky deity.

It was not difficult to adapt the myth to agriculture, although there are still incongruous elements in the names and stories of rice-field maidens hinting at a mountain or marine shamaness background. In either case, there was a sense that the act of creativity required a union of the local and the alien; the regional maiden and, following the usage of matrilocalism, the god from afar off who visited her. Before the union was accomplished, a hindrance of some kind, like the broken bridge or the dragon Susano-o slew, must be overcome, either by the visitor or the father of the bride. The successful consummation of the union amounts to a test of the genuineness of both partners.

There are then two kinds of *kami* basically, the local and the visiting. This would correspond in principle to the ancient twofold division into *amatsu kami* and *kunitsu kami* (heavenly and earthly *kami*) and also with Prof. Hori's more recent distinction between *hitogami* and *ujigami*. The latter are the stable patronal *kami* of the clan who are always in its area. The former are the more man-like, because more mobile and spontaneous, *kami* who come as visitors mysterious and creative to possess mediums, consecrate the harvest and new year, or in a more terrible aspect to work vengeance. They come from far away, heaven or *tokoyo*, the other world, and are assimilated to returning spirits of the departed, the free and immortal aspect of the human soul (Sukuna-hikona), and also to the active, militant principle in human and divine psychology which is the grace of warriors and rulers as well as the power of working nature, the *ara-mitama*.

The clan *kami* is generally celebrated twice a year, spring and fall, but the great festival, the *Niiname* or *Daijō-sai* with its harvest and new year overtones, is really an occasion of the meeting of both, and the consummation of the marriage. We shall look at the *Niiname* in more detail in a moment.

It appears that this division of ancient *kami* into visiting and local deities is the most pertinent. Other kinds of distinction are less meaningful. Oka's distinction between vertical and horizontal cosmologies, for example, does not seem to be fundamental, for both in myth and cultus, as at Ise and Kumano, both descending *kami* and *kami* who come in from out at sea and return, coexist. The important thing is that like the two brothers of the *Kojiki*, Hiko-hoho-demi and Hoderi, one with 'mountain-luck' and one with 'sea-luck', they are both bearers of *sachi*, 'luck', from the Other World. Moreover, the more one studies the mythologies, the more it appears that all the important themes are really represented in the stories as we have them from all the major ancient areas, Kyushu, Izumo, Yamato, Ise. Not too much of more than specialist interest can be made of regional variations, compared to the fundamental unity of the mythical pattern and the cultus that goes with it.

Of course the position of the *kami* may change. Very many of those who are now local shrine deities or clan *kami* began, according to the stories, as active visiting *kami* of another place who, after completing their work subduing the land or defeating enemies in mythical time, settled down in one place to protect it. Often this was accomplished by marriage to the local maiden, by which they acceded to the place of land *kami*, as well as being *kami* of the Other World, through the matrilocal principle. In other cases, as with the triadic Munakata and Sumiyoshi *kami*, a single mighty act seems to exhaust their active, *ara-mitama* spirit, and causes them to fall into a more passive and benign role.

However, it is usually most helpful to think of the *kami* in terms of their most notable role. Thereby they can be classified on the basis of the mythical structure. These types appear in all the fundamental myths regardless of the cosmological or regional particulars.

Among the heavenly *kami*, there are two kinds: first, the 'high god' type of Takami-musubi and the other, more shadowy 'musubi' *kami*, who do not themselves descend to earth but send the descending *kami*, often sons of Takami-musubi, down as envoys; second, the descending *kami*—Susano-o, Ninigi, Ame-waka-hiko, Hiko-hoho-demi, Ame-no-hiwaki, etc.

Next, there are the land *kami*. Ōnamuchi, Ōkunitama, Tenazuchi, and those whose daughters Ōkuninushi married, and whom the Emperor Jimmu met, are male *kami* who play this role in many myths. The clan *kami* is either such a land *kami* or a heavenly *kami* who has acceded to the role of land *kami*. The earth maiden, like Toyouke, Inada-hime,[7] and the many '*hime-gami*' (consort *kami*), is either herself the earth-deity or his daughter. The male earth *kami*, like Ōnamuchi or Chimata or the later Kōshin and Daikoku,[8] may have a potent and phallic sexuality which fructifies the fields, but there is a permeating rather than dynamic quality to it, and the offspring does not have special individual importance, or right of sovereignty (whch is a gift of heaven).

This brings us to the last major type, the child of the union.

---

[7] One wonders whether the element *ina* in such divine names as Inadahime, Inari, etc., certainly the same as *ine*, 'rice-plant', may not be connected with the Polynesian 'Hina' (variants: 'Hine', 'Ina'), a word meaning by itself pale white light such as that of the moon, or 'falling, declining', or, in composites, 'woman', as in *wahine*, and in the name of Hina, the great mythological mother and maiden, who was mother of the hero Maui. If so, we would see an interesting example of the adaptation of the same myth to very different conditions of agriculture. For an intriguing philosophical discussion of the Hina-Maui myth, with lexicographical references, see S. Langer, *Philosophy in a New Key*, pp. 150–8. She emphasizes that Hina is a personification of the moon.

[8] Kōshin 庚申 and Daikoku 大黒 are imported medieval and modern folk-religion deities, described in Yanagida Kunio, *Minzokugaku jiten*, and in the *Shintō daijiten*.

He has power to go between heaven, earth, and the underworld, and to die and return to life, and is archetype of the King. He himself also succeeds to the role of descending heavenly *kami*, marrying daughters of the land to beget new heirs. Examples are Ōkuninushi, the most developed in the *Kojiki*, Mitoshi, the emperors, and of course Susano-o, Ninigi, and Hiko-hoho-demi in their capacity as children of heaven and earth.

There are many combinations of these types, particularly in Shinto as it has developed in historical times. Inari, whose shrines are everywhere, appears to be a union of the male land *kami* and the female earth maiden and mother, the principal deity of the Inari pantheon being allegedly Ukemochi (Toyouke), but sometimes represented as an old man with a sheaf of grain and possessed of earth-animal messengers. The very numerous Hachiman and Hikawa groups stemming from Kyushu and Izumo respectively offer triads of *kami* who usually, in one combination or another, represent the whole of the myth—heavenly male, earthly *hime-gami* consort and mother, marvelous child. Generally (in Hachiman) the roles are played by the legendary sovereigns Ōjin, Empress Jingū, Chūai, or Nintoku. To worship at these shrines, which represent almost half the total number today, is thus to reverence the whole of the basic myth symbolically presented. Other *kami*, like Saruta-hiko, have ambivalent histories.

The major festival in Shinto since the introduction of agriculture—both court and popular, archaic and historic—is the harvest festival, the *Niiname*. All the other fundamental institutions of Shinto, including its connection with the sovereign and the state, revolve around the *Niiname* just as the Christian calendar revolves around Easter.

The *Niiname* is basically a marriage feast—a celebration of the union of two forces, conceived of as male and female, to produce the harvest and renew the cosmos and with it the state. Several divergent themes combine to create the fulness of the festival, of course, but in both the mythology and the most archaic ritual forms the concept of the marriage of heaven and earth dominates the rest. Heaven is male, the earth is female; at harvest time the male descends to the earth, and for their nuptials a new house and banquet are provided at night, and singing and dancing take place. Of the union a child may be born who is perhaps the harvest itself or perhaps the king or future king. The first lines of the *Nihonshoki*, and of the preface to the *Kojiki*, telling us that in the beginning the *yin* and *yang* had not yet been separated and the distinction between Heaven and Earth had not yet appeared, certainly derives from Chinese philosophy, but the view of cosmic dynamics which underlies it was by no means alien to ancient Japan.

The myths and mythical elements which are related to the *Niiname* provide a basic scenario which interprets the rite. As we have indicated, four roles recur in the myths: the fecundating heavenly male *kami*; a 'disruptive' force which attempts to destroy the union but is finally repelled; the female earth *kami*; and the child of the union who in time may become a hero, ruler, or clan ancestor, and who may have affinities with heaven, earth, and underworld.[9]

III   THE NAKATOMI NO YOGOTO

IN THE *Daijō-sai*, the ancient *yogoto*, or words delivered to the new emperor by the Nakatomi priest, contain mythical allusions which vividly reinforce this kind of world-view in the case of our topic, especially as imperial motifs unite with the fecundative.

The rites of the next morning are of almost equal importance in sealing the legitimacy of succession as the nocturnal offering. On this occasion, in the Heian period members of the two major Shinto priestly houses of ancient Japan, the Nakatomi and Imbe, would each perform a traditional function of the greatest symbolic weight. The Nakatomi priests, whose family was ancestral to the all-powerful Fujiwara, and who in Heian Japan were in control of the Ministry of Official Shinto, usually read the *norito*, or prayer, in the Shinto rites of the Court and here read the *yogoto*. Then a member of the Imbe, a priestly house which shared the Ministry of Official Shinto though in subordinate position, and which customarily was responsible for the presentation of the tangible offerings in rites, gave the sovereign the Imperial Regalia, the mirror and sword. In the words of the *Engi-shiki*, the Court Ritual of A.D. 927:

> In the 2nd quarter-hour of the dragon, the Imperial carriage approaches the Buraku-in and the Sovereign progresses to the *yuki* curtain. The disposition of the various guards is as for ordinary ceremonies. The Heir Apparent enters from the gate on the northeast side. (From Imperial Princes on down, their highnesses wait until ranks have been conferred and then enter.) Those of 5th Rank and above enter through the south gate and each goes to the posting-

---

[9] These matters, and especially the concept of the 'disrupter', are discussed more fully by Ono Sokyō in his 'Nihon shinwa to Niiname no Matsuri', *Shintōgaku*, No. 8 (August 1956), pp. 31–41.

board. Those of 6th Rank and below make their entrance in double
file. They stand in their places and the *Jingi-kan* Nakatomi bear
the *sakaki* branches and carry batons. They enter through the south
gate and go to the posting-board. They kneel and recite the congratulatory words to the deities of heaven. The Imbe now enter and
present the items of divine regalia: the sacred mirror and the sacred
sword. When that is done they withdraw. (If rainy or wet, they may
present them while standing.)   (53; *1274*)

This then is the situation at which the *yogoto* was recited. A
translation of the formula which was used for the *Daijō-sai* of the
Emperor Konoe in the first year of Kōji (1142), virtually the only
text which has survived, follows:[10]

> In the presence of the Emperor, the Root of Great Yamato,[11] who
> sustains this many-island nation as manifest deity, I am honored to
> recite the Blessing of the Heavenly Kami.[12]
> By command of the imperial ancestral *kami* male and female who
> have their session in the High Plain of Heaven, the eightfold myriads
> of *kami* were assembled together. They were instructed: 'The Im-
> perial Grandson,[13] leaving the High Plain of Heaven,[14] is serenely
> to rule the land of fruitful lush plains[15] and marvellous grain to
> make it a peaceable land, and to reign in the highest heavenly seat
> of the heavenly succession,[16] and serenely and peacefully[17] to partake

[10] This translation is made from the text presented with extensive commentary in
Tsugita Uruu, *Norito shinkō*, pp. 531–57. The translation is offered with some diffidence
since a version by the master translator Donald L. Philippi appears in his *Norito: A New
Translation of the Ancient Japanese Ritual Prayers*, pp. 76–9. Philippi's rendering and his
succinct notes originally drew my attention to the importance of this text. However, as an
aid to study I have devised an alternative, inspired partially by the above translation, but
also embodying personal preferences and an interest in pointing to certain problems and
possibilities. For the *Engi-shiki* equivalent, see Bock, p. 92 and n. 418.

[11] This title, Ō-Yamato-neko, is an ancient imperial epithet, occurring in the names of
three legendary sovereigns in the *Kojiki* and *Nihon-shoki*. It is used as a title rather than
a name by the emperor in the promulgation of the Taika Reforms (A.D. 645); W. G. Aston,
Nihongi, II, p. 210. Yamato is the ancient name for Japan, or rather that central part of it
around Kyoto which was the seat of the ancient imperial state.

[12] *Ama-tsu kami no yogoto*. This expression is as common as *Nakatomi no yogoto* for the
title of the piece, and perhaps to be preferred since it is evidently more ancient.

[13] This expression refers to Ama-tsu-hiko-hiko-ho no Ninigi no Mikoto, said in the
Nihon-shoki and *Kojiki* to be son of the son of Amaterasu and the daughter of the high
god Takami-musubi. He was sent down by these two to establish sovereignty on the earth,
together with the primal ancestors of the major families such as the Nakatomi, Imbe,
Ōtomo, Mononobe, and Sarume, who proudly served as his attendants.

[14] This is a stock epithet in the mythology and liturgical formulae for the celestial world
of the *kami*.

[15] This is a corresponding stock phrase for the earth, specifically Japan. Although commonly translated 'Reed-Plains', it seems that the term *ashi* is here more adjectival than
nominal, and referring as it does to the kind of fast-growing vegetation which shoots up
along the banks of streams, may be intended to symbolize more a quality of luxuriance
than of swampiness.

[16] This term, *ama-tsu-hitsugi*, would literally mean 'heavenly sun-succession', but as
Philippi (citing Kaneko, pp. 403–7) points out, the terms *ama-tsu* and *hi* are mere formal
modifiers having no essential relation to *tsugi*, 'lineage' (p. 88). The word *hitsugi* is used
simply for succession as far back as the *Nihon-shoki*, as in *hitsugi no miko*, 'crown prince'.
In any case, it is quite possible that the *hi* originally referred more to fire than to the sun.

in the Sacred Court[18] of the marvellous grain as heavenly, everlasting, eternal oblations, for a thousand or five hundred autumns.'

After the heavenly descent, the primal ancestor of the Nakatomi, Ame-no-koyane, who served before the Imperial Grandson, sent [his son] Ame-no-oshikumone up to the two peaks of heaven to speak before the imperial ancestral *kami* male and female. He [Ame-no-koyane] said, 'Ask them to add heavenly water to the water of the visible world for the offerings of the Imperial Grandson.' In accordance with this instruction, Ame-no-oshikumone rode on a floating cloud, and climbed up the two peaks of heaven. When he spoke before the imperial ancestral *kami* male and female, they presented him with a heavenly *tamagushi*,[19] saying, 'Stand up this *tamagushi*

Succession among the *kuni no miyatsuko* of Izumo was referred to by the same term, and was symbolized by the passing on of a sacred fire-drill. Words for fire (*ho, hi*) occur with great frequency in the names of the divine bearers of sovereignty, including Ninigi. See Shibata Minoru, *Chūsei shomin shinkō no kenkyū*, p. 40. But fire was also considered a *bunrei*, or spirit separated from the sun.

[17] The characters of these two adverbs could be read together as Heian, the name of the ancient capital.

[18] That is, the sacred space set apart for the *Daijō-sai* rites.

[19] This word presents a couple of possibilities, as Tsugita indicates (op. cit. pp. 537–8).

1) The characters used in the *yogoto* would literally mean 'jeweled comb', and that is how Philippi translates it. In this case it would presumably mean a comb having some ritual significance. Combs do have mythological importance. Susano-o turned Inadahime (or Kushi-inada-hime) into a comb when saving her from the monster, and stuck it in his hair. Earlier, Izanagi, when he had descended to the underworld to see his wife, broke off and lit the main tooth of the comb in his left hairlock to make a torch. In his retreat from the underworld, Izanagi, trying to stop the pursuing Ugly Females, first threw the ritual vines in his hair (*kazura*); it turned into fruit, which they ate. Then he threw down the comb from his right hairlock. It became young shoots of bamboo, which they also ate, but the two gestures sufficiently delayed the Ugly Females.

The bamboo shoots in conjunction with the comb immediately remind us of the *yogoto* situation. It may be that study of the *Kojiki/Nihon-shoki* usage would cast light on the *yogoto*. The combs of Izanagi and Susano-o in both sources are called *yu-tsu-tsuma-kushi*. *Tsu* would be either genitive or a part of *yutsu*. *Tsuma* apparently is 'tooth'. *Kushi*, as here or in *tamagushi*, means 'comb' or 'stick'. (Other ancient meanings are 'marvelous', and a kind of grass mentioned in the *Izumo fudoki*.)

Three meanings seem possible for the *yu*.

a) *Yutsu* is an archaic equivalent for *ihotsu*, literally 'five hundred', figuratively 'many'. This is the meaning used by the major Western translators, and is preferred by Tsugita Uruu in his *Kojiki shinkō*, Tokyo, 1943, p. 58. Thus, 'many-toothed comb', an appellation comparable to the 'eightfold' or 'manifold' which occur almost as *makura-kotoba* all through the *Kojiki*.

b) *Yu* may mean sacred, a meaning suggested as an alternative for the comb usage in Kurano Kenji's *Kojiki taikei*, Tokyo, 1960, p. 25. It is interesting that in the *yogoto* the shoots of bamboo which will spring up are modified to read *yutsu-iho-taka*, either 'five-hundred five-hundred bamboo' or 'sacred, five-hundred-fold bamboos'. The duplication may suggest as more sensible the latter meaning for the *yutsu* (though one cannot be sure in archaic Japanese). If that is the case, the parallel association with bamboo might suggest the 'sacred' sense of *yu* for the Izanagi story.

c) *Yu* may also mean hot water, including the water of hot springs. Indeed, the character used in both the *Kojiki* and *Nihon-shoki* has that meaning. But as far as I know it has never been suggested that it be taken as other than phonetic. The *yogoto* combines two elements also found in the Izanagi story, the 'comb' and bamboo, with a third, heavenly water from underground springs. Yet the Izanagi story takes place underground, and as we shall see, water from underground springs, especially hot springs, was of great importance and thought to be marvelous renewing water from the 'other world', *tokoyo*. Emperors bathed in it, and it had a sacramental power to purify and make divine. Renewal against the powers of night, decay, and evil is indeed the basic theme of both the Izanagi story and the *yogoto*.

from sunset to sunrise, saying the great invocation words [*futo-norito-goto*] of an invocation [*norito*] of heaven. When you speak thus, as an omen five hundred young shoots of bamboo will come up, and from under them eight wells of heaven will gush out. Take this [water] and present it as the water of heaven.'

In consequence of this commission, the marvellous grain of the Sacred Court is prepared. The Urabe[20] have made the Great Divination and have determined that the Yuki [field] is to be in [the district of] Yasu in the province of Ōmi and the Suki [field] is to be in [the district of] Higami in the province of Tamba.[21] The men of the Mononobe,[22] the sake child, the sake woman, the sake selecter, the

Given the Japanese love of word-plays, it is not impossible that all three meanings as a set of associations were intended.

2) But besides the 'jeweled comb' possibility, *tamagushi*, meaning 'jewel' or 'spirit' stick, as such has a very great ritual importance in Shinto. In this usage it is a branch of the sacred *sakaki* tree, or perhaps a plain stick, ornamented with strips of cloth or (later) paper, set up before shrines or offered in rituals. Its antecedent in the mythology is the headdress worn by Ame-no-uzume dancing before the cave in which Amaterasu hid herself.

To return to the Izanagi and Susano-o myths, it is noteworthy that if one character could be assumed to have been miswritten, we would have instead *yu-tsu-tamagushi*, 'sacred *tamagushi*', an implement which complements the previously mentioned *kazura* in the ancient rituals of Ise and elsewhere, and which would be understood in light of the headdress of Ame-no-uzume. This correction is made by Inoue Shunji in his rather eccentric translation (*Kojiki*, Fukuoka, 1966, p. 26). However, we must be cautious of a rendering supported by no evidence save its compatibility with a theory.

But nonetheless, perhaps the idea allows one to realize that the 'comb' and ritual *tamagushi* ideas are not necessarily inconsistent, but may rather point to a single ritual device, or concept. The *kazura* thrown down first was not just a 'headpiece' but vines worn in the hair in many rituals, particularly rites of spring and harvest. The 'comb' too, even if it be toothed and worn in locks on either side of the head, was clearly not an ordinary comb if one tooth of it could provide a torch, and if it could turn into a grove of bamboo.

Evidently, the Izanagi story is a mythological statement of a ritual scenario. It is significant that all these basic references to *tamagushi* or *yu-tsu-tsuma-kushi*—Izanagi, Susano-o, Ame-no-uzume, the *yogoto*—relate to it a performance at night, or at the gates of a cave or the underworld, or both, and in it the instrument serves to repel the powers of darkness at a moment of great crisis. It is an instrument of the renewal of sovereignty and the harvest festival which is the setting of the *yogoto*. In both the Izanagi story and the *yogoto* the emergence of bamboo is a sign of this renewal.

Thus one feels that the *tamagushi* of the *yogoto* was a ritual implement with these kinds of associations. Whether it looked like a comb or a branch is perhaps of no great moment, although to my mind the 'setting up' of the latter sounds rather less ridiculous, especially since it is actually done in many rites to this day. But whatever the exact ritual, its purpose was, together with the *norito* or invocational words, to engender heavenly waters which would fecundate the land, power manifested in the growth of bamboo, and to allow the renewal of life and sovereignty.

[20] The Urabe was the third family attached to the Ministry of Official Shinto. Their special function was divination. They were not as ancient as the Nakatomi or Imbe, receiving no mention before the Taihō Code.

[21] In pre-Meiji times, these two provinces were virtually always the Yuki and Suki provinces respectively. D. C. Holtom, *The Japanese Enthronement Ceremonies*, pp. 99–100 (new ed., pp. 75, 77), provides a vivid account of the divination procedure. (See Chapter IV below.)

[22] The Mononobe were a clan of great importance in archaic times who, as retainers of the emperor, had a traditional place in the *Daijō-sai*. They put up the emblematic shields and weapons around the enclosure and participated in the guarding of the gates. The *Jōgan-gishiki* of 872 indicates that the servants at the sacred fields in addition to those listed above were selected from among the Mononobe, as does the *yogoto*, but in the *Engi-shiki* they are simply called 'minor servants' rather than Mononobe. This change doubtless reflects the declining importance of the Mononobe in the Heian period and it is perhaps a mark of its antiquity that the *yogoto* formula perpetuates the older situation.

Fire Attendant, the Firewood Cutters, the Assistants, the Lord of the Rice Harvest,[23] have entered reverently bearing [the rice] into the Sacred Court of the *Daijō* banquet.[24] On the middle day of the hare of the eleventh month of this year, [the rice] being taken with sacred care and strict observance, has been, with awe, purified and presented. The day in the middle of the month being selected, the Emperor, the Root of Great Yamato, has partaken of the great sake, the black and white sake of the Yuki and Suki, with a radiant aura, as his heavenly, everlasting, and eternal oblation, for his liquor and grain-harvest.[25] Let the imperial deities, shining with rich light, who are praised with this Blessing of the heavenly *kami,* numinously gather in this communal banquet of a thousand and five hundred autumns, and sanctify him as a firm and eternal rock. Let them prosper him for a majestic era beginning from this first year of Kōji. Let him shine and radiate together with heaven and earth, sun and moon.[26]

As if taking the middle of an awesome spear, without favoring top or bottom, I the Nakatomi high priest, greater 4th court rank, higher official rank, assistant minister of the Ministry of Official Shinto, Ōnakatomi Ason Kiyochika, present this Blessing.[27]

Again I speak. You who serve in the Emperor's Court, princes, nobles, various officials of the hundred departments, common people of the four quarters under heaven, gather together, see, feel reverence, rejoice, hear, and pray, that the awesome reign of the Emperor's Court may prosper like luxuriant branches. Thus presenting this Blessing with awe, with awe, do I speak.

This formula, or similar words, were also used at the *sokui-rei,* or civil enthronement based on Chinese models which took place shortly after the new emperor's actual accession, before the long preparation required by the *Daijō-sai* could be completed. It also came to be recited at the New

---

[23] The duties of these persons will be explained, as far as can be, later. The list differs slightly from that of the *Jōgan-gishiki* and *Engi-shiki.*

[24] The rice used for the *Daijō-sai* offerings of rice and sake was carried from the two fields to the capital in a colorful procession. The sacred children, the priests, children, *sakaki* branches, and the attendants would all be part of it. After its arrival in the capital, the rice would be enshrined and venerated as a deity until the rite.

[25] Notice that a careful reading of this passage shows that the emperor is said only to partake of the grain in the form of sake, not cooked rice. This is indeed the case; Holtom errs in this respect. The emperor raises rice, millet, white and black sake each three times to his lips without consuming any of it, then finally drinks once of each kind of sake.

[26] The images of this paragraph suggest medieval rather than ancient Shinto. The *Kojiki* and *Nihon-shoki* do not suggest founding on rock, or coequal heaven and earth, sun and moon, but the *Shintō gobusho,* for example, tells of the dynasty being founded on everlasting rock, and makes the deities of the two shrines of Ise, Amaterasu and Toyouke, as sun and moon respectively, jointly ruling the universe. (Cf. the text in Jingū Shichō, *Shintō gobusho,* pp. 58–9, where the 'Go-chinza hongi' makes these associations, asserting that Amaterasu and Toyouke, like sun and moon or *yin* and *yang,* rule with the dynasty, which like the Grand Shrine is built on a divine pillar and eternal rock. The same characters are used for the last as in the *yogoto.* The 'Go-chinza hongi' dates from 1356.)

[27] Perhaps the spear is an *axis mundi* symbol. Certainly the Nakatomi priest's seizing it in the middle indicates his mediatorial position. There may be a play on the word *naka,* middle, which appears also in the name Nakatomi, the name probably meaning mediator. In any case, the imagery of this passage, unlike the above, recalls one again to the world of the *Kojiki* and the spear dipped down from heaven to churn up the island on which Izanagi and Izanami descended.

Year's rites. But clearly its native home is in the context of the *Daijō-sai*, and its allusions and meaning relate to it.

The dates for its use are somewhat problematic. The only version of the text we have derives not even from the *Engi-shiki*, but is found in the Diary, or *taiki*, of the Minister (*sadaijin*) Fujiwara no Yorinaga (1120–56). This document records the formula above read in the year Kōji 1, or 1142, at the very end of the Heian period.[28]

However it is evident that the tradition represented by the 1142 *yogoto* has roots going back to the earliest days of Court Shinto. Its history is one with that of the development of the *Daijō-sai* as the major accession ceremony. Reference to the presentation of a *yogoto* by the Nakatomi in connection with accession may be found consistently in the chain of documents dealīng with this matter, though without a text. It cannot then be proven that the wording was regularly similar. That seems likely, however, if two presuppositions be granted: the conservative nature of liturgical language, above all in the case of closely-guarded oral tradition; and the presumption that the obviously archaic language and mythological references of the *yogoto* of 1142, so unlike the formal Chinese style of original Heian eulogies but rather breathing the atmosphere of the *Engi-shiki norito* and the *Kojiki*, bespeaks a continuing tradition rather than a reconstruction.[29]

First, however, we will present a few citations concerning the Nakatomi history of the offering of *yogoto*. While references to the Nakatomi family as of political and religious consequence is a recurring theme of the *Kojiki* and *Nihon-shoki*, the earliest important instance of the distinctive function of that family is found in the *Nihon-shoki* account of the reign of Temmu, ninth year (681), third month, ninth day. According to Aston's translation, 'Close to Miwi, on the mountain, Shintō places of worship were laid out, and offerings of cloth distributed to them. The litany was pronounced by Nakatomi no Kane no Muraji.'[30] The function of the Nakatomi in making the verbal offerings—literally *norito*—reminds us of his function with the

---

[28] See Philippi, pp. 12–3. For discussion of this document, and comparison of it with a secret version preserved in the Urabe family when custody of Court Shinto fell into the hands of the Yoshida branch of the Urabe, see Nishida Nagao, *Shintō-shi no kenkyū*, II, pp. 669–90. Clearly, the contents of this prayer were considered particularly sacred and secret, like much of the ritual of the *Daijō sai*, and for this reason were not written down in any of the earlier books. The recording of it by Yorinaga may be regarded a fortunate chance; this version was first presented to the learned world by Motoori Norinaga in 1794 (Nishida, ibid. p. 670), although its existence was known to Kada no Azumamaro, who first revealed the rituals of the *Daijō-sai* more than fifty years before. The Urabe (Yoshida) version, from a manuscript found in the Yoshida family library by Nishida and Miyaji Naokazu, was used by the Yoshida priests in the rites of the fourteenth-century Northern Court. Apparently after this period this *yogoto* fell into disuse, although the sacred *yogoto* offered in the modern *Daijō-sai* is probably descended from it, even if not said by Nakatomi. The Urabe version is characterized mostly by a random omission of words found in the Yorinaga version, and is of less value.

[29] The phraseology of the *yogoto*—ancestral gods and goddesses, the Imperial Grandson, the thousand and five hundred autumns, and the like—parallel stock terms of the *norito* in the *Engi-shiki*, echoed in the *Gobusho*. They might have been written by the same hand. But if we compare the *yogoto* with the *Toshigoi norito*, for example, we observe that both present, after the stylized introduction, an element from a different stratum. In the case of the *norito*, it is the reference to the offering of the three white animals, the horse, boar, and cock. These are explained in a myth found in the *Kogoshūi*, the apologia of the Imbe. In the *yogoto*, it is the myth of the ascent to heaven for heavenly water.

[30] Aston, *Nihongi*, II, p. 293.

yogoto. Moreover, the fact that this presentation was made at Miwi, Sacred Well—a well near Ōtsu where, as Aston notes, the Emperors Tenchi and Temmu and the Empress Jitō were washed at birth—is remarkably suggestive in light of the water symbolism of the *yogoto* and the connection of the Harvest Festival with imperial succession.

From this time on, the position of the *yogoto* and the Nakatomi as its reciters is tied to the emergence of the *Daijō-sai* as an accession ceremony distinct from the annual palace *Niiname*, or Harvest Festival. Nishida properly observes that prior to the time of Tenchi (661–71) and Temmu (673–86) no real distinction is apparent,[31] although the mythology is replete with general association of the harvest rite and succession and contains certain allusions which suggest *Daijō-sai* paraphernalia and action. In fact, archaic Japan did not observe New Year as an occasion separate from Harvest and Spring rites, but these tended to merge together in the continuing celebration of harvest and renewal. Perhaps the use of the *yogoto* at New Year in the Court when, under Chinese influence, special commemorations were kept, is associated with this.

The major reference illustrating the emergence of the later pattern is provided in the *Nihon-shoki* record of the accession of Jitō, the widow of Temmu who became sovereign Empress in 686, though, owing to the requisite period of mourning, her accession was not celebrated until 690. The *Nihon-shoki* says:

> 4th year, Spring, 1st month, 1st day. Mononobe no Maro no Ason set up great shields. Nakatomi no Ohoshima no Ason, Minister of the Department of the Shintō religion, recited (a prayer invoking) blessings from the Gods of Heaven. When this was over, Shikofuchi, Imbe no Sukune, delivered to the Empress-consort the divine seal, sword, and mirror. The Empress-consort accordingly assumed the Imperial Dignity. The Ministers and public functionaries ranged in order, made obeisance in rotation, and clapped their hands.[32]

In the original, the 'prayer' is *yogoto*. This usage was codified in the Taihō Code of 701, which provides:

> On the accession day, the Nakatomi shall read the divine ritual, the Imbe shall present the divine tokens, namely the mirror and the sword.[33]

These refer to the accession rite, the modern *sokui-rei*, rather than to the *Daijō-sai*. Although the *Daijō-sai* is also mentioned in the Taihō Code and other Nara period literature,[34] it is not until Heian period *shiki*, or Court Rituals and Regulations, that enough information is given about the *Daijō-sai* ceremonial to isolate its use in it. The *Jōgan-shiki* of 872 and the

---

[31] Nishida, ibid. p. 663.

[32] Aston, ibid. p. 395.

[33] Sir G. B. Sansom, 'Early Japanese Law and Administration', *Transactions of the Asiatic Society of Japan*, Second Series, XI (1934), p. 125.

[34] For a list of references to the *Daijō-sai* in Nara period sources, such as the *Shoku-nihongi, Man'yōshū*, etc., see Umeda Yoshihiko, *Jingi seido-shi no kiso-teki kenkyū*, pp. 290–2.

Engi-shiki of 927 both show its use, as in the citation from the latter given above.

The three most important ritual buildings of the ceremonial site are the Yuki and Suki lodges and the Kairyū-den (literally, 'Eternal Flow Hall') where the emperor takes his final purificatory baths. He first enters this hall at 8 p.m. Here he bathes again in hot water presented by the officials, who in Heian times would have been Fujiwara, in turn descended from the Nakatomi. Afterwards he puts on the white linen robe called the *hago-romo*, 'feather-robe'. He then proceeds to the lodges on a carpet which is rolled up behind him as it is unrolled before him. No one else is allowed to step on it, nor may his bare feet step off it to touch the ground. The procession is intended to imitate the descent of the Imperial Grandson. We have spoken of the private act of worship and communion which he makes successively in the two lodges.

The emperor within the lodges again receives ablutions of hot water from the two maidens who accompany him before he spreads the food-offerings and sips the sake in communion. After the rite in the Suki-den, he withdraws to the Palace until receiving the *yogoto* and the regalia the next morning. This was followed in Heian times by two days of ceremonial banquets presented by the two provinces.

The maidens were 'daughters of the Nakatomi', and the officials were also of that family. Indeed, most of the officials who had part in the rite, except the Crown Prince and the Imbe, would have been considered members of it, since the Nakatomi were ancestral to the Fujiwara, who held all key positions in the Heian Court. Thus, when one high in the clan told in the *yogoto* of the presenting of water of heaven by the mythical ancestor of his family, he was speaking in the context of what they did in the present.

IV   THE MYTH IN THE *yogoto*

WE MAY now turn back to the *yogoto* itself and endeavor to understand its meaning in the context of the *Daijō-sai* action. We shall primarily engage attention upon the first half of the passage with its mythological references. Clearly, the point here is to justify the actions of the emperor and the Nakatomi, outlined in the second half, by showing how they emulate a mythological model. The actions of the gods in the time of the descent of the Imperial Grandson who established the Imperial Line is invoked as the action which the Nakatomi and the sovereign actually repeat, or are united with, in the present. The sacred time of the myth and the present are made one.

The mythological narrative consists essentially of three actions:

1   The deities sent down the Imperial Grandson to partake of the grain of earth as his heavenly and eternal food.
2   After his descent, his servant, the ancestor of the Naka-

tomi, sent his son back up to heaven to the double-peaked mountain to request heavenly water to add to the water of the visible lands (earth) to present to the Imperial Grandson.

3   The Heavenly Gods then gave the Nakatomi son a *tamagushi* telling him to stand it up from sunset to sunrise, and recite words. Then, they said, bamboo shoots would spring up like young water plants, and underneath them springs would gush forth, and that water would be heavenly water.

Within these three actions appear two themes: ascent and descent from heaven, and the virtue of the heavenly water. These seem to be both related to the consummation of the union of heaven and earth which is necessary for the establishment of sovereignty and the assurance of fecundity on earth. They derive from a time when sovereignty and fecundity were believed to be related and both assured through the rites of the sacred king.

The theme of ascent and descent between heaven and earth— and the underworld as well—is fundamental to the mythology of the *Kojiki* and *Nihon-shoki*, and particularly to the concept of kingship. The ability to execute kingship is in effect the ability to integrate these three realms.[35]

The motif of heavenly water appears to be an expression of the inception of a new reign. The adding of heavenly water to earthly is a token of the union of heaven and earth in the sovereign. Hence doing this will renew sovereignty and prosper the land. The heavenly water theme in the *yogoto* seems to be related to the association of water from underground springs with water from the 'other world', *tokoyo*. This concept and its relation to sovereignty is in fact far more prominent than any association of heavenly water with the opening of channels for wet-rice irrigation. For while the *yogoto* speaks of the emperor receiving and partaking of the fresh ears of grain and so on, the heavenly water is not cited in connection with its production. Instead, the heavenly water seems to have no relation to agriculture, as though the idea were a memoir of pre-agricultural centuries. It is simply to be mixed with the water of the visible lands at the emperor's meals, and at

---

[35] One is reminded of the Chinese idea presented in the Han period *Ch'un-Ch'iu fan-lu* (Sec. 44), which compares the ruler with the central vertical line of the character for 'king', and the three horizontal lines to heaven, earth, and man, the great triad. 'Occupying the center of heaven, earth, and man, passing through and joining all three—if he is not a king, who can do this?' Wm. T. de Bary (ed.), *Sources of Chinese Tradition*, I, p. 163.

night to cause young bamboo plants to spring up and underground wells to gush forth.

According to Origuchi Shinobu, hot water, in hot springs and (symbolically) in the emperor's bath at the *Daijō-sai*, was especially believed to come from the 'underworld' (*yomi*), which in turn was continuous with *tokoyo*, the 'other world'. Both were the lands of the dead and of marvelous and dread powers.[36] Water believed to be from the 'other world' had an almost sacramental importance in the religion of archaic Japan. Well and water *kami* were prominent, and sacred children were assigned to their service, just as the Nakatomi son was sent on the commission to fetch heavenly water. One of the most ancient sacred dances, the *yudate*, consists of the sprinkling of sacred water from branches by maidens for purification.

We have mentioned that emperors were bathed in sacred springs at birth. This practice has an intriguing relation to the *yogoto*. In the *Nihon-shoki* we read that the Emperor Hanzei (Mizuhawake) was so washed. 'Now there was a well called Midzu no wi (the beautiful well) from which water was drawn to wash the Heir to the Throne. A tajihi flower had fallen into this well and it was accordingly made the name of the Heir to the Throne. . . . Therefore he was styled the Emperor Tajihi no Midzuhawake.'[37] There was also an ancient family with this name of Tajihi. In the early Heian register, the *Shinsenseishi-roku*, we read under the name Tajihi that a member of that same family, descended from Ame-no-oshio-no-mikoto, had performed this same washing of the prince Mizuhawake, and on the occasion had offered a *yogoto* of the heavenly *kami*, and this was why the prince was called Tajihi no Mizuhawake. Moreover, we read there that after this washing, in the hot water (*miyu*) of the marvelous spring (*mizui*) of Awaji, members of that family had performed this function for princes in various places.[38] Nishida Nagao suggests, noting that prior to the Heian period documents mention the *yogoto* of the Nakatomi only at the accession, not the *Daijō-sai*, that anciently the Tajihi may instead have given it at the latter time and that the hot-water or heavenly-water motif united it with their birth-washing func-

[36] Origuchi Shinobu, 'Daijō-sai no hongi', originally published in *Kokugakuin zasshi*, xxxiv, Nos. 8 and 11 (1928), in *Origuchi Shinobu zenshū*, iii, p. 178. On p. 208, Origuchi discusses the *yogoto* and the implied rite by which the emperor fertilizes the land, pointing out that the Nakatomi was the house which must bear the water.

[37] Aston, *Nihongi*, i, p. 310.

[38] *Shinten*, pp. 1752–3.

tion.[39] In any case, we see that marvelous water brings together the renewal of sovereignty represented by an imperial birth and by actual accession, perhaps as though the accession were a mystical kind of rebirth.

After his bath at the *Daijō-sai*, the emperor puts on a robe of pure white silk which he wears throughout the rest of the ceremony. As indicated, this garment is called the *hagoromo*, 'feather-robe' or 'wing-robe'.[40] The use of that term is most interesting, for it turns up in Japanese folklore and literature as the garment of *tennyo*, heavenly maidens in the service of the moon *kami*. The most famous is the story of the *hagoromo* of Miho. A fisherman named Hakuryo put to shore on the strand of Miho and found a *hagoromo* hanging on a pine tree. He was about to carry it off when a beautiful *tennyo* appeared and implored him for it, saying that it was hers and without it she could not fly back home to the moon, where she was an attendant of the lunar deity. Hakuryo finally returned it to her, but not until he had made her promise to show him one of the dances unknown to mortals. Draped in the feather-robe, she did the dance, then, caught by a breeze, she soared up to the moon.

Many variants of the myth are found. In Tamba, it was said that the man who tried to steal it was the father of Toyouke of Ise. The putting on of the *hagoromo*, Origuchi said, is distinctly related to the bath in hot water. The hot water, like that of hot springs, is sacred life-giving water from *tokoyo*. But the moon maiden wearing the robe becomes human when she takes it off to bathe in the spring or the sea—that is, in water of the visible world—and hence is then in the power of the man who robs her of it. When she puts it back on she is then divine and able to fly to the moon. Thus by analogy the emperor, when he bathes in the earthly water, restores his human life, but insofar as heavenly water has been added to it (probably from a sacred well) he assumes divine stature and becomes the deity when he then puts on the *hagoromo*. Moreover, the maidens who attend him in the rite, Origuchi wrote, are like the *tennyo*, or moon maidens.[41]

---

[39] Nishida, pp. 664–9. In connection with this practice and the eight underground wells mentioned in the *yogoto*, it is interesting to note that one of the princes born of the Emperor Jimmu was named Yawi, 'eight-wells', and another Kamu-Yawi-mimi, according to the *Kojiki* (*Shinten*, p. 72).

[40] The term *hagoromo* is not used in the *Jōgan-gishiki* or the *Engi-shiki*, but does occur in this connection in the late Heian rituals *Hokuzanshō* and *Gōkeshidai* (*Kojitsu sōsho*, IV, p. 422, and XVII, p. 420).

[41] Origuchi, p. 225. See also his 'Ama no hagoromo' in 'Mizu on onna', *Minzoku*, II, No. 6, and III, No. 2 (September 1927; January 1928), published in *Origuchi Shinobu zenshū*, II, pp. 102–3. The version of the story here presented was told me by Prof. Ono Sokyō.

This leads to a final point to be presented: the *yogoto* presents evidence, supported by other material, that in archaic Japan the sovereign was believed to be descended from the moon rather than the sun. This suggestion may seem surprising to one conditioned by the official ideology of the historical period. But much comparative material could be adduced from other cultures to establish its tenability. Evidence such as that assembled by Mircea Eliade or M. Esther Harding[42] points to a widespread typology of an archaic male moon god who is the husband of all women, the controller of woman's mysteries who waxes and wanes in imitation of pregnancy, and the giver of rain and harvests, and who goes through benevolent and destructive moods in accordance with the phases. This male lunar deity may predate the better-known moon goddess in many cultures.[43] In Japan, the unusual emergence at a similar stage of a feminine rather than masculine solar deity as font of sovereignty should not obscure the possibility that previously the common lunar pattern prevailed.

It may be noted that the moon also has important connections with the development of human culture. The lunar cycle, and perhaps the primitive custom of holding tribal conferences by the light of the full moon, must have had significant interaction with the development of counting, for in many languages, including our own, the word for 'moon' has affinity with words for mind and

---

[42] See especially M. Eliade, *Patterns in Comparative Religion*, Ch. 4, 'The Moon and Its Mystique', and the less carefully documented but highly suggestive material presented by the Jungian writer M. E. Harding in *Woman's Mysteries,* especially Ch. 7, 'The Man in the Moon'.

[43] In some cultures both solar and lunar symbolism of kingship seem to coexist. As we have seen, this may be the case in Egypt in the parallel Re and Osiris royal ideologies. Polynesian myths associate chiefly ancestry both to sun and moon from one island to another. The Altaic shaman wears discs representing both heavenly orbs. In India both traditions exist, in some cases in different dynasties, in others together with a certain poetic freedom. Kings are compared to the sun, Āditya, who destroys the darkness of earth, but also, like Brahmans, are given the epithet 'moonlike'. In this they are compared with the marvelous plant, *soma,* which is also moonlike and mysterious and 'other', the giver of ecstasy. 'Moonlike' also suggests bringing luck, and mildness and gentleness (Gonda, pp. 25–6). The *sammaya* offering is mystically identified with royal dignity, and is made to Indra, the universal monarch and prototype of the king. It is made on the new moon, of milk taken from a cow on the eve of the new moon, and mixed with clarified butter. The texts make mention of Indra's victory over Vṛtra, the primordial monster (ibid. p. 54).

Dr Harding believes that the lunar pattern, founded on 'the man in the moon', husband of all women and the recurring victor and giver of rain, generally preceded the moon goddess and the solar descent of kings. The material which she cites is admittedly selective and perhaps controversial as a basis of generalization. For example, she tries to show that in Mesopotamia Sinn, the male moon god, was more and more superseded by his daughter Ishtar, and the son became the image of the king as Marduk or Nebo. But it does appear that the Japanese evidence, which she does not seem to be aware of, supports her contention of an original lunar model of kingship later suppressed and replaced with a solar, though without her late feminization of the moon and masculinization of the sun!

measure.[44] In Japanese one may compare the name of the lunar deity, Tsukiyomi, with *yomu*, to read or reflect on, and *koyomi*, calendar.[45]

The culture hero and original sovereign, like Ōkuninushi or Osiris, who develops the land, teaches the arts of government and agriculture, and sets the pattern of kingship, has in much archaic myth a career, in his movement between the three worlds and his dying and rising, full of lunar symbology. This is also what the moon does, and one may suggest that as he is, in fact, the moon on earth, so also he gives (as does the moon) rain, fertility, time, and culture. This he is together with the fact that he is son of heaven (the moon?) and earth. Often, like Ōkuninushi, he seemingly dies but is restored by female, that is earthly, power; he is connected with lunar and rebirth animals like the hare or the snake; and he is the husband of many women, especially princesses of the clans he unites under his kingship. Kings, following after him, will have such lunar symbols as the horned headdress. They must make rain, accept blame for disaster, and announce times of planting and harvest. These roles may culminate in his taking the part of the moon in the ritual enactment of the marriage of heaven and earth, consummated at harvest or the New Year.

If this pattern obtains in Japan in the case of the imperial line, it should be especially evident at the *Daijō-sai*. This seems to be the case. It is true that its liturgies, like the official mythology written after the triumph of solar symbolism, are almost too silent in explicit references to the moon—an oversight hard to accept considering the great prominence of the moon in popular folklore in both China and Japan.[46] But if the *Daijō-sai* is an expression of solar descent and sovereignty, one wonders why it takes

---

[44] Eliade, *Patterns* . . . , p. 155.

[45] Concerning the association of *yo* meaning 'age' or 'world', *tokoyo*, and *tsukiyomi*, see also Tsuda Sōkichi, *Jindai-shi no atarashii kenkyū*, originally published in 1913, in *Tsuda Sōkichi zenshū*, I, p. 138.

[46] The central place of the moon in the Chinese Harvest Festival is well described by L. Hodous in his *Folkways in China*. The moon, associated with *yin*, the dominant force the last half of the year, is 'congratulated' for the harvest. It is also the abode of the immortals, and hence is connected with the return of the dead, a part of harvest in China as in many cultures. Altars are set up in courtyards and streets with a pagoda on the top terrace and decorations said to represent palaces of the moon. Round moon-cakes are made of flour and brown sugar and decorated with the moon and its palaces. On the night of the festival, tables are spread in the courtyards, and it is said that beautiful flowers fall from the moon at this time, and that whoever sees them will be blessed with fruitfulness and men with prosperity. Divination is done as the moon rises (pp. 179–83). Hodous also presents several Chinese legends about the moon, including one of the hare in the moon, and a couple representing the moon as male but the giver of pregnancy and the matchmaker. It will be noted that certain of these Chinese rites and stories have entered Japan, but are associated more with the August *tsukimi*, or moon-viewing, than with the indigenous autumn Harvest Festival.

place in the middle of the night, on the day of the hare, and is replete with such symbols of alternation as white and black lamps and rough and smooth cloth.

In my view, though, the most persuasive support for the lunar concept is found in the *yogoto*, particularly in the lines concerning heavenly water. That the moon is the giver of water is an almost universal archaic notion. In the *yogoto*, we see explicitly that the *tamagushi* was to be set up from sunset to sunrise, suggesting that something most powerful at night rather than in the day was to be invoked. The *Man'yōshū* speaks of 'water which is held by Tsukiyomi, that is water which will rejuvenate'.[47] During this time, sacred manifold bamboo would sprout forth. Bamboo is a plant especially connected with both water and the moon. In the *Taketori monogatari* the marvelous princess from the moon was found by the old bamboo cutter inside a bamboo stalk. The final line of this section of the *yogoto* concerning heavenly underground springs makes no sense except in connection with an implicit lunar symbolism. Water and the sun could only be polarities, but the moon is everywhere the custodian and giver of water.[48]

The power of the moon is not limited to the sky only. It controls very chthonic things: women through their cycles, the sea through tides, snakes through their seeming rebirth. As the celestial bow it is believed to send arrows to impregnate women and animals. It could easily release the wells of the underground. The moon, in fact, travels to the underworld and rules there, as the myth of Susano-o hints. The virtual identity of 'Tsukiyomi' and 'tokoyo'—*tukuyo*—and also the root *yo* in *yomi*, the underworld, suggest that what belongs to the moon is not really so much the sky, which after all must be shared with the sun, as everything wherever found which is mysterious, numinous, nocturnal, extraordinary, running to extremes, yet fecundating and necessary, and

---

[47] *Man'yōshū*, Vol. 13, No. 3245. At the Mt Kurama temple in Kyoto there is a ceremony in May in which water is drawn and sipped from silver ladles under the full moon, and this is said to rejuvenate.

The relation of kingship and the moon is found in Polynesia. Dr Harding says, 'The Chief of Einu in the Polynesian Islands was called The Lord of the Moon, and in Samoa when the Chief died they said, "The Moon was fallen," while in other tribes watch is kept for the first rising of the crescent moon, and as soon as it is seen they cry to the king, "Your life has been renewed!" It is as though they feared that if the moon did not come again the king could not continue to live.' (Harding, p. 85)

[48] The whole pattern is eloquently stated in the names of the three sacred mountains of Yamagata prefecture called the Dewa Sanzan: Haguro (Hagoromo?), Gassan (Moon Mountain), and Yudono (Hot Water Lodge). The last has a hot springs which has been a famous place of pilgrimage for ascetics of the Shugendō.

fresh and renewing and marvelous.[49] This might be the under-world with its springs, or the land of spirits, or rain, or the renewal of life and sovereignty. The sun, on the other hand, belonging to the world of day and labor and hence of the ordinary, attracted less archaic religious attention and was thought of simply as continuous with the world of man. It was the moon and night which were on the other side, strange and powerful, and hence the alien fecundating energy working through fresh and wondrous water able to bring the works of man to harvest and renewal.

The most suggestive of all items in the *yogoto* is the ascent of the Nakatomi son to the heavenly double-peaked mountain. It is from this heavenly double-peaked mountain that the son of the Nakatomi is to obtain the heavenly water, and it is here he meets the imperial ancestral *kami*, suggesting that whatever this double-peaked mountain in the heavens is, is what the imperial line descends from. Immediately the image of the waxing crescent moon, its horns tipped upward as if holding water, springs to mind.

This interpretation is admittedly not favored by conventional Shinto scholarship. However, interpretations which are given do not suggest great antiquity. Tsugita Uruu compares, no doubt rightly, this *heavenly* double peak with the two references in the *Nihon-shoki*, on the occasion of the descent of the Imperial Grandson, to the preceding descent of Ame-no-oshihi, ancestor of the Ōtomo, 'as far as the floating bridge of heaven, which is on the two peaks of Kushihi of Takachiho in So of Hyuga'. Significantly, this line occurs just after the mention of the *Daijō-sai* symbol of the wrapping of the Imperial Grandson by Takami-musubi in the

---

[49] The *Kojiki* and *Nihon-shoki* provide many other possible glimpses into this theme, particularly in the old songs. The Japanese language allows much scope for word-play in poems and songs, perhaps so much as to make it overly risky to talk about its significance. None the less it is interesting to speculate about a song like one presented in Jingū third year, third month, fifth day in the *Nihon-shoki* (Aston, *Nihongi*, I, p. 239; *Shinten*, p. 370). It begins, in Aston's translation, 'Beyond the river is the rough pine-clad plain—to that pine-clad plain let us cross over, with bows of *tsuki* and stores of sounding arrows.' 'Pine' is *matsu*, which also means 'to wait', and as we have seen may be the root of *matsuri*, the festival, originally thought of as an occasion of waiting for the descent of spirits. Thus, the pine here is symbolically associated with shrines and festival places and the descent of spirits in many places. The 'rough pine-clad plain'—*araramatsubara*, reminding one of the name of the Aramatsuri shrine at Ise—could be a place of waiting upon 'rough spirits', *ara-mitama*, mentioned so much in the Jingū passages. Finally, the 'bows of *tsuki*' (or *tsuku*, ibid. p. 370, but according to the *Kogojiten*, p. 715, the same word, meaning 'mulberry') is *tsukuyumi*, reminding one of the prevalence of the bow as a lunar symbol, and indeed suggesting a play on *tsukiyomi*. Very speculatively, I think, the whole passage, *Ochikata no araramatsubara, matsubara ni watariyukite, tsukuyumi ni mariya o tague* . . . could be translated, 'Let us cross over to the waiting-field, the waiting-field of the rough spirits on the other side of the river, and bring arrows to *tsukiyomi*, the celestial bow . . .' Crossing the river, of course, suggests the preliminary purification, *misogi*, before the *matsuri*. *Tague* may mean 'lining up', suggesting a kind of ritual action, perhaps like the emperor's standing up the *tamagushi* in the *yogoto*.

ofusuma coverlet, and in the other instance just after another
variant which contains the presentation to the Imperial Grandson
by his wife of rice and sake from two fields chosen by divination
in an episode which is undoubtedly a mythical counterpart of the
Daijō-sai.[50] It is also significant that the two peaks are here also
connected with the imperial descent, and with an ancient retainer
family, for the Ōtomo are in this respect comparable to the Nakatomi.[51]

However, in the *yogoto* the two peaks are reached by ascent
rather than descent, implying the above two peaks of Kushihi in
Hyūga are rather an earthly model of the heavenly, discovered by
virtue of the establishing of an earthly kingdom parallel to that
of heaven. But it is only from the heavenly original that the heavenly water could be obtained to give renewed life to the earthly
model. Hence after the descent there must be a return above.

Tsugita also speaks of reference in the *Man'yōshū* to double
peaks on Katsuragi mountain and in Etchū province. Katsuragi is
one of the most important mountains in ancient Japanese religion,
the training-place of shamanistic ascetics, and the place where the
Emperor Yūryaku, in the *Kojiki*, encountered the great *kami*-of-
one-word (Hitokotonushi). It has had much ritual connection with
the Palace. According to Tsugita, its double peaks were considered
respectively male and female, and by analogy he feels the two peaks
of heaven in the *yogoto* were related to the mentioned male and
female ancestral *kami*.

However, I do not think that great antiquity can be ascribed
to this concept. The supposition that the deities of Katsuragi were
male and female is alien to the *Kojiki* story, and to the general
world-view of archaic Japanese religion. The fundamental dynamic
was the union of heavenly male deities with earthly females. A
mountain *kami* might be one or the other, presumably depending
on whether it is thought of as on the earthly side or the transcendent, but the image of two peaks as a sexual harmony suggests the
assimilation of Taoist ideas rather than the *Kojiki* independent
of such outside influence.[52]

---

[50] Aston, *Nihongi,* I, pp. 70, 87. Tsugita Uruu, pp. 536–7.

[51] In the *Nihon-shoki* account of the accession of Keitai, which traditionally took place
in A.D. 507, the Ōtomo rather than the Imbe presented the regalia. Aston, ibid. II, p. 3;
and see Nishida, p. 659.

[52] This kind of pattern suggests the obviously Taoist order of the Empress Suiko, shortly after the promulgation of the Shōtoku Constitution, to 'do reverence to the Gods of
Heaven and Earth' that thereby 'the male and female elements become harmoniously developed' (Aston, ibid. p. 135; the alleged date is A.D. 607). It is certain that such Taoist
elements have penetrated Shinto from perhaps the Shōtoku period on, and much more
subtly than Buddhism. But in the mythology a reasonably careful reading can easily dis-*

Rather, it seems unnecessary to look for terrestrial patterns for the heavenly double-peaked mountain of the *yogoto* when the point is that it is heavenly rather than earthly, and the source of a blessing which is not to be found in the visible lands. Should it not be one with Tsukiyomi, whose two horns contain the waters of rejuvenescence?

Thus the reference to the two peaks of heaven, together with the nocturnal, water, and bamboo allusions of the *yogoto*, seem to hint at an archaic world in which the moon rather than the sun was the source of fecundity and sovereignty. It is perhaps not an accident that finally, using the imported calendric system, the *yogoto* speaks of the *Daijō-sai* as taking place on the day of the hare, the animal of the moon in Chinese and Japanese and in much other folklore.

It is evident that the idea of imperial descent from Amaterasu, the 'Sun Goddess', is eclipsed on this level. This raises a question of where that idea derived from, and what relation it has to the *Daijō-sai*.

V AMATERASU

Now WE must add a few words about the development of the concept of imperial descent from Amaterasu. It is perhaps imprudent to enter into this complex matter when limitations of space prevent the assembly of the great mass of material necessary to an adequate treatment. Yet the matter is cogent enough to our present topic, the background of Court ritual, to make some gesture necessary. First some observations:

1 Amaterasu has no real place as solar goddess and source of sovereignty in the Court rituals integral to their fundamental structure. She is not mentioned at all in the *Daijō-sai*. Of course she is given formal mention in the preface of some of the *norito*, and allusion in the mention of the Ise Deity in other places. But while the myth and cultus of Amaterasu is archetypal for the whole of

*tinguish the flavor of this sexual harmony theme from the dynamic marriage of heaven and earth of the archaic myths. The rather embarrassed handling of the antecedents of the Heavenly Grandson in the *Kojiki* and *Nihon-shoki* is a case in point; clearly, changing ideology forced the writers to make him a grandchild of Amaterasu as well as Takami-musubi, but they knew that the masculine should be in heaven and the feminine on earth, and could not bring themselves to make a straightforward and convincing story of his heavenly descent on both sides. The account is ambiguous, and in any case Amaterasu is in turn the daughter of Izanagi on earth, of his washing in the sea. A formula like 'imperial ancestral *kami* male and female who have their session in the High Plain of Heaven', which may be conventional by the time of the *norito* and *yogoto* introductions, is not characteristic of the *Kojiki*.

archaic Shinto, one does not find that the explicit myth and cultus of Amaterasu, or Ise, or a solar-sovereignty motif, dominate the Court pattern. Rather, the important *kami* are those of the Eight Gods of the Ministry of Official Shinto, Takami-musubi, Ōmiya-no-me, Ōnamuchi, etc., or of the other palace shrines, and these tend each to have a special relation to one of the ancient Yamato hereditary guilds, or *be,* the Imbe, Nakatomi, Mononobe, etc.

2   Amaterasu is related to the Empress Jingū and the Ise tradition, which emphasized ecstatic dancing, divine possession, the *ara-mitama* ('rough spirit') concept, and both marine and solar *kami.* Perhaps this tradition began to permeate the Yamato Court in the reign of Bidatsu (572-85), when the establishment of a *hinomatsuri* (sun or fire worship) *be,* or hereditary guild, is reported. This might possibly refer to a group like the Sarume Maidens or certain branches of the Imbe who had roots in the Ise-Kii region. We may see its influence in the spear-pounding part of the *Chinkon-sai,* related to the Ise myth and performed by the Sarume Maidens. But as is the case with most later accretions to a religion, the later influence changed the intellectual and mythical conceptualization more readily than the morphology of the cultus. It may be that the apparent dual parentage of the Imperial Grandson by Takami-musubi and Amaterasu reflects the merging of these traditions.

3   The myth and cultus of Amaterasu, in my view, suggests basically the pattern of the earth mother over against the sky god, but with the whole of the action projected into heaven. What Amaterasu does in heaven—celebrate the *Niiname,* plant fields, hide in a rock cave—are activities which more normally would be done on earth. She does not do what heaven properly does in contrast to earth—send rain, fecundate the crops, mysteriously visit at the *Niiname.* Susano-o rather plays this role opposite Amaterasu. She seems to be, in a perhaps paradoxical but important distinction, not a heavenly *kami* but a heavenly model of the earthly *kami,* or of the earthly activity of man over against heaven.

4   The solar aspect of Amaterasu should not be overemphasized. She is solar only in the cave myth, and then only by implication, not in the Jingū or imperial descent passages. But even insofar as she is solar, this does not seem to be inconsistent with her essentially representing a heavenly model of the earthly. The sun and day seem often to have been thought of by archaic man as on this side, the side of earth, the sun being one with the fields and the labor of man. It was the moon and night which were on

the other side, strange and numinous, and hence the source of rain and the alien fecundating power necessary to bring the works of man to harvest. Thus until the idea of a heavenly model of the earthly and human—not excluding death and rebirth—emerged, the sun had remarkably little religious importance. As illustrating this union of sun and earth mother on the one side, it is striking that in a song of the *Chinkon-sai* shamaness, discussed later, Amaterasu is called Toyohirume, 'flourishing noonday maiden'. This title combines a common epithet of the terrestrial grain mother, *toyo*, found of course in Toyouke, the name of Amaterasu's companion at Ise, with *hiru*, noon, a name more or less solar. The *Kojiki* itself in one place calls Amaterasu Ōhirume, 'great noon maiden'. In fact, one is tempted to feel that a title like Toyohirume really belongs simply to the Ise Deity before Amaterasu and Toyouke were well distinguished. The element '*me*', incidentally, would tend to indicate a female consort deity to a male *kami*. One is reminded that certain Kofun pictures, and the abortive Hiruko of the myths, suggest a forgotten male solar deity. On the other hand, the name Amaterasu, unlike most *kami* names, does not indicate sex. We recall that in certain myths Amaterasu put on male garb.

5   A comparison of the Ise shrines and the major ancient Yamato shrines, such as Kamo, Ōyamato, Mitoshi, Miwa, etc., reveals a significant difference in approach to the celebration of the marriage of heaven and earth. In Yamato it seems the point was to capture the male power when it descended and hold it for the community. In these shrines the heavenly *kami* virtually became an earth *kami*, shared by the shrine on the sacred hill to which he had primordially descended, as at Kamo or Miwa. Like an arrow or a snake he then reached out from this shrine to fecundate the surrounding country. A consort *hime-gami* was generally provided, and may even have been there first, to attract him, and shrine maidens served the *kami*, but the dynamic focus was on the male deity. At Ise, on the other hand, the shrine was a palace of the female terrestrial *kami*, the home in which she received the heavenly visitor. The male consort does not share the main shrine as an equal with the goddess. Groups of females minister to Amaterasu and Toyouke as handmaidens who wove the new cloth, the *mono-imi* who prepared the feast. A new house was built for his arrival and the banquet spread, but the visitor himself has no shrine made by hands at the Grand Shrine of Ise since he comes from far away, at night, and is held rather by the attractive power

of the female.

We may here cut a complex matter short by admitting that we do not know how the special relation between the emperor, Amaterasu, and the Ise shrines developed. We do not know how any of these three came to be specially connected with the other two. We can say that the developed concept antedates the written documents of Temmu Shinto, but not by very much. Of course it has remote antecedents of some sort, and various intriguing hints of these exist, but we have not space here to explore them any further.[53] We have hoped, rather, to suggest the kind of religious situation out of which it grew. That the sovereign should be a representative, and hence, descendant, of life-giving heaven is understandable. That this should be celebrated by *hieros gamos*, which was no doubt originally the union of the king and his queen emblematic of the union of heaven and earth, is natural. Perhaps one should say rather, of the queen with her king, if suggestions of at least a matrilocal and shamanistic female sovereignty are to be depended on. The *kami*, at least, appear to have lived with their mothers, or with a rather mobile band of brothers, until they went to the house of their brides, and as for the sky *kami*, it was they who descended to earth, to the place of their terrestrial mates. (However, the 'shamanistic queen', such as Pimiko or Jingū or, for that matter, Amaterasu, is always presented as having a powerful and awesome but exceptional kind of regime.)

VI   THE MYTHOLOGICAL BACKGROUND OF THE *Daijō-sai*

THE BASIC topic in the history of the *Daijō-sai* is the matter of its separation from the *Niiname-sai*. That the sovereign, as high priest, should first partake of the new grain in union with the deities on behalf of the nation is certainly understandable. This is the extent of the meaning of the annual *Niiname-sai*, held in the Palace the night of 14-15 November every year. It differs from the *Daijō-sai* in the following ways. The rite is celebrated by the emperor in the Palace shrine (Kashiko-dokoro); this is the shrine where the most important of the Imperial Household Shinto rites are held, and no special new and duplicated buildings are put up to greet

---

[53] For example, the myth of Yamato-takeru, in some respects a secular retelling of the Susano-o myth, seems to me to be quite suggestive. It is not only the explicit references to Ise and Yamato-hime which are important, but also the role of Yamato-takeru, as imperial scion who is visiting consort to the terrestrial goddesses of imperial shrines such as Atsuta. The poems he exchanged with Miyazu-hime at Atsuta in fact contain interesting lunar allusions. The myths of Yamato-takeru in the *Kojiki*, *Nihon-shoki*, *Kogoshūi*, and *Owari fudoki* may be compared.

the new grain. The rice for the *Niiname-sai* is not grown in special fields chosen by divination and marked by special growing and harvesting ceremonies such as those provided for the *Daijō-sai*, and has not been since the end of the Nara period. The rice is selected by government officials (today the Ministry of Agriculture) on the basis of its quality. Finally, the *sechie*, or banquet held after the festival, is on a much smaller scale in the case of the *Niiname-sai*.

Moreover, Japanese commentators usually point out that the objects of the *Daijō-sai* and *Niiname-sai* are different. The *Niiname-sai* is said to be just a thanksgiving for the fruits of that year pure and simple, while the *Daijō-sai* partakes of a larger perspective, offering thanks for a whole dynastic period. However it was conceived of then, some such idea of a different object must have accompanied the ancient differentiation of the *Daijō-sai* and *Niiname-sai*. Other ideas, such as those we have discussed previously, likewise dictated the close conjunction of royal succession and harvest festivity.[54]

The Harvest Festival is central to the most ancient stratum of information on Shinto worship available. In the Divine Age sections of the *Kojiki* and *Nihon-shoki* we read that Amaterasu was celebrating this festival at the time of the incursions of her brother which caused her to retire into the cave, and moreover that she was in a 'New Palace' for the occasion. The *Kogoshūi* records also that when the goddess left the cave, Ame-no-tajikara-no-kami (whose name may signify the sheaves of grain placed at the door of a house at the Harvest Festival) opened the door for her, and the *kami* led her to a *new palace* they had constructed for her.[55] It is interesting that in the narrative of these events, the *Kojiki* speaks of the rite using the same characters as for *Daijō*, the *Nihon-shoki* using the same characters as for *Niiname*.

A little further on, at the time of the descent of the Imperial Grandson we read that Kamu-ataka-ashi-tsu-hime (Kamu-ata-tsu-hime or Konohana-no-sakuyabime), wife of the Imperial Grandson Ninigi, determined by divination two rice-fields named Sanuda and Nunada from which she prepared for him sake and boiled rice. Ths rite is suggested by Aston[56] and others to be parallel to the

---

[54] Origuchi, 'Daijō-sai no hongi', pp. 178–80, reviews the difference between *Daijō-sai* and *Niiname*, including material from the *fudoki, Man'yōshū*, etc. He also discusses the *Daijō-sai* as an imperial act, *matsurigoto*, a priestly function of the emperor towards the *kami* on behalf of the *osukuni*, 'food-land', which is an archaic term equivalent to 'land ruled by the emperor'.

[55] Katō and Hoshino, *The Kogoshūi: Gleanings from Ancient Stories*, p. 22.

[56] Aston, *Nihongi*, I, p. 86, note.

Niiname-sai.

Another very interesting set of allusions to the *Daijō-sai* as the occasion of the testing, sacred marriage, and birth of the sovereign is found in the Divine Descent passages of the *Nihon-shoki*. The key to their meaning is found in the word *matoko ofufusuma*, adequately rendered by Aston as 'coverlet spread on the true couch'. The covering of raw silk laid over the *shinza*, or Sacred Bed, placed in the *Daijō* Yuki and Suki lodges to this day, is called the *ofusuma*, and one may suppose that the couch in these myths is connected with that of the *Daijō-sai*. Thus we read that, when the heavenly *kami* sent down scions to rule the earth, one of the first was Amewaka-hiko, who however forgot his heavenly mission and died of a 'returning arrow' when 'lying down' after *Niiname*. He had apparently failed of some test which involved reclining, presumably on a couch, at the First-Fruits.[57] But therewith Takami-musubi took the *matoko ofufusuma* and wrapped the Imperial Grandson Ninigi in it, and sent him downwards.[58] Apparently this wrapping authenticated his legitimate sovereignty. In many archaic societies, such as the Polynesian, the father by some act of picking up a child or clothing him accepts him as his proper son and heir. The 'true couch' also becomes the place of divine-imperial nuptials, conception, and birth, and shortly after we see that Prince Ninigi, after his wife Toyo-ata-tsu-hime had given him two heirs, became estranged from her and sang a song which said, in effect, 'The true couch is impossible to you.'[59]

The two heirs are Hosuseri-no-mikoto and Ho-ori-no-mikoto, also called Hiko-hoho-demi-no-mikoto. Like Ōkuninushi and other true heroes born of heaven and earth on earth, they range amidst all the cosmic levels, and the latter goes to the submarine realm of the Sea King where, as though this were a second descent, the testing drama of the true couch and coverlet is repeated. The attendant of Tamayorihime, daughter of the Sea King, having met the Heavenly Grandchild (Ho-ori-no-mikoto) by a well on the beach, took him below and reported his presence. 'When the Sea-God heard this, he said:—"I will try him and see." So he prepared a threefold dais. [The original has the character usually read *toko*, 'bed,' the interlinear *kana* in the *Shinten* is *yuka*, raised area in a house where a bed is commonly placed.] Thereupon the Heavenly Grandchild wiped both his feet at the first step of the

[57] ibid. p. 66.
[58] ibid. p. 90. Other references to the wrapping occur in variants within the *Nihon-shoki*, found ibid. p. 70, 86.
[59] ibid. p. 91.

dais. At the middle one he placed both his hands to the ground; at the inner one he sat down at his ease [i.e. with legs crossed] upon the cushion covering the true couch [*matoko ofufusuma*]. When the Sea-God saw this, he knew that this was the grandchild of the Heavenly Deity, and treated him with more and more respect.'[60]

Clearly, the *shinza*, or Divine Bed, of the *Daijō-sai*, which has three levels of mats, is in mind. Clearly, too, then, sitting on this couch is a kind of test as to whether one is a true 'Heavenly Grandchild', a true sovereign with the power to bring forth a true heir. True, the *Niiname* situation alone may not be involved; probably the 'true couch' was simply the throne in archaic times. But, on the other hand, the Divine Descent passages point to a particular event, as does the fact that the Sea God *prepared* the dais, as a 'new palace' was prepared for Amaterasu.

Moreover, the 'true couch' has to do with the bringing forth of an heir in this story. The Heavenly Grandchild mated with the daughter of the Sea God, Toyotamahime, probably as a result of his passing the test. Perhaps the mating was on the 'true couch', though this is not stated. But when the child was born—as though the house of the 'true couch' had become the parturition hut of many of the myths—she took the 'coverlet of the true couch' (*matoko ofufusuma*) and wrapped the child in it. This child was an imperial heir, too. He married Tamayorihime and their son was the first (legendary) emperor, Jimmu.[61]

---

[60] ibid. p. 106.

[61] ibid. p. 107. Perhaps the names of the *kami* involved give a clue to another symbolism of succession. Ama-tsu-hikone-ho-no-ninigine, Hosuseri, and Ho-ori all contain the word *ho*, which is a variant of *hi* and means fire. Shibata Minoru, in pointing this out, states that the idea of fire is connected with succession, and that in the use of *ho* or *hi* the meanings of 'fire' and 'sun' are merged. He believes that the *himatsuribe* must have then had a function concerning succession and new fire, that perhaps its orientation was to fire rather than to the sun (op. cit. p. 40). We can see what this may mean from the case of Izumo. The accession of the *kuni no miyatsuko* is called *hitsugi*, perhaps 'transmission of the sacred fire', a term also used for imperial succession. The possession of the 'original' fire-drill given by the gods is the test of incumbency in the office at Izumo, and in the succession ceremony this drill is used to make a new fire. The accession new-fire rite, though now held at any time of the year, has obvious connection with the Izumo *Niinae*, which also centers around the making of a new fire to cook the new rice, and certain other ritual accoutrements, such as a sacred animal-skin, are used only at these two cere-monies. W. L. Schwartz, 'The Great Shrine of Idzumo', pp. 543–4. One could suppose that this rite of renewal and succession of sovereignty is pre-agricultural, since it is clearly independent of the agricultural aspects of the *Niiname* and *Daijō-sai*, as is the couch ele-ment.

Origuchi finds still another symbol of succession in the *Daijō-sai*: moving into a room of a house, that is, into the throne-room represented by the Yuki and Suki-den. Succession is to take the emperor's room, he believes. He also emphasized in this connection that the *Daijō-sai* contains no element of mourning. There is *ōharae*, or purification, which in-cludes purging the pollution of the death, but the ancient Japanese would have considered mourning for the deceased sovereign inappropriate, since the same spirit which animated*

We noted that the *Niiname* offerings, where mentioned, were presented by a woman, Amaterasu or Kamu-ataka-ashi (consort of Ninigi), and in every case the male is a visitor, who may be violent like Susano-o or, passing the test, turn out to be a sovereign.

Another early story of the *Niiname* is found in the *Hitachi fudoki*.[62] According to the account of 'an old man', long ago an ancestral *kami* was going around to meet various other *kami*, and arriving at Mt Fuji of Suruga in the evening of the day, asked the *kami* of that mountain for lodging. But the *kami* of Fuji replied that since that night he was celebrating the *Niiname* of new millet, the interior of the house was taboo. The visiting *kami* resented this, wept, and cursed that mountain, saying that henceforth it would be cold, covered with ice and snow winter and spring, and would provide no food. The *kami* then went on to Mt Tsukuba (north of modern Tokyo), climbed it, and again asked for lodging. The *kami* of this mountain answered also that tonight was the *Niiname*, but that he would not act against the *kami*'s august pleasure. Food and drink were prepared and worship done together. The visiting *kami* then blessed that mountain, saying that its *kami* and his descendants forever would be always happy, and that boys and girls would climb it to pick its flowers in spring, and with sake and song in the fall when the leaves turn. It speaks of the mountain as having a 'divine palace' (*jingū*). Men and women meet on it in spring and autumn to exchange odes, an idea probably influenced by Chinese literature.

The *Man'yōshū* also contains very intriguing glimpses of early *Niiname* customs:

> Though it be the night when I make
> Offerings of the early rice of Katsushika
> I will not keep you, darling,
> Standing outside the house. (XIV: 3386-7)

> Away, you who rattle at my door,
> On this sacred night of new rice-offering,

---

*him entered by this rite the body of the new emperor. It had been shared by Ninigi and all past heavenly grandsons (Origuchi, 'Daijō-sai no hongi', p. 194). Doubtless this theory represents an aspect of the archaic view (and an aspect of it which appealed to modern nationalists), but it seems also to overlook important aspects.

We should also note the story of the new festival house discovered on a hill by a river in the Suinin section of the *Kojiki*. On seeing this house in Izumo, the imperial prince, who had been dumb, began to speak, and another new palace was built for him.

Sasatani points out that in the *Nihon-shoki* and *Kojiki* the title *hitsugi-no-miko* was sometimes given the heir to the throne; e.g. in Richū 2, Spring first month, Mizuhawake-no-miko, who became the next emperor, was made *hitsugi-no-miko* (Sasatani, pp. 62–3).

[62] *Shinten*, p. 1834. Translated by Kōno Shōzō and Sakai Atsuharu, 'The Hitachi Fudoki', *Cultural Nippon*, VIII, No. 2 (June 1940), pp. 177–8.

When I've sent my man out
And worship in the house alone.   (XIV: 3460)[63]

These poems suggest that on the night of *Niiname*, the husbands left the house and went out, leaving their wives within to make offerings of new rice. Later, 'mysterious visitors' arrived and banged violently on the doors. Of course these were the menfolk, perhaps disguised as gods and perhaps not at their proper home. No doubt in time they won admittance by proving they were gods, and renewed the seasons with feasting and orgy.

VIII   CONCLUSIONS

WE SHALL now attempt to unify the above material concerning the archaic *Niiname* and *Daijō-sai* before proceeding to the strictly historical material, which begins with the Temmu period.

First one is struck by the atmosphere of the *Niiname*. It is a critical time from which acceptance or rejection, blessing or curse, may derive. The setting is that of a marriage feast. A newly married couple needs a new house, new food, new wedding garments, a nuptial couch. These are provided. In time, as in any proper marriage, a child is born, and is wrapped in the white coverlet of the couch.

The orientation is matrilocal, and at the marriage the bride is in her new house or purified house. She prepares for the nuptials by weaving new garments and spreading the feast of new food. There is a male visitor at night.

But, as in any marriage, things may go wrong. The hostess may mistake the guest or be inhospitable, and he may leave with a curse instead of a blessing. Or the wrong visitor may appear and, like Susano-o (who, we must remember, was also Amaterasu's consort and the father of her children) instead disrupt and destroy. But there is also a true bridegroom, or perhaps one should say the bridegroom in his true and tractable nature. The situation is thus also a test for the bridegroom. If he is true, he wins the nuptial

---

[63] Translations: Nippon Gakujutsu Shinkōkai, *The Manyōshū*. These are said in the original to be poems of Shimofusa, which is in Azuma, and thus happens to be near Hitachi.

Pierson (*The Manyōshū, Book XIV*, p. 113) translates the second:

Who is it who pushes and shakes the door of the house?
I have sent my husband to the Niiname matsuri;
That purified door!

He comments that the idea of the last line (*iwanu kono to wo*) is 'Imagine someone trying to violate a sanctified door!'

For the relation of other *Man'yōshū* material to the New Harvest and New House, see Nishitsunoi Masayoshi, *Kodai saishi to bungaku*, especially pp. 361–2.

couch and will beget a son, who in turn will be a true heir, the one wrapped in the true coverlet, who later at such a time will also prove true.

Thus there are three figures, the male sky *kami* who is the true bridegroom, the female earth *kami*—often daughter of a local male land *kami*—who receives him, and the disruptive influence. This last in one way or another, as we have seen, appears in all of the *Niiname* myths and adds to them the strong note of a time of crisis. There is the violence of Susano-o, and later the dragon which he slew before consummating his marriage with the daughter of the land *kami*. Every myth of descent and marriage with *Niiname* overtones (as most of them have) contains the Disrupter, whether it is personified, or is subjective like the marriage problems of Ninigi or Ho-ori-no-mikoto. One is reminded of the fact that to this day in some parts of Japan young men traditionally make a play at disrupting the nuptial procession by throwing dirt.[64] But the disturbance is quelled by the kinfolk of the bride so that harmony and the hope of new life can be restored. So in the marriage of the sky and earth *kami*, there is a third male element which seeks to intrude and disrupt the mating, and must be dispelled. But, interestingly, in the case of Susano-o, both male elements, the fructifying and disrupting, are combined in one male person. In the same way, the mysterious visitors at harvest in the ancient villages were both the husbands of the village and lordly intruding *kami*. In the end, of course, the disturbance passed, and the harvest was celebrated and the new child brought forth.[65] The purpose of the festival is to tame this disruptive male force, to cause the sky power fruitfully to unite with the maiden and become a reliable guardian of the land and father of a child.

In a story of the Emperor Yūryaku in the *Kojiki*, the emperor was seated under a *tsuki* tree (mulberry; but note the play on words, since *tsuki* also means 'moon') beside the Harvest Festival hall at the time of the festival. A court lady from Mie, an *uneme* from Ise province, was offering him a wine cup when a large leaf fell from the tree into the cup. The emperor became very angry and was about to kill her when she soothed him with a poem. The verses related that the leaf was a good augury, for it fell from the

---

[64] G. Bownas, *Japanese Rainmaking and Other Folk Practices*, pp. 70–1, 161. For the relation of such practices to Harvest and New Year's, and the themes of orgy and renewal, see Prof. Hori's article, 'Rites of Purification and Orgy in Japanese Folk Religion'.

[65] On the mysterious visitors or *marebito*, and other ancient folk religion practices cognate to the *Niiname* and *Daijō-sai*, see Hori's 'Mysterious Visitors from the Harvest to the New Year', in R. M. Dorson, ed., *Studies in Japanese Folklore*, pp. 76–103.

top of the tree through the middle and lower branches, and the upper part of the tree represented heaven, the middle part the sovereign's more remote provinces, the lower his nearer provinces, and it landed with a curdling like the heavenly spear in the far-off divine age. In passing, we are reminded of the custom of drinking sake out of oak leaves in the *Engi-shiki Daijō-sai.* But principally we see in this myth a beautiful recapitulation of the archaic theory of sovereignty, derived from heaven, with a hint of lunar origin, renewed at the *Niiname* after an apparent disruption which almost results in the death of a maiden but is resolved by soothing the imperial spirit with a correct rendering of his divine legitimacy.[66]

Thus the emperor, after almost killing the handmaiden in his rage, at the *Niiname* was pacified when she (and later his empress) sang songs expressive of the meaning of the festival. These songs were called *shizu-uta,* or calming songs. The same intent of course attaches to the *Chinkon-sai* for the soul of the sovereign, and the whole of the *Niiname* could be viewed as an attempt to assist the bride to make the marital taming of the sky god successful.

But in the earliest myths as well as in the later ritual usage, two strains emerge in the *Niiname*: what might be called the popular and the imperial; that concerned with the renewal of the crops, and that concerned with the renewal of sovereignty. The two themes are not merely casually connected; they are rather intimately interwoven and we may even say the one is necessary to the other. There can be no harvest without the social order achieved by the state and its sovereign, and no sovereignty without that continuity of legitimacy which, in the face of the decay and mortality wrought by time, must be brought about by renewal. Moreover, the same themes animate both, but with a different though parallel meaning. On the popular side, the descent of the sky *kami* could be interpreted naturalistically; it was the action of heaven in fertilizing the land to produce the crops. On the other, it must be interpreted humanly or, rather, divinely; it was the mating of the *kami* with an earthly maiden to generate a visible line of rulers. Yet the action is the same action. The distinction is not made; the marriage is at once heaven with earth and the sovereign with his (womanly or spiritual) consort; the child is at once the harvest and the next heir to the throne.

When the sovereign enters successively the two lodges of the

---

[66] We might observe that just after this episode, the *Kojiki* presents under the Emperor Seinei a Harvest Festival held by a provincial governor at which the identity of two princes, one of whom became emperor, was revealed. The same story is told at a different place in the *Nihon-shoki.* The basic motif is no doubt significant.

Daijō-sai in the middle of the night, each furnished as a residence with lamps and the couch of testing and tables for food, surely he is the other-worldly sky-descended visitor, and his purpose is the fructification of the land, the proving of his legitimate sovereignty and the renewal of the life. He is the new child, the Imperial Grandchild—hence washed with heavenly water—and the begetter of the next one. He surpasses the state of the priests of Ise and the envoys. Of course he is decorous in all things; he does right what Susano-o did wrong in intruding on Amaterasu, and he passes the test.

We may ask, though, why the special *Daijō-sai* was made to occur only in connection with the accession when anciently both the harvest and sovereignty themes may have been present equally in every *Niiname*. One reason is that like the rebuilding of the Ise shrines, which before Temmu probably occurred at every *Kanname-sai*, though with buildings of a much smaller scale, the building of the Yuki and Suki lodges with each new reign was intended to be a ritual continuation of the pre-Nara practice of rebuilding the Palace with every reign. This was to erase the impurity of death and to signify a new beginning of human affairs, the birth of a new Imperial Grandchild.

Another reason may concern the empress. We have seen that the Imperial Grandchild of the myths, when he descends to earth, marries a daughter of the earth *kami*. Now it is interesting that the marriage of the Emperor Jimmu supposedly occurred only a year before he assumed the imperial dignity, and, moreover, that he 'honored his wife by making her empress' on the occasion of his enthronement at Kashiwahara.[67] The Emperor Temmu did the same in his case,[68] no doubt the precedent for the Jimmu account. However, it is also true that it is not his visible empress whom the sovereign meets in the *Daijō-sai* as we know it, and, in fact, she has significantly little part in it.

In some of the areas which submitted to the Yamato line and became part of the Empire of Japan it seems the divine king married a different consort every year, this being part of the *Niiname-sai*. This may have been the case in Izumo, and may lie behind the story of the earth *kami* there with eight daughters who were sacrificed one each year to the dragon, apparently at the *Niiname-sai*, until Susano-o slew the dragon and married the last.[69] We do

---

[67] Aston, *Nihongi*, I, p. 132.
[68] ibid. II, p. 321.
[69] ibid. I, pp. 52–3.

not know if this custom obtained in any form in the Yamato tradition, but if so, it may be in reaction against it that by the time of Temmu the union of emperor and empress, and with it the *Daijō-sai* as a special and unique level of union between the sovereign and the *kami* of the land, was restricted to an act done in conjunction with the accession.

The divine marriage framework does not deal with all theoretical questions which arise in connection with the *Daijō-sai*. There is, for example, the matter of why the sacred fields, the lodges, and the rite are duplicated. This certainly has some relation to the many examples of duplication of the parallel *Kanname-sai* rite at Ise and the alternate location of the buildings there. It does not bear any obvious relation to the sacred marriage theme, but is another of those subtle and intractable mysteries which lie beneath the seemingly simple surface of Shinto. Certainly, if the present theory is at all correct, the Yuki and Suki lodges do not, as Holtom thought, enshrine the souls of the past and present emperor respectively.[70] It is rather a visit to female *kami*. The rite, however, nowhere gives the name or names; we will not enter into the considerable but fruitless speculation by which Shinto writers have tried to elucidate what it is. It is enough to suggest that it is the great earth maiden, whose heavenly model is Amaterasu, but who, throughout Japan and the world, has gone under many names.

---

[70] Holtom, p. 146 (new ed., p. 117).

CHAPTER III

The Background of the
Engi-shiki Daijō-sai Ritual

W
E ARE now at the moment of movement from myth and
preliterate rite to the perpetuation of the same forms in
writing and the usages of a Court. The *Daijō-sai* itself
receives but the scantiest reference in the writings of the period,
partly because of deliberate secrecy, like that which surrounded
the Chinese emperor's rite at Mt T'ai, partly because such old
Shinto things were of little interest to most persons of culture.
But by reflecting on the general shifts in the structure of religious
life, we can provide a counterbalancing backdrop to the mythical.
The forms which the Ministry of Official Shinto (*Jingi-kan*) put
to paper were a perpetuation in form of what was already passing
away as spirit, but the very fact that it was desired not to lose their
appearance is also significant. In a time of rapid transition, it was
necessary to encapsule the power of the past—even if in the guise
of crystalline ritual—in the heart of a very different culture, and
thereby to unify the two.

The next stage after the mythical was precipitated almost too
rapidly by the stabilization of agricultural society, the influx of
continental culture, and the effective unification of the state. At
once Japan had to discover itself as historical, that is, as living in
a present obviously different from a concretely remembered, non-
mythological past. Yet the situation had to be interpreted reli-
giously in order to preserve its equally obvious continuity with the
theocratic past.

What changes in orientation occurred? First of all, the emergence of the historical era produced an upsurge of masculine supremacy in the political and spiritual orders. Neither the Confucian
state nor the Buddhist church could abide the archaic experience
that, in the world, genuine power could center in female sexuality.
The Taika and subsequent reforms destroyed matrilocalism as an
official institution, no empress reigned after the Nara period, while
the Saiō at Ise and the *mikannagi* remained as purely Shinto offices. This 'patriarchal' transformation, of course, is one which

most cultures have undergone at the inception of their historical period, and which commonly effects a solar symbology for royal descent, as in Babylon, Egypt, India, Peru, and elsewhere.

Second, increased bureaucratic organization and ideological pluralism in the Court decreased its effectiveness as an unequivocal theocratic center.

Third, the tendency to locate the heavenly and earthly deities in permanent shrines, rather than in the palace or the field or mountain, led to a loss of a vital appreciation of their dynamic quality.

Fourth, the more complex social and political organization led to a greater emphasis on the role of families (both native and immigrant) who had special occupations or special roles in the political hierarchy, that is, the various *be*, *miyatsuko*, *tomo*, etc. Thus, careful attention was given to their divine origin and relation to the imperial family in the written mythology. This was paralleled by a need to show the properly subordinate relation of the clan *kami* of the various localities and clans to the imperial line.[1]

In sum, this critical transitional period was informed by a sense of a 'fall' of society into the secular, for which appropriate compensation had to be made.

The sovereign's formal function, as representative of the heavenly deities in fecundating the earth, was not changed, but the locus was. *Hieros gamos* within the palace, whether human or divine, was no longer explicit. Neither female spiritual power nor theocracy nor the dynamics of divine descent could any longer conveniently govern day by day, or year by year, practical affairs.

The requirement was then for a religious construction which would affirm the new state of affairs without denying all of the more matricentric past, and preserve at least ritually the theocratic ideal without refusing place to the new world of Chinese idea

---

[1] For a discussion of the principal families and of the immigrants, and their relation to the development of religion, see Nakamura Toshikatsu, 'Yamato seiken no saishi kōzō'. Nakamura points out that the main families cited in the Amaterasu myth are the Nakatomi, Imbe, Sarume, 'Mirror-makers', 'Jewel-makers', and Ōtomo. (We may observe that, if the cited forgers and craftsmen be connected with the Mononobe, these would also be the main families who had traditional roles in the ancient *Daijō-sai*.) For the background of the Nakatomi, whose name means 'mediator', see ibid. pp. 45–51. For the ritualized role of the naturalized immigrants, especially to what extent shamanism was imported from Korea through them, see ibid. pp. 51–3. The Urabe are a special problem. Since they later shared the Ministry of Official Shinto with the Nakatomi and Imbe, one could ask why they are not given divine-age antecedents like the others, but they are not mentioned until the Taihō documents. It has been suggested that they are actually of immigrant background or are a branch of the Nakatomi. Nakamura inclines to the latter theory, ibid. pp. 53–5. For a more technical study of the Taika and pre-Taika clans, see Naoki Kōjirō, *Nihon kodai kokka no kōzō*, especially the charts pp. 44–5 and 62.

systems and the new fact of historical nationhood. It is easy to see how the Amaterasu-Ise ideology provided a cumbrous, but remarkably viable, way of handling these problems. The solar goddess is presented as being at once heavenly-ancestral and agricultural. As we have seen, her fields are the celestial model of the earthly, but her role is that of the earth mother offering the first fruits. In a word, she blesses the present heaven-descended patriarchy while preserving the memory of the sovereign queen. She unifies the former dynamic tension of heaven and earth by removing the action to a heavenly place which is a model for earth, thus liberating the emperor to play the role of male fecundating power below in reciprocity with both heaven and earth, with both the Amaterasu and Toyouke shrines at Ise. As the Sujin-Suinin accounts suggest, the movement of the imperial cultus to Ise was the result of the breakdown of a previous concept of kingship and the ritual preservation of its ideology in another place, Ise, and in a special ceremony, the enthronement *Daijō-sai*. But in the earlier sources the deity of Ise is not called Amaterasu, but merely the Ise-no-ō-mikami, the great *kami* of Ise, nor is any name given even today to the deity whom the emperor meets in the *Daijō-sai*.

The archaic society in the mythology was matrilocal. As Motoori recognized long ago, the man went to the place of the woman in the marriages, divine and human, of the *Kojiki*. This of course affected the concept of divine dynamics. It also affected the workings of Japanese kingship.[2]

The ruler consolidated his position by marrying one woman of each tribe subject to him, usually the daughter of the *kami*, or chief.[3] If the wanderings of Ōkuninushi, Yamato-takeru (though the official myth makes him a prince, not a sovereign), and certain mythological emperors are any guide, at first this practice may have retained matrilocal character also, and the charismatic office of kingship, like that of the male *kami*, was ambulatory—the monarch came as a visitor.

Of course, then as ever since, the Japanese emperor has had essentially a priestly rather than a practical political function, which explains the continuance of the dynasty. He has, like certain Paramount Chiefs of Africa, or leaders of tribal confederations in North America, served to create unity sacramentally whether

---

[2] For an extensive and recent study of Japanese matriarchical systems, see Takamure Itsue, *Bokeisei no kenkyū*. Here I have used pp. 23–34.

[3] In the matrilineal period, naming the child was also the responsibility of the mother, as is shown in the Suinin account. See Shibata, pp. 29–30.

or not it was a political reality: the achieving of the latter is left to other hands, other voices speaking in his name. Whatever the latter do, whether in the course of history they rise or fall in power, the emperor's function is to ratify it; but just as sun and rain fall on the just and unjust without blame, so he is without moral responsibility for the practical decisions of those who hold temporal power.

We may thus understand the language which speaks of the emperor as 'manifest *kami*', 'sun', and the like. He, or rather his office, is one with the universal *logos* by which all destinies natural and human are fulfilled. This theory of sovereignty, while probably similar to that of the Chou and earlier periods,[4] may be contrasted with that which obtained in China under Confucian influence. There, 'heaven' was to be distinguished from the monarch, who held political power only as long as he enjoyed the 'mandate of heaven', meaning theoretically as long as he ruled virtuously, practically as long as he could enforce his rule. When one dynasty succeeded in overthrowing that in power, it was presumed that the mandate had been passed to it. In Japan, on the other hand, the point is that the emperor *is kami*, or heaven. It is his office which, tacitly and impersonally, through the signing of edicts which ratify the workings of historical fate, sanctions the course of events. Thus in Japan it is not the dynasty which changes, but the viceregal and shogunal families which, analogously to Chinese dynasties, rise and fall 'under heaven'. In both cases 'heaven' amounts to impersonal *logos*. Although of course there are strong traces of the 'mandate of heaven' theory in the *Kojiki* and *Nihon-shoki*, as in the account of Buretsu,[5] the basic principle of hereditary legitimacy is never lost sight of.

The archaic emperor, then, unified the state through marriage. In time the matrilocal principle disappeared and the sovereign had court ladies, *uneme*, brought from the various provinces. At about

---

[4] For a valuable study of early Chinese kingship, see Wm E. Soothill, *The Hall of Light*.

[5] Buretsu (supposedly r. 498–506), according to the *Nihon-shoki*, 'worked much evil, and accomplished no good thing. He never omitted to witness in person cruel punishments of all kinds, and the people of the whole land were all in terror of him' (Aston, *Nihongi*, I, p. 399). He is the only sovereign of whom such an adverse generalization is made. Moreover it seems obvious that his reign is intended to mark the end of a dynasty or line, since his successor (Keitai, which means 'continuing the line') is made to come from a far place and to be only a distant relative of the preceding sovereign, being a fifth-generation descendant of the Emperor Chūai, the husband of Jingū. While the story is probably a fabrication as far as particulars go, it may be intended to represent some dynastic upheaval which was remembered to have taken place just before the beginning of the historical period, at the beginning of the sixth century (Keitai is dated r. 507–31). It is interesting that something like the Mandate of Heaven theory is resorted to as an implied explanation.

the same time, the shamanistic and theocratic elements of kingship, as practically important matters, declined. The archaic king was apparently close to a female shamanistic medium, like Ainu chieftains and Okinawa kings to very recent times, who gave oracular advice on matters of state in trance.[6]

This shamaness might be the wife, sister, or other female relative of the sovereign, or a woman of lower class chosen by divine election; we see both of the last two types in the Sujin accounts. The 'shamanistic queen' like Pimiko or Jingū was doubtless simply a person in this office, always a Court fixture, who through an especially powerful and charismatic personality caused the kingship to be eclipsed during her lifetime.[7]

There is reason to think that, at least symbolically, the removal of the dynastic cultus from the Palace and the sending of Yamato-hime to Ise in the legendary Sujin-Suinin period marked a beginning of the decline of the Court power of shamanism and archaic theocracy. Of course all throughout the Nara and Heian periods, the Court was not uninfluenced by prophecies, oracles, and omens of all sorts, but these came from a variety of sources and not especially from an institutionalized shamanism of the archaic type. On the other hand, certain very interesting and important institutions of the *Engi-shiki* religion, the *mikannagi* of the Ministry of Official Shinto and the Saigū princess, are clearly closely related to the ancient institution. If no longer genuinely shamanistic, these persons are a sort of petrified 'ritual perpetuation' of the forms of the theocratic past.

The movement against archaism was stimulated by contact with continental culture and found its initial climax in the Kōtoku and Taika reforms of the middle of the seventh century. They implicitly rejected matrilocal and matrilineal institutions in favor of

---

[6] See Kindaichi Kyōsuke, *Ainu Life and Legends* and Wm P. Lebra, *Okinawan Religion*, pp. 110–14. The Okinawan *chifijing*, or chief priestess, was customarily an elder sister or the eldest daughter of the ruler. She lived a restrictive and ceremonial life with female assistants in some ways comparable to the Heian Saiō, but she was mature or elderly rather than a child. The shamanistic power of the office seems to have slowly given way to a purely ceremonial role under Confucian influence. At one time she could even force the abdication of a sovereign on the basis of her oracles, but in the reign of Shō Shin (1477–1526) her shrine was removed from the palace to the other side of the city (an action comparable to that of Sujin?) and thereafter her role in affairs of state became much less important. On this see also pp. 102–3, where Lebra shows that early Chinese and Japanese visitors to Okinawa reported that women held more power than men on both state and local levels, and that until more recent years the *noro*, or priestesses, often had judicial roles, which they exercised partly by magical and shamanistic means.

[7] For a fuller discussion of archaic shamanism and kingship in Japan, see J. M. Kitagawa, *Religion in Japanese History*, Ch. 1, and his 'The Prehistoric Background of Japanese Religion', pp. 292–329.

patriarchal and were designed to put government on a different footing from that of marriage, shamanistic theocracy, and a clan organization of society with the imperial house holding a mere paramountcy. The official priesthood, simultaneously, developed (on paper) from the hereditary functions of certain families to a bureau of the government, although the same families continued to dominate it and even increased their influence.

The beginning of the crisis period was the introduction of Buddhism. According to the *Nihon-shoki*, this was accomplished in A.D. 552 when the Korean kingdom of Paekche sent an image of Buddha to the Japanese emperor.[8] The emperor, Kimmei (r. 539-71), was impressed with the new doctrine but indecisive. Immediately, if we believe the *Nihon-shoki*, a division was formed. In answer to the emperor's question whether the Buddha ought to be worshiped, his leading ministers answered as follows:

> Soga no Oho-omi, Iname no Sukune, addressed the Emperor, saying:—
> 'All the Western frontier lands without exception do it worship. Shall Akitsu Yamato alone refuse to do so?' Okoshi, Mononobe no Oho-muraji, and Kamako, Nakatomi no Muraji, addressed the Emperor jointly, saying:—'Those who have ruled the Empire in this our State have always made it their care to worship in Spring, Summer, Autumn and Winter the 180 Gods of Heaven and Earth, and the Gods of the Land and of Grain. If just at this time we were to worship in their stead foreign Deities, it may be feared that we should incur the wrath of our National Gods.'[9]

Thus the lines were drawn between an attitude of international openness and conservative nationalism, not for the last time in Japanese history. We see on the one side the Soga family, soon to rise to supremacy on the early fortunes of Buddhism, and on the other the Mononobe and Nakatomi, both houses connected with Shinto affairs. The apprehension of the Nakatomi, as the official priests of the traditional religion in the Court, is easy to understand. That of the Mononobe may be a little more complex. As a guild of metal-workers and armorers, they had certainly profited from those earlier waves of cultural influence from the continent which had introduced these arts to Japan. While the advanced technology practiced in Japan was that of Korean and Chinese immigrant artisans, the Mononobe must have represented the native house most abreast of such developments. Perhaps indeed it

[8] Aston, *Nihongi*, II, pp. 65–6.
[9] ibid. pp. 66–7.

was a sense of rivalry in the same field which led them to begrudge the spreading influence of their religion as well as their art. Moreover, the Mononobe seem to have had a peculiar special relation to Shinto which is not explained solely on the grounds of their trade, as well as a high place in the councils of state. The special relation to Shinto may be understandable in light of the sacred aspect of metal and metal-working. It may also have to do with a different vocation they seem to have held, that of controlling and pacifying spirits.[10] In any case, we see in the Jōgan and Engi *shiki* that they had a special role in the *Daijō-sai*. In the Jōgan period (859-76) they were still said to be widely distributed through the provinces. The string-tying (*musubu*) part of the *Chinkon-sai*, or spirit-pacification rite of the Palace, is attributable to them, and one feels they had a special interest in the cultus of the high god Takami-musubi. The Mononobe always came down on the conservative, if not reactionary, side of every question, and always favored Shinto and the Yamato tradition thereof.

During the reign of Kimmei, each of these families practiced their preferred religion on a more or less experimental basis, and the prevalence of pestilence or prosperity were adjudged tests between them. The verdict was, as might be expected, doubtful, but Buddhist influence clearly continued to increase. The following reign, that of Bidatsu (r. 572-85), may have witnessed something of a Shinto reaction. The emperor himself was apparently of two minds on the matter of Buddhism, and issued contradictory edicts concerning its encouragement and suppression with every word of advice given him from the Soga or Mononobe side.[11] It was also in this reign that a sun-worship (or fire-worship) guild (the *hino-matsuri-be*) and a guild for the empress's service were established. In the light of later developments in Shinto, this may suggest that Shinto was taking new forms in response to the threat of Buddhism.[12]

---

[10] Origuchi Shinobu believed that the 'mono' of Mononobe meant 'spirit'. The word *mono* used in this way often meant the spirit of an animal or a 'lower' sort of malevolent or queer *kami*, as in *tsukimono*, possession by an animal spirit, but there is also the word *ayashikimono*, which suggests a strange, marvellous, and radiant spirit, as well as one queer or uncanny. Origuchi thought that the Mononobe originally were not armorers but their function was to handle the 'Spirit of Yamato', that they were priests of the national-imperial deities and hence custodians of the emperor's spirit. Thus their function at the *Chinkon-sai* or Spirit-Soul-pacification and in the Jimmu account can be understood ('Daijōsai no hongi', p. 197). This theory probably has much truth to it, though certainly the treasury of their Isonokami shrine shows they had a great interest in weaponry too. But more recently Uemura Seiji has stated that the name refers to military armor (*Jimmu Tennō*, p. 31).

[11] See Aston, *Nihongi*, II, pp. 102–3.

[12] ibid. p. 95.

In the next reign, that of Yōmei (r. 585-7), the Nakatomi and Mononobe were defeated in battle as the debate reached the point of violence, and Buddhism continually grew in importance in the subsequent periods of Sushun (r. 587-92) and Suiko (r. 592-628). Temples and monasteries continually sprang up. Confucian ideas and Chinese court practices likewise flourished, as did vigorous dynastic quarrels.

The first landmark of the new age was the so-called Constitution of Prince Shōtoku traditionally dated 604, attributed to the remarkable prince who served as regent under Empress Suiko until his death in 621. He was a man of brilliant mind, deep Chinese learning, noble character, and devout Buddhism, as well as of a firm mastery of matters of state, if half the tales of him be true. However, the 'Constitution' is held by most scholars actually to date from a generation or so after his time.[13]

The 'Constitution' is really a set of ethical and moral maxims for civil servants. They represent an idealism which would seem most lofty in any age, all the more so in comparison with the realities of seventh-century Japan. But they are significant in representing the kind of ideas which were current among the small number of intellectuals. The second, 'Sincerely reverence the three treasures', etc., is clearly Buddhist. The other sixteen articles actually follow the ideology of Han Confucianism,[14] admixtured as it was with Taoism, stressing the four seasons, the duties of master and vassal in a hierarchical society, the example of antiquity, and virtues such as good faith, moderation, honesty, public spirit, avoidance of envy, and making important decisions only with the advice of others. But the supremacy of the sovereign is made clear, and the 'Mandate of Heaven' theory is avoided.[15]

The great landmark of the seventh century, however, is the Taika Reform. It took the form of a Court edict, and like all such in Japan in some instances it was only ineffectual idealism, in others meant only paper changes, and in still others was unenforced.[16] But it would be a great mistake to feel it did not reflect a

---

[13] The Constitution was supposedly issued in 604, and just before, in 603, 'Cap Ranks', the Chinese gradations of officials, were said to have been instituted. Again it is not certain whether the ranks were established then or forty years later at the Taika Reform, where the matter is repeated, but this is of no great importance to our study. On the date of the Constitution, see Sansom, *A History of Japan to 1334*, pp. 52-3.

[14] It is noteworthy that this element of Chinese thought had greater early explicitly political influence in Japan than Buddhism.

[15] Text in Aston, *Nihongi*, II, pp. 129-33.

[16] Nakamura suggests that, to see the effect of the Taika Reform, Yamato may be contrasted with Izumo, where the *kuni no miyatsuko*, both chief priest and civil ruler, continued in power in wide areas despite nominal submission to the throne. The office was*

period in which 'winds of change' were blowing strongly. It was a period which can only be compared with such times as the Taira or the Meiji eras in Japanese history, when fundamental structures and symbols were being rapidly and radically transmuted, whether social, political, or religious. The half century from the Taika Reform of 645 to the Taihō Code of 702 saw the consolidation of a new concept of sovereignty and government—patriarchal, rational, appointive, bureaucratic, centralized—on the one hand, and the emergence of institutional Buddhism (of the Nara schools) and of what we will call Temmu Shinto on the other.[17]

During the reigns of Saimei (r. 655-61) and Tenchi (r. 661-71), which followed the Taika period, Buddhism continued to flourish. Attempts were made to put the provisions of the Reform into practice, but owing to internal and external difficulties, this goal was not fully accomplished. Perhaps the most important disturbance was the so-called *Jinshin no ran* of 671, the dynastic civil war which followed the death of the capable and pro-Buddhist Emperor Tenchi. The party favoring the late emperor's son was defeated by the forces of Temmu, a brother of Tenchi. Whatever his personal beliefs, Temmu seems to have been supported by conservative, pro-Shinto, anti-Reform nobles. Especially significant is the important support he received from the province of Ise.[18]

The civil war and Temmu's victory served the purpose of delaying the full implementation of the Reform, and the perhaps more memorable purpose of allowing Shinto a breathing spell adequate to force institutional forms sufficient to preserve its spiritual heritage in the very different new age.[19] We may now note that the major institutions of official (in contrast, of course, to popular)

---

*transmitted in the Seng family, and its incumbent long continued to exercise a local quasi-magical sway unrationalized by bureaucratic organization. But he notes also that the Taika Reform itself had not too great an effect on ritual, which was not radically reconstructed until Temmu (op. cit. pp. 55–8). For the kind of powers which the Izumo *kuni no miyatsuko*, as an *ikigami* (a priest of divine charisma, or living *kami* for whom the secular and religious realms were one) held locally up to the time of the Meiji Restoration, see W. L. Schwartz, 'The Great Shrine of Idzumo', pp. 543–7 and appendix. The Taisha-kyō sect still preserves something of its ethos—as do certain 'New Religions' about their charismatic founders.

[17] It is interesting that, as happened in the half-century preceding the Meiji Restoration, and as often happens in times of social crisis and incipient radical change, popular ecstatic, shamanistic, and quasi-apocalyptic movements seem to have flourished as heralds of the Taika age. Under the reign preceding it, that of the Empress Kōgyoku (r. 642–5), the *Nihon-shoki* presents a number of portents. Most impressive are those concerning prophets and ideas arising from among the common people. See Aston, *Nihongi*, II, pp. 188–90.

[18] Tsuda Sōkichi pointed out that the extension of imperial power to the east, consummated in the triumph of Temmu, is also important. 'Nihon jōdai-shi no kenkyū', *Tsuda Sōkichi zenshū*, III, pp. 156–7. See pp. 80–132 of this essay for a discussion in detail of the implications of the various decrees and their economic background.

[19] See Kawasaki Tsuneyuki, *Temmu Tennō*, Tokyo, 1962 and 1966.

Shinto up to modern times—the imperial ideology based on the *Kojiki* mythology, the special place of the Grand Shrine of Ise, the Saigū, the enthronement *Daijō-sai*, the regulation of shrine matters and local shrines by the Crown through the Ministry of Official Shinto, the sending of extensive Court offerings, especially at the *Toshigoi*—all these either effectively originated in the Temmu period or received extensive modification in it. These rites are the foundation of the Ministry of Official Shinto part of the *Engi-shiki* and thus are precisely those central to our study.

However, only two of the above can be assigned to Temmu on the basis of the *Nihon-shoki*. In 673 a princess was selected to purify herself in preparation for going to Ise as Saigū princess.[20] In 677 'The emperor gave orders to the Shrines of Heaven and the Shrines of Earth that the sacred rice-tax should be divided into three shares, one of which was to be set apart for the offerings to the gods and the other two given to the Kannushi [priests],'[21] thus setting a precedent for the imperial regulation of such matters. According to the preface of the *Kojiki*, it was Temmu who ordered its compilation. Temmu also celebrated the *Niiname*, or Harvest, festival, according to the *Nihon-shoki*, but its relation to enthrone-ment is not so clear as in the case of his successor Jitō (r. 690-7). Later and less historically reliable sources attribute also the first *Toshigoi*, the separation of the *Daijō-sai* and the *Niiname*, the institution of the periodical rebuilding of the Grand Shrines of Ise (*shikinen-sengū-sai*), and other such matters to Temmu. Since many of these are found institutionalized in the Taihō Code of 702, or soon after, but yet are very problematic as institutions of great antiquity in their courtly form, certainly the attribution of this whole complex of institutions to the Temmu-Jitō period and its Shinto revival is correct in principle, and probably in historical fact.

Historically important references to the *Daijō-sai* do not begin until the reign of Temmu. Although not absolutely certain, it seems a likely hypothesis that the Temmu period was responsible for the direction the *Daijō-sai* was to take. According to the *Nihon-shoki*, the *Niiname-sai* was held in the fall of the second year of Temmu, the first year he ruled in peace, for on the fifth day of the twelfth month of that year presents were given to all in atten-dance at that feast: that is, the Nakatomi and Imbe, the *kamuzu-kasa*, or *kanzukasa* (predecessor of the Ministry of Official Shinto)

[20] Aston, *Nihongi*, II, p. 322.
[21] ibid. p. 336.

officials, and the district governors of Harima and Tamba (clearly the Yuki and Suki provinces) and the laborers under them. Before, a Great Purification (which may or may not have had a special connection with the *Niiname-sai*) was commanded on the sixteenth day of the seventh month. On the twenty-first day of the ninth month the *kamuzukasa* announced the Yuki and Suki provinces. On the first day of the tenth month a 'wine feast' was held for the ministers; this may or may not have had a connection with the following. On the third day of the tenth month an *Ainie* was held, and offerings of cloth were presented to the *kami*. This was an ancient harvest festival, also called *Aimbe*, *Aimube*, or *Ainame*— clearly a variation of the *Niiname*. It was celebrated in the eleventh month before the *Niiname*. The emperor partook of new sake offered to the *kami*, and sent imperial offerings to certain shrines. The *Engi-shiki* lists seventy-one shrines to which *Ainie* offerings were sent; they and the offerings are carefully listed (*Shinten* text, pp. 1045-61). Why the *Niiname* and the *Ainie* are distinct is not clear; apparently somehow two divergent traditions are represented, perhaps in a phenomenon not dissimilar from the divergence of the *Niiname-sai* and the *Daijō-sai*.[22]

In the fifth year of Temmu (675) we do not have specific notice of the holdings of the *Niiname-sai*, but under the date of the first day, eleventh month, it is said that because of the *Niiname-sai* the first of the month was not announced. (Announcing the beginning of each month was a borrowed Chinese Court custom.) Then, in the sixth month, eleventh day, twenty-first year of Temmu, it is recorded that the *Niiname* was held, and on the twenty-third a meal was given for all of rank, and on the twenty-seventh presents were given to the *kamuzukasa* and provincial officials who had helped with the *Niiname-sai*.

However, it is not until the reign of Temmu's widow and successor, Jitō, that association of the *Daijō-sai* with enthronement becomes evident. It is as though the concept was developed with the progress of Shinto thought during the Temmu period, applied in the Jitō period, then codified in the Taihō legislation promulgated shortly after her abdication. In the spring of her fourth year (689) the *sokui-rei*, or accession ceremony, was held, with the Nakatomi no Ōshima no Ason, minister of the *kamuzukasa*, reading the

---

[22] Origuchi believed that the *Ainame* was a rite just of the Home Provinces, and that the relation of the Court to the Ise *Kanname-sai* and the national *Daijō-sai* represent expanding waves of imperial influence, gauged by the distance to which offerings were sent and received ('Daijō-sai no hongi', op. cit. p. 185).

norito, and Shikofuchi, Imbe no Sukune, delivering to the empress the divine seal, sword, and mirror, and the ministers making obeisance. The delay after the actual accession is explained by the Chinese custom then obtaining of a three-year mourning period following the death of the previous sovereign. Then, as we would expect from the timing provided in the *Engi-shiki,* the next year, twenty-fourth day of the eleventh month, the *Niiname-sai* was held, and again the same Nakatomi and Imbe presented the *norito* and the mirror and sword. A few days later a banquet was given as usual for the *kamuzukasa* officials and the governors of the Yuki and Suki provinces. This is the first clear instance of the later pattern, however ironic it may be, in view of the basic theory of the rite, that it was performed by an empress.

As stated, the practice of the reign of Jitō corresponds with the provisions of the Taihō Code enacted early in the next reign. In principle this Code represents the final resolution, so far as formal Court organization and practice is concerned, of the crisis which had continued acute since the introduction of Buddhism a century and a half before. Of course in practice major changes arose, such as the virtually plenary power of the Fujiwara and later of the shoguns, but these potentates were usually circumspect about observing the ceremonial forms of the Taihō Code with the primacy of sacredness and honor it accorded the emperor. It remained theoretically the fundamental law of Japan until the Meiji period; later enactments in its spirit, such as the *Engi-shiki,* were regarded as emendations or casuistic application.

No text of the original Taihō Code issued in 701-2 is extant. We have only two early Heian period commentaries, the *Ryō no gige* of 834 and the *Ryō no shūge* of *c.* 880-920. The effect of Chinese law and scholarship is evident, both in the wording, that is, the characters, used in the text, and in the syntax and allusions of the commentaries.

The dependency of the Shinto sections of the Code on the Chinese T'ang dynasty rituals has been illustrated recently by Kashihi Tanaka.[23] It is noteworthy that the chapters of the Japanese Code which treat of the *Daijō-sai* have no parallel in the Chinese source, even though other chapters are almost verbatim transcription. This indicates that the Japanese writers understood the differences in the concept of kingship implied by this religious rite and wished not to minimize the distinction from the more civil Chinese usage.

---

[23] Tanaka, *A Comparison of the T'zu-Ling and the Jingi-ryō.*

But Article 11, which defines the conditions of abstinence before a ritual, follows quite closely Article 38 of the *T'zu-Ling*, even though comparable concepts of ritual purity—abstinence from death, blood, and sickness, and the use of 'separate' food and fire, as well as washing—certainly obtained in Japan very anciently. The pattern seems to be one of borrowing foreign language for what one already has, and using parallel language for the rest, or simply assuming knowledge of it.

The law and state organization of the Taihō Code is often called the *ritsu-ryō*, that is, roughly, 'the laws and administrative ordinances'. The Empire of the Nara and Heian periods may be called the '*ritsu-ryō* state' so far as its political theory is concerned. Its foundations are the Taika and Taihō codes, its culminating expression the *Engi-shiki*; but as the '*ritsu-ryō* state' lost political meaning it preserved power as an ideal not without force even in the Meiji period and the twentieth century. The '*ritsu-ryō* state', grafting Chinese forms onto archaic Japanese institutions, is in many ways a unique construct.

It is not, first of all, a method of practical government but a symbolic expression of the meaning of the state. The former could be handled by other means, and usually was, although in the early *ritsu-ryō* period especially the powerful members of the Fujiwara family who held practical power did also occupy high office within the structure. But the meaning of the structure as such was the presentation of the state as ritual, and therefore meaning and order. The central figure, of course, was the sovereign, the continuing incarnation of the powers of archaic theocracy. The state, then, by Court structure perpetuated both the meaning of the archaic world to some degree and absorbed the foreign contact which had introduced the history that destroyed its reality.

The Code provides for no fewer than four variations of the Harvest Festival: the *Kanname-sai* of the Grand Shrines in the ninth month (apparently, as far as palace ritual is concerned, the dispatching of the imperial envoys with imperial offerings, as provided in the Regular Festival Section of the *Engi-shiki* (*Shinten*, p. 1043), the *Ainie* Festival mentioned above, the *Niiname-sai* or *Daijō-e* of the eleventh month, and the *Daijō-e* of the accession. The *Chinkon-sai* is cited. The Taihō provisions are slightly vague concerning the distinction between the enthronement and the annual *Daijō-e*, partly because separate terminology had not yet emerged, but since it is clear that some distinction is intended, it appears we are safe in allowing later developments to assist in elucidating the meaning.[24]

However, in Nara the format of the accession and annual ceremonies was probably similar to a greater extent than obtains today. The divination of the Yuki and Suki fields appears to have continued for the annual *Niiname-sai* until the reign of Kammu (A.D. 781-806) which began the Heian period, and perhaps the building of the Yuki lodge and Suki lodge was annual as well. But by the time of the Jōgan Ritual of 872, which contains a full *Daijō-sai* ritual in vols. 2-4 of its ten surviving volumes and is presumably based on the fragmentary Kōnin Ritual[25] of 819, the distinction is clearly made in much the same terms as in the *Engi-shiki* and the modern rite. The enthronement rite is called the *Senso Daijō-e* (or *-sai*), the annual simply the *Daijō-e* or *Niiname*. It is only since the Meiji rituals that the terms *Daijō-sai* and *Niiname-sai* have been used strictly and exclusively to refer to the enthronement and annual festivals respectively.[26]

The shape of events after the Taihō period was one of steady development along the lines laid down by the Code. The basic issue was the relation of Shinto and Buddhism. Pressures from both

---

[24] The Taihō Code states in Article 10 of the section devoted to the Ministry of Official Shinto: 'Upon the accession of an emperor, all the gods shall be worshipped. There shall be partial abstinence for one month, complete abstinence for three days. The offerings shall be made ready within the three months preceding the *Daijō-sai* ceremonies.' Articles 11 and 12 give further details concerning the two types of abstinence, discussed earlier in this chapter (section 2).

Then Article 13 provides for the accession ceremony proper, such as the modern Civil Enthronement (*sokui-rei*) and the Jitō period ceremony: 'On the accession day, the Nakatomi shall read the divine ritual, the Imbe shall present the divine tokens, namely the mirror and the sword.' (The regalia jewel, which never receives as much mention in earlier writings as the mirror and sword, is not named.)

Article 14 reads: 'The great food festival (*Daijō-e*) shall be celebrated once in each reign by provincial officers. Other festivals shall be celebrated annually by officials of the Department (of Religion).' (Translation by Sansom in 'Early Japanese Law and Administration', p. 125. In the same place, Sansom comments: 'This appears to mean that when the *Daijō-e* was celebrated in connection with the enthronement ceremonies, special officers were appointed in each province to carry on observances which were a counterpart of those at the capital. But the ordinary *Daijō-e* was to be celebrated, together with other festivals, by the usual officials.' Thus, in the fact that provincial governors were required to celebrate the *Daijō-sai* (same as *Daijō-e*) in a special way in conjunction with the accession, we can see evidence that it was doubtless special in the palace too, and also a hint that the emergence of the distinction may be related to the unification of the nation and the establishment of a centralized system of government, with a permanent capital. Of course, before the Nara period for which the Taihō Code was the legal foundation, the first *Daijō-sai* would automatically be distinct in that it would be the first celebrated at a new palace. We have seen that it may also have been connected with the marriage of the sovereign. Before the Nara period it was also one with the New Year, and replete with the kind of associations this suggests.

[25] The Kōnin and Jōgan Rituals were respectively the first and second of the major emendations and revisions of the Taihō Code ritual law, the *Engi-shiki*, or Engi Ritual, being the third and last of this series.

[26] For a list of references to the *Daijō-sai* in Nara-period sources, such as the *Shoku-nihongi*, *Man'yōshū*, etc., see Umeda, pp. 290-2.

the highest and lowest levels of society favored accommodation; against them it was primarily the Ministry of Official Shinto and the Grand Shrine of Ise (that is to say, four or five powerful families) which managed to keep the worship of the traditional gods alive within the Court, if in a rather crystallized form. But throughout the Nara and Heian periods the formal prestige of the Ministry of Official Shinto and its rites did not diminish, probably because of the family connection of the all-powerful Fujiwara with the Nakatomi, and such institutions as the Saigū even attained to some degree of spiritual vitality, at least to the extent that they could become the occasions of popular festivals and colorful parades, and from time to time appear in the literature. However, one feels that of all the religious systems current in Japan at the time, it would be to Official Shinto that one would last take his real spiritual concerns. But such a characterization scarcely does justice to its purpose in the life of the Court and the nation, which (as things developed) was not at all to meet the same needs as Buddhism.

In the Nara period, however, the balance of force and role between Shinto and Buddhism was undecided. It was indeed a high point of Buddhist influence. Even at Ise, for example, a Buddhist temple in conjunction with the Grand Shrine existed; it was built in 715, but moved outside the shrine precincts in 772 after an oracle from the lunar deity Tsukiyomi revealed that a typhoon was due to the anger of the Ise *kami* at its presence.[27] While this coincided with a certain reaction against Buddhism toward the end of the Nara period, it shows that Ise was always relatively more grudging of Buddhism than most shrines, which continued a certain symbiosis with a temple until the Meiji period, while Ise preserved not only its Shinto purity but such practices as the anti-Buddhist taboo words.[28]

The confusing nature of the evidence regarding the relation of Shinto and Buddhism reflects the fact that, as Professor Kitagawa has pointed out, there were two conflicting trends within Shinto.[29] One was toward accommodation with Buddhism, the other ex-

---

[27] Ōnishi, *Daijingū shiyō*, pp. 92–4. See also Kishimoto Yoshio, *Shintō no rekishi*, p. 26. Kishimoto believes that Buddhist influence was actually stronger at Ise in the Heian period than in the Nara, if subtler.

[28] *Kojiruien, Jingi-bu 2* quotes the *Shoku-nihongi* for Tempyō Jingū 2 (766) to the effect that a Buddhist image was placed in the Ise temple, and also gives stories of the removal of the temple (pp. 1715–16). Perhaps the anti-Buddhist taboo words of the Saigū, at least the 'Inner Seven', derive from the period of this conflict.

[29] J. M. Kitagawa, *Religion in Japanese History*, pp. 43–4.

pressed a nostalgia for the pre-Buddhist past and a desire to preserve its forms unstained. In the Temmu period, there is the first and most influential upsurge of Shinto feeling as nostalgia for something already felt, unconsciously at least, to be slipping away or past. Thereafter one can see the interplay of Buddhist and Shinto strength between the Temmu and *Engi-shiki* periods moving virtually according to a cyclical pattern, with Buddhism reaching a peak of force in the middle of the centuries, Shinto making a modest resurgence around the turns of the eighth, ninth, and tenth centuries.

The accommodation with Buddhism produced the obvious and rationalized systems of Ryōbu Shinto, with their various metaphysical ways of handling the problem. There was also the straightforward cultic alliance of the two religions, such as the famous story that the Buddhist leader Gyōgi obtained advice from the Grand Shrine of Ise to build the great Buddha of the Tōdaiji, or the story that the *kami* Hachiman was brought from Usa in Kyushu and enshrined in it. Indeed, the most powerful places for worship were often those fanes known as Gongen shrines, which were temples located on a pre-Buddhist sacred mountain whose object of worship was, in effect, a hybrid of Bodhisattva and *kami*, and the cultus a blend of the most potent elements of both religions. Such places were Kumano, Yoshino, and Dewa.

But perhaps the most telling illustrations of syncreticism are those which resulted in such subtle or gradual changes in practice that the influence of the other religion was undetected and therefore unrationalized. Thus Shinto embraced, perhaps more from popular or Confucian Chinese religion than Buddhism, ancestralist elements. Precisely to what extent original Shinto included ancestrism is disputed, but there is no doubt that outside continental influence heightened the identification of *ujigami* with ancestors and the idea that these and other spirits are powerful just because they are ancestors. Ancestrism modified the character of a whole spectrum of ostensibly Shinto culti, from the veneration of the Imperial Family for its dynastic ancestors (which no doubt helped shape the new prominence of the *Kojiki/Nihon-shoki* mythology and of the Grand Shrine of Ise) to the folk religion connected with harvest of the peasantry. Another example is pilgrimage. Pre-Buddhist *kami* had worship and power only following tribal lines, so the idea of a long journey to worship a different deity was meaningless. But after the notion of universal gods and of pilgrimage entered with Buddhism, notable Shinto shrines, including the purest, Ise, profited greatly from it.[30] (Pilgrimage to Ise by other than members of the Imperial Family did not begin until the close of the Heian period, however.) In turn, of course, Buddhism in Japan absorbed many elements from the native religion, especially shamanistic—even though this was lost by official Shinto more or less simultaneously.

We have already intimated what forms the nostalgic, conservative trend within Shinto took. It was pre-eminently the Temmu ritual crystallization of the most precious motifs from the religion of the past. It is worth noting, however, that often the conservative spirit must change precisely what it wishes to preserve in order to preserve it. Thus not only had Shintoists to capsulize what had been vague, oral, and diffuse in single symbols, such as the Grand Shrine of Ise, and written myth, but they had also to appeal precisely to the power of the Court. Precisely to keep what represented a less centralized age, they had to depend on the authorization of the central government, and hence also become a pillar of support for it. The preservation of the spirit of the pre-literate age with its shamanistic religion and untamed tribes became the function of that most bureaucratic of offices, the Ministry of Official Shinto, and of those most tediously legalistic and bureaucratic of documents, the Taihō Code and its supplements leading up to the *Engi-shiki*. In this connection we may note that official Shinto served the Court as a way of manifesting imperial authority in the provinces, as in the *Toshigoi*. As time went on, the rituals adjusted themselves to the fact that the dispersion of prominent families through the provinces, such as the Mononobe, decreased, and the importance of appointive officials—of course members of important Court families—increased.

As has been said, around 800, the time of the establishment of the Heian capital, there was a certain resurgence of interest in Shinto. Of course from an overall point of view it was minor compared to the other religious and political concerns of the time, but

---

[30] Tsuda Sōkichi points out that the spirit of the departed Emperor Tenchi (r. 661–71) is spoken of as a *kami* in the *Man'yōshū* (II). He says that the emergence at about the same time of the term *jingū* (*divine* palace) under the influence of Chinese, derives from the association of imperial ancestors with the shrines so designated. In the *Man'yōshū* the word is especially found in the *Azuma uta* (Eastern songs), hence from the direction of Ise ('Nihon jōdai no kenkyū', op. cit. pp. 357–61). Hence there is some general relation between the movement of imperial authority toward the east, imperial ancestrism, and the rise to prominence of Ise. For the developing relation between ancestral *kami* and *ujigami*, the ancient clan *kami*, see Shibata, pp. 30–40. Virtually all the prominent shrines with many branch affiliates became such in large part because they became *ujigami* shrines of important families—of the Imperial Family at Ise, the Fujiwara at Kasuga, the Minamoto at the Kamakura Hachiman, the Taira at Miyajima, etc.

a few books came out suggesting a feeling on the part of those concerned with it that, along with everything else being set right by the movement of the capital, Shinto should also be re-examined. The *Shoku-nihongi* containing the Imperial Edicts of the Nara period and continuing the relating of history in the generally pro-Shinto vein of the *Nihon-shoki* appeared in 797. In 804 ritual books (*gishiki-chō*) of the Grand Shrines of Ise presented, as the result of an imperial inquiry, their definitive ritual, rationale, and history. In 807 appeared the interesting and important *Kogoshūi*, the Imbe apologia against the increasingly powerful Nakatomi containing much valuable mythological and historical material. Finally in 819 the Palace Ritual of the Kōnin Period (*Kōnin-shiki*), first of the three major explications of law and ritual, stressing Ministry of Official Shinto matters, was put into effect. These three rituals, or *shiki*, those of the Kōnin, Jōgan, and Engi periods, are meant to be practical interpretations of the Taihō Code legislation and express (in their worship sections) the official concerns and policies of the Ministry of Official Shinto. (Only fragments of the Kōnin Ritual survive.)[31]

After the Heian period was well under way, for a time interest in Shinto again declined. During the middle years of the ninth century, the far more exciting and glamorous Buddhist developments at Kōya and Hiei, and the eager reception of new ideas from China, attracted far more attention. However, toward the end of the century and into the next a moderate reaction against Chinese influence set in. The official missions to China ceased as early as 839, although unofficial cultural exchange continued. But the evident decline of the T'ang dynasty leading to its collapse in 907 lessened China's effective cultural power. Japan acquired a new confidence to emphasize its own language, literature, and even religion. Again, the Shintoist aspect of the reaction was minor against the total scale of things, and produced no particular popular movement in favor of the ancient cultus, but was apparently sufficient to create an atmosphere conducive to the writing of the classic statement of Ministry of Official Shinto religion, the *Engi-shiki*.

The first half of the tenth century, the period which lies in the background of the *Engi-shiki*, was—despite the idealization of it by later Heian writers—not only a time of the resurgence of Japanese letters, but also a time of increasing social disillusion and con-

---

[31] On the *jingi* (Shinto ritual) content of the major legislation from the Ōmi Code of Tenchi 9 on down, see Umeda, pp. 53 ff.

fusion. The all-powerful Fujiwara strove to suppress the other clans but were forced to contend with rebel uprisings in the east and north and in the Inland Sea. Disturbance and banditry were everywhere, even in the capital and the Palace. It was often recognized that the exploitative social system had something to do with the problems, and rulers like Fujiwara no Tokihira (in power 899-909) seriously attempted reform, but without real success. What wealth there was in an island nation poor in natural resources and transportation was too much concentrated in non-productive hands, noble or ecclesiastical. Like many another leisure class, Heian Japan was to leave a glowing cultural legacy, but could not avoid its own inevitable self-destruction. A vivid picture of the situation is given in the Statement of Opinion (*Iken fūji*) of 914 of Miyoshi no Kiyotsura, a distinguished Confucian scholar and statesman, who was a member of the committee which compiled the *Engi-shiki*. He presents in detail the deterioration of public finance and morality which, in his view, had continued since the introduction of Buddhism. He shows moreover that the increasing poverty of the nation is due to the capricious desire for luxuries on the part of the upper classes. He makes special point of the corrupt and lazy lives of the Buddhist and Shinto clergy, and the low standards of learning.[32]

However, as Miyoshi conceded, the picture he draws is partial. Heian society had still more than two centuries to run before it reached its lowest point of decline and its eclipse. Culture continued to flourish in the capital, and even if corrupt, Buddhism and to a much lesser extent the other religious orientations and the glory of Court life still evoked profound and creative visions of man. The greatest literary works, such as *The Tale of Genji*, still lay in the future. As Sansom observes, though reduced to powerlessness in the political order the sovereign 'is looked upon as the protector of learning, the guardian of a ceremonial tradition that is wearing thin'.[33] His primary concern was the promotion of great literary undertakings, including the compilation of laws and precedents, the writings of histories and literary anthologies. The production of the *Engi-shiki*, in which of course the emperor is ceremonially central, is a part of this vision of the imperial function. It may thus be seen as the final expression of the *ritsu-ryō* model of the state, and a lasting memorial of a society which, caught between an archaic past which it knows can never live

---

[32] Sansom, *A History of Japan to 1334*, pp. 147–8.
[33] ibid. p. 148.

again except in ritual and a present at once glorious and corrupt, seeks to immortalize on paper and in forms where it has been and what it sees as its spiritual essence, even as its exterior fabric slowly crumbles.

The writing of the *Engi-shiki* was commanded in Engi 5 (906) by the Minister of the Left Fujiwara no Tokihira, who, as we have seen, was by intention a reformer. (Since it was commanded in the Engi calendric period it is called the *Engi-shiki*, or 'Ritual of Engi'.) The purpose was to compare, revise, and amend the previous rituals into a definitive edition. A committee of eleven names was entrusted with this task. As listed in the preface of the *Engi-shiki* (surname first), they were, with their major office:

> Fujiwara no Sadakuni, Dainagon (second to the Minister of the Left)
> Fujiwara no Ariho, Chūnagon (second to the above)
> Taira no Korenori, Sangi Ōkura Kyōshō (ranked below the above; in Stores Ministry)
> Ki no Haseo, Sangi Sadaiben (equivalent in rank to above)
> Fujiwara no Sugane, Shikibu no Taifu (vice-minister of the Bureau of Rankings)
> Miyoshi no Kiyotsura, Monjō no Hakase (Doctor of Letters; the Confucian scholar discussed above)
> Ōkura no Yoshiyuki, Mimbu no Taifu (vice-minister of the Census Bureau)
> Fujiwara no Michiaki, Go no Sashōben (an Assistant Minister of the Left)
> Ōnakatomi no Yasunori, Jingi no Taifu (vice-minister of the Ministry of Official Shinto)
> Mimune no Masahira, Dainaiki (a Palace Affairs official)
> Koremune no Yoshitsune, Myōbō no Hakase (Doctor of Laws)[34]

Doubtless the more exalted of these persons regarded their appointment to this task as more or less honorary and left the drudgery to subordinates. On the other hand, we see the name of at least one serious reformer, and have reason to believe the work was undertaken as a project necessary and culturally important.[35] Only one Ministry of Official Shinto person appears in the list, but it may be significant, in view of the fact that that Ministry's sections of the book are the longest, most thorough, and most researched parts, that he is the only one who seems to have remained with the project to the end twenty-one years later.

---

[34] *Shinten*, pp. 1003–5.
[35] Haseo Ki was also a courtier noted for scholarship, according to the *Kampyō ikai* of the Emperor Uda, but was relegated in time to a sinecure at Tōdaiji by Tokihira. Sansom, *A History of Japan to 1334*, pp. 142–3.

Changes occurred, as we would expect, before the *Engi-shiki* was finished in 927. In 913 the Dainagon Fujiwara no Tadahira, who finally wrote the preface, and the Udaiben (Ministry of the Right Official) Tachibana no Sumikiyo were added. In Enchō 3 (925) the Dainagon Fujiwara no Kiyotsura was added. At the same time Ōnakatomi no Yasunori of the original list together with Ki no Hisanaga and Ato no Tadayuki were entrusted with the final editing. The preface was signed by Tadahira, Kiyotsura, Ōnakatomi no Yasunori, Hisanaga, and Tadayuki, indicating that perhaps only these five were the effective members of the committee by the time the project was completed, and as we have noted only one of these, Yasunori of the Ministry of Official Shinto, was an original member.

The Introduction to the *Engi-shiki*, before the preface which supplies the above information about the compilers, was written by Tadahira and gives the sort of philosophical and historical rationale which was thought necessary to grace and explain a work of this sort. It is written in most ornate language, and provides an interesting insight into the formal thought of the period, even if the Chinese literary and philosophical atmosphere may seem contradictory to our understanding of the meaning of the rites here introduced. It begins by saying, 'When we reflect seriously and with detachment, we perceive that heaven overshadows earth. After its example the sacred emperor instructs the people. In the *yin* there is pathos, in the *yang* alleviation. The wise kings patterned themselves after this and so guided customs.' However, 'rectifying legal principles and conferring discipline, by way of encouragement and admonishment, can bring to agreement the barbarian and the noble.'

Then there is praise of the good influence of the Emperor Saga (who promulgated the Kōnin Ritual) who in his day reversed this deterioration, and of Seiwa of the Jōgan Ritual, who in the same way 'preserving the lack of frivolity of the Chinese kings, led the people with rich words'. He is especially honored for (in his laws) 'heaping up praise and lightening penalties', as did the virtuous emperors of antiquity—that is, the sage-emperors of China. 'Like the virtue of refreshing rain his blessings spread everywhere; blowing with a pure wind it cleansed the dust of the whole earth.'

However, 'the benefit is no longer widespread,' and the people have fallen into recalcitrant ways. But once again, by imperial word, the dykes are to be repaired by adjusting the law code. What was lacking even in these two previous noble systems of law is to be supplied. A new code is to be issued, carefully selecting and emending the best from the previous works. It is to be a moderate work, not envisioning radical change but based on thorough study of the 'old books' of the Kōnin and Jōgan codes and the books of the Han dynasty.

It is stated that the twenty-two books of the *kyaku* (emendation of the civil code, now lost) were early finished and presented, and now 'at last the fifty volumes of the *shiki* are selected and gathered'. This Introduction would have been formally intoned at the presentation of the work to the sovereign, and there are at the end apologies for the fallibility of the officials who prepared it.[36]

We see then, finally, that the preparation of the *Engi-shiki* is explained as another high point in a history viewed as deterioration and renewal, in a world governed by the alternation of *yin* and *yang*, the renewals being attributed to the acts of the sacred sovereign to recover the glory of past moments of repristination. Hence, finally, the theory which produced the *Engi-shiki* itself is not inconsistent with the profoundest theme of its rituals, the renewal of the world in each year and each age of man with heavenly waters brought to earth by the heaven-descended emperor.

---

[36] Text in *Shinten,* pp. 1001–2.

CHAPTER IV

The *Engi-shiki* Text of the
Accession *Daijō-sai*

I INTRODUCTION

THE *Senso Daijō-sai*, or First-Fruits Festival as performed by the emperor as a part of his accession ceremonies, is regarded by the *Engi-shiki* and all other standard Shinto writings as in a class by itself as the most sacred of the worship which Shinto has to offer. Unquestionably, this is because it unites in the most explicit way the otherwise twofold foci of Shinto piety, the emperor and the harvest, the image of the representative man and the image of abundant food. The *Daijō-sai* is also a ceremony virtually in a class by itself for the student of Japanese religion, for there is no other rite of comparable importance which has preserved intact so much from such remote antiquity. Those usages of the Ise shrines, such as the *shikinen-sengū* ('twenty-year rebuilding') and the *Kanname-sai* (harvest festival at Ise), which doubtless approach it in age of continuous tradition and certainly breathe the atmosphere of the same late pre-Buddhist Yamato period, have not quite the archaic purity of the *Daijō-sai*. Even the oldest stratum of Ise usages reflects a mixture of indigenous and Yamato elements which can in fact be attributed rather precisely to the Temmu period, and whether in the *Gishiki-chō* (ritual book of the Grand Shrine of Ise) or the present we see nothing at Ise untouched by Temmu's assertion of the alliance of the Grand Shrine and the Yamato Court.

This is the case even when both the Ise and Yamato elements of the Temmu amalgamation would be older than Temmu, as most of them were, since the alliance was meant to be a conservative gesture. Like the *Daijō-sai*, they are rituals which encapsule the world of late Neolithic Japan, the Japan of the Yayoi and Kofun periods. These ceremonies received their crystallized form just as the old was passing away as Chinese or Buddhist ideas permeated the Court. Just because the Court felt itself becoming more Chinese than Yamato, the power of its past was entombed with the imperial ancestors in the rites of Ise, and Ise seemed to remain the same only because its status, purpose, and administration changed.

But in the *Daijō-sai* we have remarkably preserved, as in amber, an intact memoir of the Yamato Court. Even in the *Engi-shiki*, it stands apart in its archaic integrity. The other rites, of course, are also written down with the intention of preserving the Shinto tradition of the Court and the Grand Shrine. But yet the others, the *Toshigoi*, Saigū, and the like, while rooted in antiquity, depend heavily for their Engi-period operation on post-Taihō institutions: they are talked of in the language of Court ranks, imperial offerings, the Ministry of Official Shinto itself. A glance at the *Daijō-sai* text reveals a different world, one in which these elements, though present, are distinctly more peripheral. One need not pick out the thread of archaic ritual action from admixed ponderous lists of offerings and of personages with imported titles. Rather the simple line of ritual action emerges clearly of itself.

A further advantage is that the *Daijō-sai* has been the subject of a competent monograph in a Western language, D. C. Holtom's *The Japanese Enthronement Ceremonies*.[1] On the other hand, scholarly material in Japanese, despite the great intrinsic interest which ought to accrue to such an incomparably ancient survival, is remarkably slight in quantity, and for the most part dated in approach. This is apparently because there have been only three enthronements within the last hundred years, and none since 1928. Such studies as do exist have generally appeared around the time of an enthronement, with the important exception of the recent work of Professor Tanaka Hatsuo. However, to date only the first volume of his projected study has appeared.[2]

We will begin with a general outline of the *Daijō-sai*, following with a presentation of the *Engi-shiki* material with commentary. The most important fact about this rite is that, like the rebuilding of the Ise Shrines and the *Kanname-sai*, which was the climax of the Saigū's activities, it is a variation of the Harvest Festival, the

---

[1] This book makes the ceremony vivid and comprehensible, although it contains a few errors of fact and (in my opinion) of interpretation, and suffers from a lack of documentation in the historical sections. However, it is primarily concerned with the contemporary rite. R. A. B. Ponsonby-Fane also deals with the contemporary *Daijō-sai* at much shorter length, in *The Imperial House of Japan*, pp. 341–68, and *Studies in Shinto and Shrines*, pp. 56 ff.

[2] Tanaka Hatsuo, *Senso Daijō-sai no kenkyū*, I. I would also like to express my indebtedness to Prof. Tanaka for many personal conferences concerning the *Daijō-sai*. He is not, however, responsible for my interpretations of the rite.

Niiname.[3] As presented in the *Engi-shiki*, it is the Harvest Festival celebrated with the emperor serving as priest the year after his accession. It is the Court *Niiname-sai* for that year, but as celebrated in conjunction with the accession in this way it contains several elements, all very archaic, which distinguish it from the *Niiname* of an ordinary year.

The *Daijō-sai* really begins in the early spring, when two special rice-fields in different parts of the empire are selected by divination and planted in accordance with special ceremonial traditions. In the fall, also in accordance with special traditions reminiscent of the rebuilding concerning the cutting of the first wood and so on, two identical rectangular lodges together with a few auxiliary buildings are erected near the palace. On the eve of the great rite, the *Chinkon-sai*, or pacification of the emperor's spirit, is held. The next night, the emperor makes purification with hot water, then enters the first of the lodges, called the Yuki-den. The inner room of this building is furnished in the manner of an ancient throne-room, with a couch, pillow, tables, and lamps. Here the emperor, assisted by two maidens, offers new rice and sake and other food to the *kami*, and goes through the motions of partaking of the rice and drinking the sake. He then retires, changes his vesture, purifies himself again, and enters the Suki-den, the other building, at 2:00 A.M. This building is identical in furnishings with the Yuki-den, and the rite is also identical; as at Ise and elsewhere, Shinto seeks duplication, bifurcation of rites and structures. Then, on the morning after the rite, the Nakatomi read the *yogoto* ('congratulatory words') and the Imbe presented the mirror and sword in ancient and Heian times. The *Daijō-sai* buildings are torn down, and the solemn ceremony is followed by a series of banquets with sacred dance as entertainment. Thus there are basically three distinct stages: the *Chinkon-sai*, the *Niiname*, and the *enkai*, or

---

[3] During the Nara and Heian period, a virginal imperial princess, usually a child, was selected by divination upon the accession of a new emperor. She went to Ise to serve as Saiō in an institution known as the Saigū. Before arriving at Ise, however, she spent a year in a consecrated dwelling on the capital grounds, called the Shosai-in, and another year in a residence called the 'country house', No-no-miya. Her progress to Ise was an occasion of great solemnity; the emperor himself bade her farewell by placing a comb, the 'Comb of Departure', on her forehead. At Ise, the princess would live a life of seclusion and strict Shinto piety, save for three times a year (the *Kanname-sai*, or Harvest Festival, at Ise, and the two *Tsukinami*), when she would solemnly travel to the two Grand Shrines to participate in the imperial offerings. It seems evident that the Saigū is meant to show the Imperial House before the great Shinto deities as it would like to be seen by them—pure, virginal, unstained by alien Buddhism. The fourth major festival, the *Toshigoi*, is also, of course, linked to the Harvest Festival in that it is an act done in direct anticipation of it, as the *norito* makes clear. See the interesting, if somewhat dated, article by Yamamoto Nobuki, '*Toshigoi to Daijōsai to no kankei*'.

banquet with its dance. These each may be said to represent an aspect of the renewal of kingship and of the crops which is the intent of the rite.[4]

II   PREPARATIONS

WE MAY now turn to the *Engi-shiki* ritual itself. The ritual begins with a setting forth of the time:

> Whenever the accession to the throne takes place by the 7th month of a given year the *Senso Daijō-sai* is held in that year; if in the 8th month or later, then the festival is held in the following year. (This refers to accession after abdication and does not mean enthronement after national mourning for the death of a Sovereign.)   (31; *1245*)

This means that the timing of the *Daijō-sai* does not depend on the accession accomplished immediately upon the death of the previous sovereign by the private reception of the Regalia, but on the official enthronement in the Palace, the *sokui-rei*, which might not take place in fact until a year or more had elapsed. It would be held between the second and eleventh months of the year after the death or abdication of the previous emperor. Formerly three years of mourning were observed before such a rite could properly be observed; this is reflected in the fact that the public accession of the Empress Jitō (r. 690-7) did not occur until her fourth year. This seems to have begun with the impact of Chinese customs in the reign of Tenchi, but was shortly reduced to one full year of

---

[4] As indicated, the *Daijō-sai* has been an extremely conservative rite, and the usage of 1928, the last, differed in only a few significant ways from that of the Engi period. It should be mentioned also that since the beginning of the Heian period there has also been another parallel accession rite, the *sokui-rei*, 'accession ceremony'. This is held in the Shishin-den, or Great Throne Hall, of the Imperial Palace in Kyoto, and consists of a solemn proclamation by the Prime Minister of the accession in the presence of the Imperial Regalia, the enthroned sovereign and (now) the empress, and the Court. Although accompanied by a certain amount of symbolic ornamentation, and preceded and followed by processional pomp, this is essentially a simple and civil rite, thoroughly based on Chinese models, and of little interest in connection with our study. It is fully discussed in Holtom, *The Japanese Enthronement Ceremonies.* It is held before the *Daijō-sai.*

The actual accession is accomplished shortly after the death of the previous emperor through a third rite, a brief ceremony in which the three items of the Imperial Regalia, the Mirror, Sword, and Jewel, are officially transferred to the new sovereign. This rite, the *kenji togyo no gi,* was in use in the Heian period also. The Mirror and Sword were and are actually presented to the emperor three times, at the *kenji togyo no gi,* the *sokui-rei,* and the day after the *Daijō-sai.* Of course, the originals of the Mirror and Sword are kept respectively at Ise and Atsuta, so the ceremony consists of transfer of the Jewel and of making an announcement before the shrine within the Palace containing a model of the Mirror and of a transfer of a model of the Sword. Holtom, p. 58 (*47*). (Numbers in italics refer to page numbers in the 2nd ed. of Holtom's work, pub. by Sophia Univ. in 1972.)

mourning, which has continued to the present.[5] Of course, the many abdications of the Heian period would have allowed a shortening of the procedure since no death was involved. The Jōgan Ritual[6] is the same as the *Engi-shiki* here, except that it makes clear that the *sokui* rite is referred to. The *Engi-shiki* continues:

> In the given year, the officials in charge determine by divination beforehand the provinces and districts for the *yuki* and *suki*. When the announcement has been made the orders are handed down according to precedent, and then they determine who shall supervise and who shall conduct the ceremonies.   (31; *1245*)

The method of divination still used for this purpose is agreed to be extremely ancient. It is the use of bone heated and cracked which appears in the *Kojiki* and *Nihon-shoki*. Such a one as Ame-no-koyane-no-mikoto, ancestor of the Nakatomi, did this divination before the Rock Cave of Heaven, and together with Futotama-no-mikoto, ancestor of the Imbe, was commissioned to perform it by Amaterasu when they were sent down from heaven as companions of the Imperial Grandchild. These two deities are invoked in the rite. But whereas in ancient times the shoulder blade of a deer was used, by the Engi period the Chinese practice of using tortoise shell had gained favor.

When a favorable day has been determined, a temporary thatched 'Divination Shelter' is constructed before the main shrine (Shishin-den) of the Palace compound. A light blue curtain is hung about it, and within it a *himorogi*, or upright branch of *sakaki*, is hung with white streamers and surrounded by a hempen fence. As Holtom notes, the *himorogi* probably represents the earliest form of Shinto shrine.[7] Three tables for offerings are placed before the *himorogi* and in front of these a rush mat (*sugomo*) is laid. An area spread with clean sand is laid before the Divination Shelter; this area is called the Divination Garden (*uraniwa*). The *uraniwa-no-kami* are mentioned elsewhere in the *Engi-shiki*, being invoked by the Nakatomi and Urabe in the semi-annual *Gotai-no-miura* (or *mura-no-miura*), or predictions for the emperor which are

---

[5] Holtom, p. 59 (*48*).

[6] The Jōgan Ritual of 872 is the immediate predecessor of the *Engi-shiki* as a Court ritual, and is frequently referred to in the latter as the *Gishiki*, or Ritual. Its ten surviving volumes contain a full account of the *Daijō-sai* which will be frequently cited for comparison in this study since it presents an interesting, somewhat earlier version of the ceremonies. We will use the text as it is presented in conjunction with the appropriate *Engi-shiki* material in Miyagi Eishō, *Engi-shiki no kenkyū*, I. Above citation, p. 129.

[7] Holtom, p. 99 (*75*).

solemnly reported to him in the sixth and twelfth months, and
are invoked by the Saigū in preparation for the Thrice-Yearly
Festivals at which she visits the Grand Shrine of Ise. (*Shinten*,
pp. 1032, 1200)

At the divination proper, first ordinary worship is offered at the
Shishin-den, with Shinto music (*kagura-uta*) as the doors are
opened, offerings, and *norito*. Holtom describes the subsequent
rite as follows:

> Immediately following this the divination service proper is per-
> formed. The actual divining rites take place on the sanded area
> before the divination shelter. At the close of the worship before the
> Shin-den the chief ritualist and other priests pass to their position
> for performing divination. A ceremonial box made of willow wood
> and containing writing material is placed on one of the tables within
> the shelter. A *norito* is then read summoning two ancient deities of
> divination named Ame-no-koyane-no-mikoto and Futotama-no-
> mikoto to come down into the *himorogi*.
>
> Then, while soft music is played, a ritualist who has been care-
> fully prepared in mind and body by three days of special purification
> rites, kindles a fire by rubbing together two pieces of *hinoki* ('fire-
> tree'). He catches the spark of pure fire thus created on some specially
> prepared wood and then, when the flames burn up strongly, holds
> a tortoise shell over them until it is cracked by the heat. During this
> period all of those present, and particularly the ritualists conducting
> the rites, endeavor to keep their spirits calmly receptive to the divine
> influences with which the place is filled. The shell upon which the
> *kami* reveal their will is cut in a shape that roughly resembles the
> form of a tortoise. The lower part is square, the upper part is tri-
> angular suggesting the head of the creature. The shell measures five
> *sun* in width and eight *sun* at the longest dimension. The markings
> on the shell are read according to a traditional secret formula, and
> the indication of the will of the *kami* thus determined is written on
> a paper, sealed, and placed in the box before the *himorogi*. After
> this, *kagura-uta* is again rendered and the gods are returned to
> heaven.[8]

Today this rite is conducted by ritualists and officials of the
Imperial Household; in the Engi period, however, it was super-
vised by the palace retainers (*shoshi* 諸司) but conducted by the
Ministry of Official Shinto, the Nakatomi and Imbe, descendants
of the deities invoked, and the Urabe, who claimed descent from
the Nakatomi ancestors and whose special province was divination.
In the Jōgan Ritual, the palace retainers are not mentioned, but instead the Ministry of Official Shinto, at the command of the Prime

---

[8] ibid. pp. 99–100 (77).

Minister, performed the task.[9] The Yin and Yang Bureau (*ommyō-ryō*) was not involved save in the report of the results to the emperor, which required passing the paper ceremonially from one official to another up the ranks to the throne.[10] However, the secret method of reading the shell markings is based on the Chinese five-element system.[11] The wood used is taken from Mt Katsuragi in Yamato, especially from the Niho-no-ikazuchi Shrine precincts (a shrine listed in the *Engi-shiki*). Ikazuchi-no-kami was a thunder deity who also appeared as a great serpent in the *Kojiki* and *Nihon-shoki* accounts of the reign of Yūryaku (supposedly r. 456-79). A Nakatomi named after the deity was the *saniwa*, or divinatory official, for the Empress Jingū (supposedly reigned A.D. 20-169); this Nakatomi was claimed as an ancestor by the Urabe.[12] Katsuragi also had importance for the *Toshigoi* and was famous as a training place for shamanistic hermits and ascetics.

Anciently only a limited number of provinces were selected as Yuki and Suki provinces, which sent the provisions respectively for the two lodges. One was on each side of the capital. Ōmi was almost always the Yuki province, and Tamba the Suki. Now provinces from all parts of the empire are eligible.

The *norito* for the *ōharae*, or Great Purification, is found in the *Engi-shiki* collection. The rite consisted of reciting the *norito*, together with waving a *sakaki* branch and scattering salt. It was a prerogative of the Nakatomi. The *norito* suggests that also, as is done today in some places, a list of offences was attached to a piece of wood and thrown downriver. The text next says:

> At all times, there are Imperial Messengers for the Great Purification. In the first decade of the 8th month these are selected by divination and then dispatched: one to Left and Right Capital Offices, one to the five inner provinces, one for each of the seven circuits. In the second decade once more Imperial Messengers are selected by divination and again dispatched: one to Left and Right Capital, one to the five inner provinces, one each to the provinces of Oomi and Ise. On the last day of the month the civil officials residing in the capital assemble and perform purification as they do for the ceremony for the two seasons. (31; *1245*)

---

[9] Miyagi, I, p. 130.

[10] Miura Hiroyuki, *Sokui-rei to Daijō-sai*, p. 67.

[11] ibid. pp. 67–9. Yamada Yoshio, *Gosokui Daijō-sai tairei tsūgi*, p. 66. The *Kojiruien, Jingi-bu 2*, has materials and diagrams on the reading of the deer-bones, p. 1265, and of tortoise-shell oracles, pp. 1273–4.

[12] Yamada, *Gosokui Daijō-sai tairei tsūgi*, p. 66.

Much the same preparatory purification was held in anticipation of the progress of the Saiō princess to Ise. The *Daijō-sai*, and the departure of the princesses to Ise and Kamo, were the major occasions for holding great purifications on the last day of the eighth month in addition to the regular twice-yearly great purification on the last day of the sixth and twelfth months. In all these special cases, the special Great Purification has an essential connection with the harvest festival and events which, theoretically, occur only at the beginning of each reign. The 'messengers' were appointed to perform the rite at various strategic points throughout the empire, thus emphasizing that it was not just the Court or the capital which was involved, but the entire nation which must be pure before it can be brought into union with deity through the emperor in the manner intended by the *Daijō-sai*. The performance of the Great Purification was a particular privilege of the Nakatomi.

The text next states that at the same time imperial offerings are presented by imperial envoys at the Grand Shrine and the various other major shrines. The offerings are of cloth, and the same shrines participate as those which receive such offerings at the *Toshigoi*. It is interesting that it is provided that these rites take place in the eighth month, the same as in the Saigū, even though the subsequent ceremony occurs not in the ninth but the eleventh month.[13]

However, the emperor's own purification takes place at the expected time. We next read, 'the Sovereign goes down to the streamside to perform lustration in the last decade of the 10th month' (32; *1246*). A list of offerings is provided. In making this progress to the Kamo River, offerings are presented to the shrines along the way, and alms to the poor. Today, this purification is accomplished by the presentation to the sovereign of a wand which he holds and 'purification garments' which he puts on and removes, and which are then cast into flowing water. But when in the Heian period he made the journey to the Kamo River, it was an occasion of great pomp and spectacle.[14] The *Engi-shiki* notes that 'the Sacred Maidens and diviner's assistants who serve as escorts are provided with riding horses' (32; *1247*). In the Jōgan Ritual the Great

---

[13] But actually the schedule was somewhat irregular; see texts citing instances in Miyagi, p. 130.

[14] See Miura, pp. 148–50. The reason for the change in method of purification was the removal of the imperial capital from Kyoto to Tokyo at the beginning of the Meiji period; the Kamo River, of course, was not available in the new location. The old practice was not revived with the return of the *Daijō-sai* to the old capital in 1914.

Purification was done on the evening before this day, not on the last day of the ninth month as in the *Engi-shiki,* indicating in the latter an ever-increasing rigidity about the time for the Great Purification.[15]

Purification is also accomplished through abstinence on the part of the Court, and the observance of taboo words. The text reads:

> At all times, there is to be one month of partial abstinence (starting the first day of the 11th month and lasting through the last day); total abstinence is for three days (starting on the ox day and ending on the hare day). This month of abstinence is announced in advance to the officials in charge, and when the order is handed down to the inner provinces no one may participate in Buddhist fasts or maigre feasts. The language to be used is: death is called 'getting well', illness is called 'slumber', to weep is 'to shed salt', to strike is 'to caress', blood is called 'sweat'; meat is called 'vegetables', and a tomb is called 'clod of earth'. (33; *1247*)

This is the same provision for 'abstinence' which is provided in the Taihō Code and the Saigū chapter.[16]

III   THE SACRED FIELDS

WE NEXT turn our attention to the sacred rice-fields, the Yuki and

---

[15] Miyagi, text vol., p. 131. The palace ritual *Hokuzanshō* 北山抄 (Northern Mountain Scroll), written between 990 and 1020, provides a full description, comparable to that provided in the *Engi-shiki* for the Saigū purification, of the *Daijō-sai* purification procession to the river (*Kojitsu sōsho,* pp. 413 ff.). This document also reiterates the purificatory prohibitions, such as taboo words, and says that the month before the rite is a sacred (*sai*) month (p. 415).

[16] Abstinence does not mean religious asceticism, but simply the avoidance of impurity. We have cited the provisions of the Taihō Code: 'During partial abstinence (*ara-imi*) all government offices shall carry on their work as usual. But [officials] shall not pay visits of condolence upon a death, or call upon the sick, or eat flesh. Nor shall death sentences be pronounced or criminal cases be judged. No music shall be played, and no unclean or inauspicious tasks be performed' (Sansom, 'Ancient Japanese Law and Administration', op. cit. p. 125). These are based upon ancient Shinto conceptions of purity, with the probable exception of the avoidance of meat, which (like the euphemism for 'meat' in the taboo words) must have crept in from the impact of Buddhist culture despite the aversion to overt Buddhism. The prohibition of music was based on Chinese Court usage, and as we have seen, the language derives from the *T'zu-Ling.* The taboo words are the same as the 'Outer Seven' of the Saigū and the list of the Sai-in chapter, though in slightly different order, but they omit the strongly anti-Buddhist 'Inner Seven' and the two 'Addenda' of the Saigū. The Jōgan Ritual spells out what is to be avoided in the language of the Taihō Code, but lists only five taboo words, omitting 'to strike' and 'tomb' (Miyagi, I, p. 132). That the *Daijō-sai* was construed as an occasion reserved for pure Shinto is apparent from the prohibitions against Buddhist practices. This in itself shows that the 'abstinence' was not designed chiefly from a belief in the intrinsic value of asceticism, since Buddhist austerities and Buddhist 'maigre feasts' would have been more austere than Shinto, but rather is fundamentally founded on the Shinto idea of the pollution of sickness and death. Inō Hidenori states that cooking over a 'pure fire' only and eating out of special dishes was also practiced, above all in the case of the emperor's food (Inō Hidenori, *Daijō-saigi tsūran,* p. 11). This is typical of practice in the Shinto Purification House (*saikan*) before a festival.

Suki fields, in which the grain for the ceremony is raised. A number of typical agricultural ceremonies are now held throughout the growing season, and probably equivalents were celebrated in the Engi period, although only the *nukiho shiki*, the fall ceremony of plucking the grain heads, is provided in the *Engi-shiki*. It is certainly the most significant of the field rites of the *Daijō-sai*. Others now include an April ceremony of purifying the sacred fields (*saiden no shubatsu shiki*), a ground-breaking ceremony (*kuwaire shiki*), a planting ceremony (*tanemaki shiki*), and a 'water-mouth ceremony' (*minakuchi matsuri*) for purification of the irrigation waters entering the field. The transplantation ceremony is carried out around the first day of the sixth month.[17] These rites remind one in general of the rites used at the shrine fields (*saiden*) of the Grand Shrine of Ise, and indeed follow the pattern of rites used in Japanese agricultural religion everywhere, although the spring welcoming of the field-gods from the mountain or elsewhere is not officially recognized in the *Daijō-sai*. At Ise, even the official Divine Field rites contain a gesture in this direction.

The *Engi-shiki* text here begins with a rather complicated statement about taxation, which amounts to allowing the two selected districts to present the *Daijō-sai* rice in lieu of other direct taxes (*33; 1247*). It is also stated that the fields selected shall be among those operated by the capital nobility. The first part of the grain-picking (*nukiho*) ritual reads as follows:

> In the first decade of the 8th month the [*Jingi-*] *kan* is asked to send one chief diviner and three *urabe* diviners, who are to be dispatched two to each of the two provinces. One of them is named the diviner of the rice-ears and one is named priest diviner. Upon reaching the respective provinces they each go to the sacred district, where they perform purification rites. . . . That completed, they select by divination the rice paddies and the various functionaries for the sacred area. (Men and women singers are not determined by divination.) One *sakatsuko* (an unmarried daughter of the prefect or assistant prefect of that district is selected by divination for this). One honorable *sakanami*, one sifter of flour, 2 helpers, one *tametsu sakanami* (the foregoing all women); one lord of the rice-ears, one ash-burner, four firewood-cutters, 20 singers, 20 women singers.   (*33-4; 1248*)

The *tametsu* was grain to be especially presented to the emperor from the two provinces after the rite. The Jōgan Ritual adds that 15 Mononobe, 9 women and 6 men, are selected by divination.[18] These appear to correspond to the 'various functionaries'

---

[17] For the above, see Holtom, p. 103 (*79–80*).
[18] Miyagi, I, p. 133.

spoken of in this part of the *Engi-shiki* rite. This change reflects the fact that in the Nara period, whose situation is still assumed (unrealistically) in the Jōgan Ritual, the Mononobe were yet a widespread and influential clan, especially in Shinto and imperial matters. But by the Engi period they had lost prominence, and are found only in the capital rituals. We will observe the functions of these persons chosen by divination in a moment. But first the building erected in the field:

> [Then] the sacred area is propitiated. For this the symbolic offerings are . . . [list omitted] . . . For all these Treasury goods are to be used. (But the sake and food for the propitiation festivals are furnished by the respective provinces.)   (34; *1248*)

The Jōgan Ritual adds that after the pacification the harvest hall is decorated with *sakaki* in the four corners and with cloth hangings, and the officials wear white garments of linen for the purification.[19] In the *Engi-shiki*, next the specifications for several buildings which are put up are given. These are: a Shrine of the Eight Gods, a sacred house (*imiya*) for the rice grain, an official (*matsurigoto*) house for the envoys, a house for the 'lord of the rice-ears', and a house for the *sakatsuko*. The Jōgan Ritual adds a house for straw storage and a hall for the Mononobe ladies.[20] In the *Engi-shiki*:

> . . . all to be made of unpeeled wood and thatched with grasses; the side walls to be made of grasses. One well is to be dug (a roof built over it). There are to be 16 square *jō* within the compound; brushwood is to be used for the fences, and wood to make the doors. Within this sacred compound eight *kami* are to be worshipped (Mitoshiro-no-kami, Takami-musubi-no-kami, Niwatakatsuhi-no-kami, Oomiketsu-no-kami, Oomiya-no-me-no-kami, Kotoshironushi-no-kami, Asuha-no-kami, and Haigi-no-kami).   (34-5; *1249*)

We may note that these buildings are constructed according to the same very primitive architecture as the Yuki and Suki halls, of unbarked wood, straw, and reeds. The list of eight *kami* is quite interesting and has been the subject of a certain amount of rather inconclusive speculation.[21]

The text next mentions that two diviners serve the Eight Gods in each of the two districts.

Then the very interesting account of the cutting of the grain appears:

---

[19] ibid.
[20] ibid. pp. 133–4.
[21] See Appendix.

> At all times, for plucking the rice plants the diviners lead the gov-
> ernor of the province, the prefects of the districts and on down to
> lower functionaries to the rice paddies to pluck the grain. First the
> *sakatsuko,* then the lord of the rice-ears, then the *sakanami,* then the
> lower functionaries, then commoners, in succession pluck the grain.
> Then it goes to the sacred compound where it is dried and stored.
> Then they begin to divide it up, taking the first 4 *soku* which were
> plucked (4 bundles making a *soku*). They measure the amount for
> the august cooked-rice offerings, the rest they measure for the two
> kinds of sake both dark and light. Then it is all heaped into baskets,
> 1 *soku* in each basket. Two baskets make a load; supports are put
> under each load. Covers are made from woven reeds, and on them
> *sakaki* branches are inserted and bark-cloth festooned. When that is
> done workers on foot take up the loads; for every 10 loads there is
> one junior attendant to urge them on. Diviners, governors, and
> prefects lead the lower functionaries and others. Forward and back-
> ward they supervise the transportation. In the procession the rice-
> in-ear for the august cooked rice is carried first, the remainder fol-
> lows this. The lord of the rice-ears wears a bark-cloth headdress and
> shows the way. They reach the capital in the last decade of the 9th
> month. Divination is done outside the limits of the sacred area. A
> temporary shelter is built beforehand and the august rice is stored
> therein for a while.   (35; *1249-50*)

The Jōgan Ritual has the Mononobe men and women in the
procession in place of the 'lower functionaries' and gives a larger
place to the children. The Mononobe pick the grain after the ceremonial first picking by the *sakatsuko,* etc., then laborers finish
the job.[22]

The *sakatsuko,* 'sake child', a young virgin girl chosen by divination, was to be the first to pluck the sacred grains. We are reminded of the Saigū princess so far as qualification and selection
by divination is concerned (save that the sake child was not a
princess), and of the boy and girl *mono-imi* at Ise who had similar
functions in the first cutting of wood and ground-breaking at the
Ise Rebuilding. Such special functions are reserved for selected
children in festivals to this day, and certainly reflect very ancient
religious concepts. As we shall observe in a moment, the sake child
also had the function a little later of picking the first grains of rice
to be used to make sake for the *Daijō-sai,* and in the consecration
of the Yuki and Suki buildings. The sake was brewed at the Upper
Kamo Shrine, the shrine dedicated to the sky-male consort of
Tamayorihime.

The *ina-no-mi-no-kimi,* 'lord of the rice-ears', is a male, also local

---

[22] Miyagi, I, p. 134.

and chosen by divination, who apparently supervises the ceremonial picking. We do not know enough about his functions to be able to interpret the meaning of the office.[23] The third mentioned in this passage is the *sakanami*, 'sake woman', apparently an older lady, also chosen locally and by divination, who assisted the 'sake child'. An adult to assist the special child is also a common part of this concept, as for example the *'mono-imi* fathers' of Ise. We notice that a child also had a sacred function in the handling of the picked rice, and that it was conveyed to the capital in a special way.

The solemn procession of the offerings from the sacred fields to the capital is suggested in the *Engi-shiki*, which says that there is a child or 'junior attendant' in the procession after every ten loads, and that the officials have a part, including the 'lord of the rice-ears' in a bark-cloth (*kazura*) headpiece. The Jōgan Ritual gives a more adequate outline of it. Of course, 'lower functionaries' have replaced Mononobe in the Engi usage; the available evidence points to the conclusion that no other significant changes occurred, unless the four children with bark-cloth and *sakaki* branches have disappeared. They are not mentioned in the *Engi-shiki*. The Jōgan procession is illustrated in the diagram below.[24]

R.	XX	XX			XXXXX		
L.	XX	XX	X	X	XXXXX	X	XXXXX
	4 laborers (*kenji*) carrying sake	4 children with bark-cloth and *sakaki*	the priest diviner	the lord of the rice-ears	10 persons carrying rice	child with sake	5 Mononobe

Then this same order is repeated once again. Thus the inveterate duplication in Shinto is expressed in each procession, as well as in the fact that they come from the two provinces.

Other supplies for the *Daijō-sai* are procured in analogous ways, as we read next in the *Engi-shiki*:

> At all times, in the *yuki* and *suki* provinces the districts selected by divination must apportion and furnish 30 *koku* of *tametsu* rice (for *tametsu* sake), 40 short *tatami* mats, 70 seat-mats, 70 long mats, 50 split-bamboo mats, and 300 workers on foot who are sent to transport this rice and are to be urged on in the same way as those for the plucked rice plants. (35; *1250*)

---

[23] Origuchi Shinobu indicates that the 'sake child' and 'lord of the rice-ears' were essentially priests—*miko* and *kannushi*—of the Rice itself. It was itself a *kami*, and in the procession discussed below was greeted with heralding just as the emperor was ('Daijō-sai no hongi', pp. 178–80).

[24] Miyagi, text vol., p. 134.

This rice would be used for the banquets after the rite. As we shall see, mats are lavishly used in the *Daijō-sai* buildings, particularly where the emperor must tread. Likewise, timber is provided:

> At all times, the mountains where materials for the *Daijō* buildings and oak leaves for sacred food offerings are to be gotten, as well as the moors where reeds for thatching are to be cut, and ground to be used for the sacred areas, are all to be selected by divination by the members of the *Jingi-kan* and the governors of the provinces together in the first decade of the 8th month. (In divining the sacred area, first it is exorcized; required articles for this are forwarded by the respective provinces.) When that is done, the fact is announced to the *Jingi-kan*. And the prefect in whose district the mountains and moors are situated is made to keep them under taboo and prevent any defiled person from entering them. The mountain from which materials for the august *koto* for the Pacification of August Spirits are gathered is subject to the foregoing procedure; there are to be four kite-tail *koto* which the *Jingi-kan* orders the Bureau of Skilled Artisans to construct and send up.   (35-6; *1250*)

Here again we are reminded of practice at the Ise shrines, and probably not by accident, since it appears that Yamato practices such as these were incorporated into the Grand Shrine usage. We notice that everything which has an important sacred use, a use connected with spirits and offerings and the *Daijō-sai*, must have a sacred history: its origin is determined by divination, which means it is selected by the *kami* in their own mysterious way and not by man, and thenceforth is marked off as taboo to profane use or touch. We note also in all things the preference for even numbers, and fundamentally the liking for twofoldness, parallels, or opposites: mountain and moor, etc.

IV   THE NEW RITUAL BUILDINGS

THE SCENE now moves to the preparation of the buildings at the palace for the ceremony: 'The compound where the august foods are to be cooked and the food for the officials under particular taboo is to be prepared must be selected by divination at a place conveniently near the Palace. When that is done the festival of propitiation takes place'. (36; *1250*)

The 'officials under particular taboo' (the *omi*) are those officials who have prepared themselves for especially sacred functions in the ceremony. They stayed in a Purification House near the Ritual buildings, wore white linen garments, followed the usual Shinto means of preparation, such as eating out of special vessels food cooked over a special fire, bathing, and drinking no sake. No special rites were performed, nor was talking forbidden, save that the taboo words must be observed, no business not connected with the ceremony discussed, no contentious or inauspicious words raised, nor unofficial visitors received. This usage is the same as the Strict Abstinence of the Taihō Code; officials not directly connected with the rite observed it at places near their offices. All kept this abstinence, including the emperor himself.

The rites for building parallel the way a new imperial palace was built, as reflected in the *norito* for the Palace Blessing Festival. There follows a list of offerings and of payment to those who take part, ended by the note, 'For all these, products of the province are to be used.'

Next are lists of buildings put up. The first list below refers to a set of buildings erected 'near the Palace'; that is, in proximity to the site of the future *Daijō* buildings but not at that site. The supplies and personnel of the ceremony, such as the sake child, selected and brought up from the provinces, remained here for a short while until the second group of buildings was completed. The second group is divided, as we see, into two identical and parallel sections, the Yuki and Suki, and each of these has a Gai-in, a building outside the *Daijō* building enclosure, and a Nai-in within it. The lists read as follows:

> 1 shelter for food offerings, 1 sake shelter, 1 shelter for offerings to the *kami,* 1 for utensils, 1 for Palace cooks, 1 for serving the august foods, 1 for cooking the different kinds of fish, and 1 for preparation of foods (for the foregoing shelters: the number and dimensions of them may vary according to the demands of the affair). All are to be built of boards and thatched. One well is to be dug. The compound is to have a gate opening on each of the four sides. When the building of these is done, the diviners of the rice-ears enter the compound and perform exorcism. Articles required for this are sent up by the respective provinces. (34; *1251*)

Then the other buildings:

> The sacred area in the capital is set up in advance and divided in two: the *yuki* is to the left and the *suki* to the right. The two provinces are to send the plucked grain. When it has reached the capital, first the ground is hallowed. When that is done the *sakatsuko* first takes the sacred spade; then they begin to sweep the ground; then holes for the posts at the four corners of the enclosure are dug. The diviners lead the provincial governors and prefects of the districts and all those down to laborers. They go into the mountain selected by divination and cut the wood; then they worship the *kami* of the

mountain, and that done, the *sakatsuko* first takes a sacred axe and
commences to chop a tree. After this the different laborers lay hands
to the work. (Cutting the timber for the Daijō-gū duplicates this.)
[The Jōgan Ritual again mentions the Mononobe as having a part
in this rite, as well as five children.]
Again, the diviners lead the prefects and lower functionaries to the
moors selected by divination to cut the reeds. Then they worship
the *kami* of the moors. That done, the *sakatsuko* first cuts the grass,
then the various others lay a hand to it. (Cutting the grasses for the
Daijō-gū duplicates this.)   (36-7; *1251-2*)

The above buildings are only 'outer buildings' to the main Yuki
and Suki lodges, and not of great importance except for the practical matter of preparing the sacred banquet. However, this must
be done in new and special buildings ritually constructed the same
as the sacred lodges. These buildings, too, are duplicate; the Yuki
and Suki offerings must be stored, prepared, and served each in
their own separate but parallel structures. The 'sake child' and
provincial and district officials and so on are those of that province,
the Yuki or Suki as the case may be. The following places are
found in each:

The sacred enclosure is divided into inner and outer compounds,
for which brushwood is used to make the fences and wood to make
the gates. In the inner compound the Hall of Eight *Kami* is to be
built, 1 shelter for the rice-ears, 1 shelter each for dark sake and light
sake, and 1 storehouse, 1 shelter for sacred food offerings, 1 for
mortars, 1 for Palace cooks, and 1 fermenting room. In the outer
compound a shelter is to be built for *tametsu* sake, 1 storehouse, 1
shelter for cooking august offerings, 3 shelters for *tametsu* cooking,
and 1 fermenting room (dimensions of the foregoing buildings are
according to need). For all of them unpeeled wood is to be used, and
reeds for thatching. The screening is done with reeds (but, for the
fermenting rooms, walls must be painted). For the interiors, lengths
of straw matting are to be used; for the sake shelters and fermenta-
tion rooms, straw matting is used for the ceilings and bleached cloth
for the interior. For the two wells: when the divining has been
completed the *sakatsuko* commences to dig the august well and the
diviners of rice-ears commence to dig the well which is for the
sakatsuko. When the building of the two compounds is completed
the august rice-ears are gathered into the rice-ear shelter, but the
grain for the august cooked rice is separately stored on shelves built
for it. The Eight *Kami* of August Food are to be worshiped inside
the inner compound. (The symbolic offerings for this are the same
as those preceding.)   (37; *1252*)

The first well is for water for making sake, the second well for
water for cooking. The Eight *Kami*, the same as those of the field,

are now moved with their grain to the capital. The same archaic construction as in the Yuki and Suki halls, soon to be erected, is used. We can be sure that, as today, the special rice brought into this storage hall in anticipation of the Banquet was itself honored as divine.[25] Most of these buildings would not have been particularly imposing, little more than sheds, but the erection of a separate building for every function, here carried to very great lengths (far more so than today), reflects a marked tendency of Yamato religion. The same may be observed at Ise.

We are also reminded of Ise in the next matter, the weaving of the divine garments, done in preparation for the Harvest Festival just as it was done by Amaterasu and her maidens. At Ise there are two weaving-halls, called *hatadono*, where cloth presented as offerings at the *Kammiso*, or Deity Raiments, Festival is woven in the fifth and tenth (now ninth) months. Beside each hall is a shrine to the clan *kami* of the ancient weaving guild of Mikawa which performed this task. The text says:

> At all times, for the weaving of deity raiment, the *Jingi-kan* dispatches one shrine chief of the shrine of the Kanhatori in the first decade of the 9th month, and giving him a post-station bell, sends him to Mikawa Province, where he gathers together members of the deity households. Then two chief weavers of deity raiment and six weaving women and two artisans are selected by divination. When that is done, the shrine chief leads the ten persons, from chiefs downward, and carrying 10 skeins of tribute silk-thread that the Kanhatori of said province have forwarded, he returns to the sacred area in the capital. First a worship service is held at the weaving house; after that they commence to weave. For building they need: 4 axes, 4 chisels, 4 knives, 4 planes, 3 gimlets, and 3 fire-kindling sets (required for the foregoing: 3 *tei* of iron), 2 deerhides, 3 *kin* 4 *ryō* each of bark-cloth and hemp, 1 quiver, 4 mats, and 4 *tan* 8 *shaku* of tribute cloth for lustrous robes for the 10 men and women, all to be supplied from official goods. As for the halls for Kanhatori, there is 1 for each province, and 1 resthouse each for the men and the women Kanhatori, 1 resthouse for *hafuri* (dimensions of these are according to need), all to be built of unpeeled wood and thatched with reeds.
>
> (37-8; *1252-3*)

The 'deity raiment' here refers to cloth offered to the *kami*, that is, placed in the two baskets, one black for *aratae*, or 'rough cloth',

---

[25] In *The Japanese Enthronement Ceremonies,* p. 104 (*81*). Kada no Azumamaro, in his classic study of the *Daijō-sai,* discussed later in this chapter, has a drawing of the sacred rice in storage before the ceremony. Its divine status is indicated by the fact that each of the two baskets of rice, the Yuki and Suki, has before it an eight-legged table such as is used for offerings, with a *nusa,* or wand with streamers, placed upright on it. *Kada no Azumamaro zenshū,* x, p. 128.

and one white for *nigitae*, or 'smooth cloth,' set by the divine bed in each of the two lodges. It was not worn. The special cloth worn by the participants is called a *yukamono* garment, mentioned later.

There is next a discussion of the vessels used in the rite for offerings. We are told that the palace staff kept a detailed record of them. The making of various vessels and implements is contracted out to various provinces. An official of the Ministry of Official Shinto is sent to these provinces in the eighth month, first to perform a purification, then to arrange for this work. A list is provided of the responsibilities of the provinces (38-40; *1253-4*). These offerings are called *yukamono* vessels or supplies. The three provinces of Kii, Awa, and Awaji (near the Inland Sea) have special responsibilities. Three diviners are sent to them to make arrangements and supervise the work; they are called *yukamono* messengers. The goods are specifically for offerings. Those presented by Awa, where the Imbe had deep roots (as we can see in the *Kogoshūi*), were the responsibility of that priestly clan.[26] These offerings were the usual cloth and military items of imperial offerings, together with seafood and salt. The offerings of Awa included garments for the *katsukime* (diving women who presented offerings from Kii). All these offerings are presented to the Great Storehouse with the grain. The offerings of Kii are prepared by ten *katsukime* from the town of Kata and include mostly seafood—abalone, conch, etc.—and salt. Such diving women anciently and to this day ply their craft along the coasts of Ise and Kii. But one is surprised to see that ten members of such a presumably lowly social group should have such exalted recognition, quite parallel to that of the old and proud priestly house of Imbe in the neighboring province of Awa. One recalls that the Sarume Maidens, the matrilineal sacred dancing group who will appear later in the *Daijō-sai*, also perhaps came from these same coasts. One wonders if perhaps the *katsukime* in question were not members of some comparable

---

[26] According to the *Kogoshūi*, the Imbe of Awa had a definite ancient tradition of contributing to the *Daijō-sai*, even if the offerings cited are not exactly those specified by the *Engi-shiki*. The *Kogoshūi* states that the descendants of Ame-no-hiwashi-mikoto, who cultivated hemp and made *yū* out of it, migrated to Awa at the command of Jimmu. (Other branches of the Imbe clan are said to have settled in Izumo and Kii, being makers of sacred jewels and carpenters respectively, and still others settled in eastern Japan.) Of the Awa group, it is said that at the *Daijō-sai*, 'they pay tribute of the bark of the paper-mulberry, hempen fibre, coarse cloth made from them, and several other things to the Imperial House.' Later the author laments that the services of the Imbe as sacred carpenters have been wholly dispensed with, 'whether for rebuilding the Ise shrine or erecting the sacred tabernacles or pavilions for the Great Harvest Festival at the enthronement of a new Emperor'. Presumably the Kii branch, which is descended from those who built the first Palace, that of the Emperor Jimmu, is in mind. Katō and Hoshino, pp. 32-3, 47. Cf. pp. 31-2.

group of female or matrilineal specialists in the sacred as well as a craft group. The Imperial House, although based in Yamato, had a strange tendency to give great favor to shrines (Ise, Kumano) and religious specialist groups (Imbe, Sarume) based in this Ise-Kii-Awaji-Shikoku area, indicated not only in this sign of special importance given to *Daijō-sai* offerings from Kii, Awaji, and Awa, but also in the importance of Ise and Awaji myths in the *Kojiki*.[27]

The offerings of Awaji are also *yukamono* vessels, but consist only of various earthen vessels. To conclude this section, we read that:

> Messengers from the three provinces of Kii, Awaji, and Awa take the ceremonial utensils. On the day they go up to the capital, the streets in the provinces on the way are swept and a welcome is given. At all times, the rice for dark and light sake is to be pounded. The *sakatsuko* commences this and then the other women join in the pounding. When it is done the *kami* of the wells are worshiped, then the *kami* of the stoves. On the day they begin the brewing of the sake the *kami* of sake are again worshiped. (40; *1256-7*)

The *kami* of the wells and stoves were worshiped, of course, because the water of the well was used for the sake, and the kitchen was where it was made. Next, a member of the sake guild together with a member of the fire guild and five horsemen went up into a mountain selected by divination. They celebrated the mountain *kami*, then built a fire with which to refine white sake from the black (unrefined) state. One *koku*, which amounts to 180 liters, was so processed. It was used also for the banquet after the *Daijō-sai*.

Next we come to one of the major events of the *Daijō-sai*, the building of the so-called Daijō-gū, or Daijō Palace—the Yuki and Suki lodges.

> At all times, seven days before the festival, those who build the Daijō-gū, two officials, a Nakatomi and an Imbe of the *Jingi-kan*, in order of rank, lead the governor of the *yuki* province and the various functionaries, forming a single line. Again, the Nakatomi and Imbe separate from them and lead the governor of the *suki* province and those under him in manner similar to the others, all in a single file. These lines start from the east- and west-side gates of the Chōdō-in and arrive at the palace ground (in the south garden of the Ryūbi-dō), then the lines divide to left and right (*yuki* to the east and *suki* to the west). That ground is ceremonially pacified . . .

---

[27] Origuchi notes that the offerings from various provinces compare to the presents made by lesser houses to the main house, especially at the New Year ('Daijō-sai no hongi', p. 185).

[Offerings are listed] . . . The *sakatsuko* from both provinces take *sakaki* branches, deck them with bark-cloth, and set them up in the four corners of the enclosure and at the gates. When that is done they take the consecrated spades (4 for each province, wrapped in cloth bags and tied with bark-cloth). They commence to dig the holes for the posts at the four corners of the hall, 8 spades to each hole; afterwards the various workers take over the digging at one time. That palace measures 21 *jō* 4 *shaku* from east to west, and 15 *jō* south to north. In the middle on the east side is the *yuki-in,* and on the west side is the *suki-in.* In the palace fence due south there is a gate. Within it there is a brushwood fence. On the east there is a gate; outside it a brushwood fence is to be built (the *yuki* province builds this). Again, there is a gate due north, inside it a brushwood fence; and there is a gate to the west, outside it a brushwood fence (the *suki* province builds this). The middle fence between the two structures is built by the two provinces. On the south end of the central fence 1 *jō* from the brushwood fence is a small gate (built by the two provinces). For the fences brushwood is used. Spears are planted in the eight fence-ends. Into them the branches of oak (*shii*) are inserted. (In ancient language they are called *shii no wae*). The various gates are 9 *shaku* in height, 8 in width (small gate less). *Shimoto* is woven to make the doors. The Yuki Hall is to be built with one main hall (4 *jō* long, 1 *jō* 6 *shaku* wide), ridge going south to north. The 3 *ken* to the north form one room and the 2 to the south a chamber. On the south is a door. Screen matting forms the door. Across the roof-ridge are placed 8 crossbeams and the gable boards are extended. For construction unpeeled wood is to be used, and for thatching, green miscanthus. Beams of cypress are used for the ceiling, horizontal trabeation is of straw matting, and the partitions are of miscanthus. Straw matting is used over the exterior and interior. On the ground tufted grasses are spread. Added to the foregoing are coverings of split bamboo, and in the chamber straw matting is spread over the covering of split bamboo. On top of the straw matting are laid white-edged august *tatami.* On the *tatami* are placed triangular pillows. (*Tatami* and pillows are installed by the Bureau of Housekeeping; the making of them is in the procedures for that Bureau.) Curtains of ordinary cloth are hung before the doorways (to be hung by the Bureau of Palace Storehouses). On the east, south, and west sides of the building hang reed blinds on the outside, and on the inside are sliding doors of straw matting. But for 2 *ken* on the west side the blinds are furled up, leaving an open interval. In the northeast corner of the enclosure the house for the kitchen is built. (Length and width thereof are the same as for the main sanctuary.) The eaves run east to west. The eastern eaves are screened with oak brushwood. Under the east wall shelves are constructed. Along 3 *ken* of the west eaves foods are stored. On the north of the kitchen house the mortar house is built (1 *jō* 4 *shaku* long and 8 *shaku* wide). It is screened with oak brushwood and has a door on the west side. On the south and west sides of the two structures brushwood fences are to be built, making this a separate enclosure. To the southeast of the main sanctuary an august privy is to be constructed (1 *jō* long and 8 *shaku* wide). Its walls are like those of the main sanctuary. On its west side is a door.

The hall of the *suki-in* is made to conform to the foregoing. The construction of it is to be completed within five days. The Nakatomi and the Imbe lead the Sacred Maidens and others in consecrating the buildings and the gates . . . [Offerings are listed]. (41-2; *1257-9*)

The two buildings are identical, so the above instructions for the Yuki lodge would apply to either. This written description, terse and technical, is perhaps rather confusing, but with the aid of the beautiful drawings and plans which can be found in most standard books the general conception becomes clear and the meticulous details fitted into place.[28] It is important to catch from these lines the architectural flavor of the rite, for these two simple buildings are its symbolic heart. Yet how different they are, in their rough and ephemeral aspect, from the ornate metaphysical symbolism of a Buddhist pagoda, or the massive immovable testimony of a basilica. But one senses, even through these austere and official lines, tiny shelters of a very archaic and rustic beauty; one feels the solid texture of the rough unbarked timber, smells the thatch and reeds, sees the clean unadorned square lines. We may bear in mind that a *jō* is about ten feet, a *shaku* about one foot. In the Heian period, a *ken* was not a precise unit of measurement, but the space between two pillars along the wall of a building. The Yuki and Suki lodges each have one pillar in the center of the front and rear (hence two *ken*) and seven pillars (six *ken*) lengthwise. One must note the duplication of the buildings, and the fact that they are to be finished and consecrated only two days before the

---

[28] Most of these illustrations are derived from the attractive and interesting drawings made by Kada no Azumamaro. These include pictures of the interior and exterior of the buildings—which, together with his full account of the rite, got Kada into considerable trouble with the government when they were first published in 1739. The pictures are published in his 'Daijō-e zushiki', *Kada no Azumamaro zenshū*, x. The *Kojiruien, Jingi-bu 1*, p. 1410, also offers plans of the Yuki and Suki halls. A document entitled 'Dai-dairi-zu kōshō' (Construction plans of the Great Palace), in *Kojitsu sōsho*, xxvi (1951), originally written in 1804, gives in Part 3, with appendix (pp. 204–67), detailed instructions for the guidance of Court officials in the construction of the Daijō buildings, including the banquet halls. There are summaries of the usages of construction for many *Daijō-sai* from the late Heian period to the Edo, taken from original documents, together with a summary of the Jōgan and *Engi-shiki* usages. Helpful plans of the Jōgan and Engi constructions are included, and may be referred to for exact elucidation of the above, especially where the modern arrangements given in most books is somewhat different. In general only the Kyoto parts of the rite are dealt with. There are only incidental references to the rituals.

ceremony, to be torn down shortly after.[29]

Next there is instruction concerning the Kairyū-den, the main building not duplicated.

> The Bureau of Carpentry builds the main sanctuary of the Kairyū-den to the north of the Daijō-gū (4 *jō* long, 1 *jō* 6 *shaku* wide, the ridge running east to west; 3 *ken* of its west side are straw matting; doors are on the east and south). It is built of unpeeled timbers and thatched with rushes. The horizontal timbers are covered with straw matting.[30]   (42; *1259-60*)

We shall see a little later that this building is to be used by the emperor for changing and ceremonial purification before the two parts of the rite. It is divided into two rooms, one being for the emperor's private purificatory bath.[31] There is a further description of the appointments:

> 4 august shields are put up at the south and north gates of the Daijō-gū (each 1 *jō* 2 *shaku* long, upper width 3 *shaku* 9 *sun*, middle width 4 *shaku* 7 *sun*, bottom width 4 *shaku* 4 *sun* 5 *bu*; thickness 2 *sun*) and 8 spears likewise (each 1 *jō* 8 *shaku* long). The Left and Right Outer Palace Guards request these from the *Jingi-kan* in the first decade of the 9th month. The Bureau of Military Storehouses is caused to fashion and prepare them according to precedent. (Shields are made by the shield-makers' *uji* of Tamba Province; the spears by the Imbe Uji of Kii Province. After the celebration is over they are gathered up by the Outer Palace Guards.)   (42-3; *1260*)

One *sun* equals 1.2 inches, one *bu* .12 inch. Here is another interesting reference to the Imbe, in this case of Kii; the shield and spear of course were symbols of sovereign authority, like the mirror and sword. Like all other significant contributions to the equipment of the *Daijō-sai*, these derive from the south coast of Japan.[32]

---

[29] In man's religious tradition, parallel to the idea of building lasting monuments, there is a conception that, as though in defiance of eternity in behalf of the ordinary experience of continuity in time, what is made for the gods should be destroyed straightway. Examples are Chinese funerary vases and Navaho sand paintings.

[30] See also Yamada, *Gosokui Daijō-sai tairei tsūgi*, p. 132, for further information on this building.

[31] See Miura, p. 160, for a plan of this building.

[32] The shields and spears set around the Daijō Palace may well have more importance than would appear on the surface, for as Umeda remarks (in *Jingi seido-shi no kiso-teki kenkyū*, p. 291), they are emphasized in most of the documents. In addition to the *Engi-shiki* and the Jōgan Ritual, the *Saikyūki* 西宮記 (*Kojitsu sōsho*, II, p. 148) and the *Hokuzan-shō* (op. cit. p. 418) speak of them. Origuchi says that originally the Mononobe stood them up, as the *Man'yōshū* (vol. 1) tells us, and that they were magically intended to keep out evil spirits ('Daijō-sai no hongi', p. 211). In this case they would probably be essentially part of a building rite, comparable to the dramatic bows and arrows erected on the roof of new buildings in the ridgepole ceremony, each pulled taut and one pointing upward, the other downward. (This rite, intended to repel evil spirits, was introduced from China about a thousand years ago.) No doubt the same sort of significance did attach to the set-*

There is next a list of cloth prepared by the Needlework Bureau (*nuidono-ryō*), and of mats by the Housekeeping Bureau (43; *1260*). The Sarume Maidens were part of the Needlework Bureau, and since they are also connected with the Amaterasu myth, significance may not be lacking in this. However, this sewing is to be distinguished from the special ritual weaving of the *hatadono,* or weaving halls. There is next a list of offerings prepared by the Palace cooks. A prevalence of leaf and fish appears, naturally in view of the nature of the divine feast. An interesting reference to 'mountain vessels', *yamatsuki,* probably high, round offering tables, appears; when the festival is over these particular items are all put in a pure place in mountain or field, and the others divided among the various officials.

Then we read that the office in charge of preparations for the *Daijō-sai* (the *sayū no emonfu,* literally 'the office guarding the left and right gates') requests the services of members of the Mononobe, Kadobe (Gate Guards) and *kataribe* (Narrators). It must make this request through proper channels; it speaks to the government, stating the amount of participation required, which passes on the required number to the proper provincial governors. The text states how many of each are ordered from each province: of Mononobe, 40 from the capital; of the Gate Guards, 4 from the capital, 8 from Yamato, 3 from Yamashiro, 2 from Ise, 1 from Kii, a total of 18; of the Narrators, 8 from Mino, 2 from Taniwa, 2 from Tango, 7 from Tajima, 3 from Inaba, 4 from Izumo, 2 from Awaji, total 28. The Jōgan Ritual gives the same list.[33] One notes the concentration even in the Jōgan book of the Mononobe in the capital, and the strange absence of the Narrators there (44; *1263*).[34]

Next comes a listing of the clothing allotted to various participants (44-5; *1263-4*). Certain matters of interest occur. The Sarume Maidens (dancing-ladies) and the court ladies are mentioned, and it is said that the High Priestess and Sarume wear the same garments as at the Harvest Festival. Women of *miko* rating and below all wear *hikage no kazura* headpieces, literally 'sun-shade vine', an

---

*ting up of the armor about the new ritual palace, though I imagine the role of these military items as tokens of imperial sovereignty, as in imperial offerings, was more in mind.

[33] So does the *Hokuzanshō,* op. cit. p. 418.

[34] See Origuchi, 'Kataribe no rekishi' (section of *Kokubungaku no hassei,* Part 4, originally published in *Nihon bungaku kōza,* No. 4, April 1927; published in *Origuchi Shinobu zenshū,* I, p. 167–77). Origuchi does not here discuss the distribution of the *kataribe,* but states that while at first it was a male line, the people known by this title came to include Nakatomi and Sarume women, and also important members of major clans, such as the Mononobe, Katsuragi, Ōtomo, etc. There was also a line of '*saru*' reciters, mainly from Kyushu.

item which occurs fairly often in literature such as this.[35] These festal headpieces are so called because they are made of a vine which grows on the shady side of mountains. Thirty-three Ministry of Official Shinto personnel, from the Chief Minister to *koto* players, are named. There is also mention of the Imbe of Awa province, indicating representatives of them came, and the *ina-no-mi-no-urabe* and the *negi-no-urabe*.

V   THE FIRST CEREMONIES

WE NOW turn to the schedule of events of the *Daijō-sai* festival proper: '[B]efore the middle tiger day of the 11th month (if the hare day falls on the 1st of the month use the first tiger day), when the entire array of things, inside and out, is properly set in order. . . .' (45; *1264*)[36]

Following the Chinese calendric system, days were named in accordance with a continuously repeating cycle of twelve zodiacal animal signs. *Tora* (tiger) was the third, *u* (rabbit) the fourth; so if *u* fell on the first day of the month, *tora* would be the twelfth. Otherwise, the middle *tora* day would fall between the 13th and 25th. This cycle operated independently of the beginning and ending of months. The preparations to be made are like those for the *Chinkon-sai*: 'similarly to the usual arrangement at the beginning of the Pacification of August Spirits' (45; *1264*).

This ancient and most interesting ceremony was held annually the day before the Harvest Festival. Unfortunately the *Daijō-sai* chapter gives us no further information about it than the above parenthetical note. The Seasonal Festivals section provides certain further details.

Here we read that except for the garments the same worship is done for the sovereign and for the Middle Palace, that is, for the

---

[35] As shall be noted below, in connection with the *Chinkon-sai* songs, this headpiece also had shamanistic overtones.

[36] Presumably this refers to the offering of the Palace Blessing or *Ōtono-hogai*, for which a *norito* is provided, and which is mentioned in the last line of the *Engi-shiki* *Daijō-sai* ritual. In this connection, Origuchi had a theory that the Yamabito, 'Mountain People', had a traditional part in the Palace Blessing and purification of imperial buildings, including the Daijō buildings and the Palace ('Daijō-sai no hongi', pp. 218–20). These people were one of several groups of entertainer-religious specialists, like the Sarume, who had some officially recognized roles. They are mentioned often in the *Man'yōshū*, and once in the *Engi-shiki* (as leading the procession of the *Matsuno-o* Festival, *Shinten*, p. 1029). Perhaps they were a clan of non-Yamato indigenous people, pushed into the mountains together with their peculiar customs and beliefs, who were the ancestors of the contemporary Sanka. (These are a class of Japanese mountain 'gypsies' who claim not to be descended from the Heavenly *kami* but only from the Earthly, and who have certain special festivals.) Be this as it may, I am not sure there is real evidence that the Yamabito had a role in the Heian *Daijō-sai*.

empress. The Eight Gods (the Bureau of Official Shinto list is given) are honored, plus Ōnaobi-no-kami. He is said to be the deity of the correction of errors and is especially connected with this ceremony. A list of offerings including weapons, cloth, rice, food, mats, and vessels is given. The first items are especially interesting. These are a sword, a bow, two arrows, twenty *suzu* bells, twenty shells, a bolt of silk, five *kin* of mulberry cloth, ten *kin* of linen, three boxes of different kinds. These offerings are placed on a table and presented to the *kami*. They are used only at the *Chinkon-sai*, and seem to derive from the Mononobe *Chinkon-sai*, being also used at their clan *kami* shrine, Isonokami, in its well-known *Chinkon-sai* ceremony. They may be compared with the various lists of seven, eight, or ten precious divine things which occur in the *Nihon-shoki* and other ancient books, as brought down from heaven or, in the Suinin section, from Korea. These are not identical with each other or with this list, but include similar items— magical mirrors, jewels, swords, spears, and the like. Of special importance is the list of eight magical items (*yatsushiro-no-mono*) presented by the *Kujiki* as having been offered by Umashi-maji-no-mikoto (an ancestor of the Mononobe) at the time of a pacification of the spirit of the Emperor Jimmu. This list included magical gems and scarves for the warding off of various evils.[37]

To return to the *Engi-shiki Chinkon-sai*, it is stated that on this day the Ministry of Official Shinto priestesses pound rice in the sanctuary of the Bureau and winnow and cook it using special implements, and it is offered. Then in the late afternoon (monkey hour, 4:00 p.m.) all gather in the sanctuary. Various officials and participants are summoned and formally enter as their names are read, including the Sarume as members of the Sewing Office and *utame* (singing-women) of the *jibu-shō*.[38] Then the storehouse officials enter and present headpieces. Next the Chief Minister of the Ministry of Official Shinto and players on the *koto* and flute are summoned, and music is commanded. First there is a tune on the flute, then the *koto* joins, then the singers. The shrine serfs (*kambe*) clap. Then the priestesses and Sarume dance. Lastly the Ministry of Official Shinto Nakatomi and Imbe, followed by many other high officials, dance in the garden. Then all withdraw (*Shinten*, pp. 1062-4).

---

[37] Listed in Holtom, p. 110 *(86)*. Text in *Kojiruien, Jingi-bu 2*, p. 499.

[38] This office was responsible for Court (*gagaku*) Music, for Palace marriage ceremonies, for promotion rites to above 5th Rank, for funeral and condolence arrangements, for care of tombs, and supervision of Buddhist priests and nuns.

However, the most significant parts of the *Chinkon-sai* are not included in this ritual, valuable as it is for certain details. Holtom provides a fuller account. First two Sacred Trees (*himorogi*) are set up in a temporary shrine in the Palace, and the eight treasures (the first eight listed above, down to the boxes) and the other offerings are made. Then, in the presence of the emperor, a priest brings in two ceremonial willow boxes, one containing clothes belonging to the emperor, and one bound with a white silk cord said to represent the life of the emperor. These are set before the *himorogi*. The Palace Ritualist (*miyaji*) claps his hands thirty-two times, in four series of eight claps each. 'Then a female ritualist (*mikannagi*), holding bells in one hand and a vine-draped spear in the other, mounts an object resembling an inverted tub, called *ukefune*, and performs a dance. She strikes the tub with the spear and with each blow counts—"One, two, three, four, five, six, seven, eight, nine, ten." With each count a priest ties a knot in the emperor's life cord.' This box is then put back, and the priest takes the box containing the clothes and shakes it ten times. The same ceremony is then carried out for the empress.[39]

The antiquity of this ceremony is attested by the myth of Ame-no-uzume dancing on a tub (*ukefune*) before the cave when Amaterasu hid therein. Yamada states that the *Chinkon-sai* was originally performed by the Sarume Maidens, which fits with the tradition that Ame-no-uzume was the ancestress of this clan.[40] He also believes it was a New Year's rite originally, which would likewise fit with the suggestion of renewal in the myth and the pounding of the spear as a spring fertilization gesture. This is not to say that its connection with the *Niiname* is not ancient; it is also indicated in the myth that the ancient *Niiname* was at once Harvest, New Year, and Spring rite. But the *Chinkon-sai* and *Niiname* are also discrete; as Miyagi suggests, the *Chinkon-sai* is related to sovereignty, the *Niiname* to agriculture.[41] At least the two have developed in these directions; the *Chinkon-sai* is private, not to say secret, the *Niiname* is more public in principle, even on the imperial level.

The spear and tub rite clearly has roots in the Ise-Kii region from whence the myth of Amaterasu and the Sarume derived; this is suggested by the fact that it alone is mentioned in the *Kogoshūi*.[42]

---

[39] Holtom, p. 111 (87). The *Saikyūki* seems to be the earliest document to refer to the tub rite in the *Chinkon-sai*. See Honda, *Kagura*, p. 247. He shows it is also mentioned in the *Gōkeshidai* of the later Heian period.

[40] Yamada, *Gosokui-rei Daijō-sai tairei tsūgi*, p. 121.

[41] Miyagi, II, p. 551.

[42] Katō and Hoshino, p. 22.

However, there is a Palace tradition of such a rite separate from the *Chinkon-sai,* suggesting a lengthy tradition. Since before the early Heian period, a shrine to a Sono and Kara *kami* (the former is said to be the same as Ōmononushi, the palace deity of the Sujin account) had protected the Palace, and at this festival in the eleventh month a *miko* offered a spear, bow, sword, and *sakaki* on a tub, and one dance used was called *torimono,* suggesting the spear may have once been taken up.[43]

None the less, one feels that the spear and cord rites are distinct practices fitted together. It is easy to conjecture, together with most scholars, that the cord rite is a contribution of the Mononobe. As stated, it is performed today at the Isonokami Shrine in Yamato, near the present Tenri City, on 22 November. This is the ancient *ujigami* shrine of this Armorers Clan, whose ancestor submitted to the Emperor Jimmu and according to one tradition performed the rite for him. They represent a tradition deeply associated with the Yamato Court. At Isonokami on the 22nd of the eleventh month, the Chief Priest ties together ten strings—two each of purple, red, yellow, white, and green—in the darkness of the sanctuary while reciting magical words. The sacred object (*shintai*) of this shrine is an ancient sword, and several other old weapons of great value are possessed by it.

To the part of the Mononobe, then, is attributed the cord rite, perhaps also the offering of weaponry, and probably the incorporation of the Eight Gods headed by Takami-musubi, whose very name suggests trying as well as birth-giving. These are set over against Ōnaobi-no-kami in the ritual, and one is inclined to feel he is equivalent to the Omoikane-no-kami of the myth, before whom Ame-no-uzume performed her tub rite, and who seems to be the classic high god of the Ise mythological tradition.

Nishitsunoi in a recent study has investigated the *chinkon* theme in the *Man'yōshū,* with its allusions to the pacification of spirits in life and after death (and concluding that the first, typified by the ritual under consideration, is earlier), and feels that the Mononobe element was added to the *Chinkon-sai* only in the Man'yō period.[44] This would mean, as the evidence of the shrine to the Sono and Kara *kami* suggests, that the Sarume ritual was probably performed at the Palace for the emperor some time before the Mononobe part was added, even if it ultimately may have been an import also. But the Mononobe would have performed their ritual for

---

[43] Kurabayashi Masatsugu, *Kyōen no kenkyū, girei-hen,* p. 562.
[44] Nishitsunoi, pp. 314–15.

themselves at Isonokami long before lending it to the palace.[45]

The medieval work *Nenjūgyōji hishō* has preserved some songs used by the *miko* at the *Chinkon-sai*. They are of considerable interest, for they are obviously of very ancient derivation and express a most archaic understanding of the rite. Translation of these verses is extremely difficult, but it is hoped the following will give something of their spirit:

I   We want to bring down the Great Soul
    Of the *kami* Toyohirume
    Who resides in Heaven:
    The Root is a gold halberd
    And the Branch is a wooden halberd!

II Oh! the August Umbrellas
    That stand on the Mountaintop of Mount Miwa!
    If they do not flourish now,
    When shall they be able to flourish?

III Oh my sister

---

[45] Origuchi believed that three strands united the *Chinkon-sai*: the Sarume, or High-Plain-of-Heaven tradition; the Mononobe, or Isonokami shrine tradition; and an Azumi tradition. The first two were joined first. Then, a little before the Nara period, the Azumi tradition of a Kyushu sea-people, which brought in the element of pacification (*shizume*) rather than shaking (*furi*) of the soul, was added ('Daijō-sai no hongi' p. 192). This contrived explanation may not be necessary, since the indicated change in the meaning of the control of the soul achieved by the rite probably infiltrated from several sources. But a significant point is dealt with. The *Chinkon* as interpreted by the *shizume* idea was that symbolized by tying, at least later—the pulling together of elements of a soul conceived of as dispersed over several directions and perhaps strayed to great distances. The *furi* idea rested on the premise that the soul was disturbed but that its elements were only in a detached and disconcerted arrangement in the general vicinity of the body and need to be, as it were, shaken down and settled. This is typified by the spear pounding, insofar as it is like an effort to drive the restless soul-parts back home, and by the symbolic shaking of the boxes of magical trinkets and imperial clothes.

Perhaps all the *torimono* sacred dances, those which involve holding and shaking something, a spear, sword, or *suzu* bell, or shaking a box, contain this idea. Honda, in his recent work *Kagura,* divides indigenous Japanese sacred dance into two main streams, the Izumo, or *torimono* (holding something), and the Ise, or *yudate,* in which the central point is offering and sprinkling hot water with leaves. He includes the main Court dance tradition, insofar as it is indigenous, in the former—this, of course, includes the main dances of the Grand Shrine of Ise, in contrast to native dances of the Ise region, since the former were mostly introduced from the Court.

The dance used at ordinary worship at the Izumo Shrine, which consists mainly of shaking a bell and counting from one to ten, and is archetypal of the Izumo tradition, is said, according to Schwartz (op. cit. pp. 516–17) to represent the dance of Ame-no-uzume; certainly, whether dance or myth came first, the present-day ritual dance at the Izumo shrine is like that of Ame-no-uzume in essence.

The *yudate* tradition is, according to Harada Toshiaki (*Kodai Nihon no shinkō to shakai,* p. 40) older in the Yamato Court tradition than the *torimono,* as the emphasis on water and leaves in the *shizu-uta,* or pacification songs, of the *Kojiki and Man'yōshū* may indicate, and was done by a girl to pacify evil by shaking and scattering hot water with a bamboo or oak leaf.

If these hints are reliable, then the dancing myth of Ame-no-uzume holding her spear may not really be indigenous to Ise. There is no suggestion of the *yudate* tradition in the *Chinkon-sai,* but perhaps remnants of it survive in the *Daijō-sai* and other Palace rites in the use of leaves for plates, drinking, and headwear, and in the symbolism of hot water and bamboo in the rite and the *yogoto.*

> At the mountain-foot of Mount Anashi,
> You must wear mountain-creepers as a crown
> Because many people look at you now!
> IV Let us take a *tamachi*
> And plant the sacred clothes in the soul-box
> Let the *kami* whose spirit has ascended,
> Whose spirit has just ascended,
> Now come!
> V Let the *kami* who holds the soul-box
> Let him [the same *kami*] whose spirit has
>   ascended and left,
> Now come!
> Let the soul [of the empress] which has left,
> Let this soul return![45]

We have previously discussed the title Toyohirume, which is taken to refer to Amaterasu but perhaps better refers to the undifferentiated Ise-no-ō-mikami. A remarkable insight is here provided into the *Chinkon-sai* ritual background of the *Kojiki* myth. Professor Hori takes the metal (or gold) halberd to mean 'substance', the wooden to mean 'shadow'.

In the second, the *kami* of Miwa is Ōmononushi, the patronal spirit of the land of Yamato, who as we see in the Sujin chapter of the *Nihon-shoki* was served by a series of shamanistic women. The umbrellas are *kasa*, or straw umbrellas, which have shamanistic associations.

In the third, the 'sister' is a shamaness; 'to be able to look at her' means 'to be able to see her as a manifestation of the *kami*'. Anashi was a sacred mountain of the Fujiwara, where their daughters served as *miko* and where that powerful house gathered in the spring for purification rites. The last two verses refer to the souls of the emperor and empress.

The *Chinkon-sai* is now interpreted as a uniting of various aspects of man's spirit in preparation for the *Niiname*. It is thus mythologically rooted in such concepts as that of the mysterious unity of Ōmononushi and Sukuna-hikona, said to be respectively the deity's *nigi-mitama* (smooth spirit) and *kushi-mitama* (marvellous spirit), the two spirits of him who was worshipped as Yamato no Ōmononushi at Miwa and as the marvellous personage from over the sea.[47] There was also the *ara-mitama*, 'rough spirit', and *saki-mitama*, 'blessing spirit'. But probably the *Chinkon-sai* should

---

[46] Text with *kana* in Hori, *Wagakuni minkan shinkō-shi no kenkyū*, ii, p. 786. See also his translation of three of these songs and discussion of them in 'Mysterious Visitors from the Harvest to the New Year', in Dorson, ed., pp. 96–7.

[47] Nishitsunoi, p. 315.

also be seen as an independent rite of renewal at New Year's, perhaps actually in part pre-agricultural and hence more ancient than the *Niiname*, for kingship and shamanism antedate agriculture.

VI   THE HEART OF THE RITE

AFTER the *Chinkon-sai*, we read that:

> At dawn on the day of the hare the *Jingi-kan* officials distribute the symbolic offerings for the various *kami* (that is, those to whom offerings are placed on top of the tables at the *Toshigoi* Festival). (45; *1264*)

This is the day after the tiger day above of the *Chinkon-sai*. A list of offerings follows, but a list of shrines is not provided. It seems to be the same as that for the *Toshigoi*. Then:

> On the appointed day the Nakatomi officials lead the diviners to the Ministry of the Imperial Household to determine by divination who from the various departments shall be under particular taboo. That done, they return to their respective quarters. They perform ablutions and don their sacred robes and gather together. Besides them, one Nakatomi and one Imbe official are sent to lead officials of the Needlework Bureau and the Ministry of Treasury in placing the quilts and unlined garments in the Yuki-den of the Daijō-gū and to lead Palace Storehouse officials in placing the divine raiment and silken coronets in the Kairyū-den. Members of the Bureau of Palace Caretakers offer the august hot water three times. One time is for personages under general taboo at the usual place in the Palace; then hot water is offered twice to those under particular taboo (both times in the Kairyū-den). The various guards stand up their staves and the various officials line up the articles for solemn presentation in the same way as for New Year's Day ceremonies. Two persons each from the Isonokami and Enoi Uji, wearing Court dress, lead 40 of the Inner Mononobe (dressed in unlined tunics of dark-blue cloth). They set up shields and spears for the *kami* at the north and south gates of the Daijō-gū (2 shields and 4 spears at each gate). (46; *1264-5*)

This paragraph contains several points both important and obscure. 'Those under particular taboo' are members of the official body selected, as we have seen, to make themselves ritually pure by ablutions and putting on new garments to perform sacred functions at a particular rite. They must be distinguished from those under 'general taboo', an expression which refers both to persons and to the light abstinence before a major festival. When applied to persons it means the whole Palace staff, when used of abstinence it is synonymous with *araimi,* the general preparatory abstinence they all undertook. To add to the confusion, both 'particular taboo' and 'general taboo' also are used to refer to the garments worn either by such persons or during such times. That of the 'particular taboo' is unique to the *Daijō-sai,* being made of a special grass and white, but designed like Court dress. That of 'general taboo' is white silk. The hot water referred to is the hot water used by the emperor in the Purification House for his ablutions before each of the two parts of the rite. He took ablutions three times, the first being called the 'hot water of the general taboo' because it was presented by people in the Palace.

The reference to the New Year's rites is significant since one may believe that the whole of the *Daijō-sai* has such connotations. So is the reference to the Isonokami Shrine and the Mononobe, since as we have seen the Mononobe had a very special connection with the *Chinkon-sai* as well. Isonokami was their patronal shrine. Perhaps the shields and spears point also to the indebtedness of the *Daijō-sai* to the Mononobe influence on Court rites—they were armorers, and their sacred objects were such metal weapons. On the other hand, the architecture and contents of the *Daijō* buildings themselves are completely lacking metal, pointing to an origin of the rite in the archaic agricultural Japan which antedated the relatively recent introduction of metal (first to the third centuries). One may speculate that the marked influence which the Mononobe had on the religious life of the early Court may stem from their having early acquired the imported skill of metalwork. That this was by no means a secular art is evidenced by the role of the mirror and sword in the mythology.

We next have a long passage dealing with the ceremonies beginning around 10:00 a.m. to prepare the buildings for the *Daijō* rite. It is not necessary to give more than a summary. The officials enter following the order given by the positioning signs (*henni*), the Bureau of Rankings (*shikibu*) as usual being responsible for its observance. The Mononobe have an important role standing under the shields and spears and guarding the gates, twenty at each of the two gates. The Hayato, a special and colorful family of Imperial guards derived from Kyushu, took places on either side of the gates also, and while waiting gave the dog-like cry with which they always marked the inauguration of an important festival or imperial progress. They also had a traditional dance they performed on such occasions. Also in the procession four shrine serfs (*kambe*) carried *sakaki* branches. At ten the Palace officials presented the 'hot water of the general taboo' to the emperor in the Palace.

At the same time the offerings of both provinces were carried into their lodges. Various kinds of cloth were included, but the climax of the procession was the 'sake child', riding in a palanquin, followed by the sacred rice itself and the 'lord of the rice-ears'. Then came the offering table, carried by eight women, and the sake table carried by four, and lastly the black and white sake, eight persons carrying each, and eight sacred vessels. These were taken of course to the Nai-in buildings, the buildings for preparing the offerings within the Daijō Palace enclosure, not at this point to the Yuki and Suki lodges themselves. Then the Ministry of Official Shinto (meaning perhaps especially the Nakatomi) offer *nigitae* ('smooth cloth') and the Imbe of Awa *aratae* ('rough cloth') in the same way. Then the Imbe and all others except a few withdraw and the gates of the Daijō Palace are closed.

The cooking of the food in these buildings is of great interest. Here we see the 'sake child' and 'sake woman', brought in from the Yuki and Suki provinces, climax their roles:

> The *sakatsuko* begins to pound the rice for the august cooked rice; next the *sakanami* women together finish the pounding without changing hands. The Court chieftains kindle the fire. Members of the Office of the Sovereign's Table lead the Court chieftains of various *uji*, who respectively assist the members of the Office in cooking the august foods. Officials of the Imperial Household Ministry divide into left and right columns and lead the members of the Office of the Palace Tables and Imperial Sake Office, who each line up in that place and make ready the articles to be offered to the *kami*.   (49-50; *1269*)

The Jōgan Ritual adds that traditional rice-pounding songs were sung during this work, which has been the practice up to the present.

Then after the day's work in the Nai-in kitchen, the food is brought into the outer room of the Yuki and Suki lodges. At the hour of the cock (6 p.m.) cooking fires are lit in the outer room of the lodges, and the lamps for illumination are lit.

At this hour also the emperor arrives at the Purification House to prepare for his part in the rite. The *Engi-shiki*, presumably out of reverence, is very sparing of details concerning the interior arrangements of the Yuki and Suki lodges, and of the movements of the central figure, the emperor. Before the Meiji period such matters were generally kept secret. The first book to discuss fully this aspect of the *Daijō-sai*, the 'Daijō-e gishiki gushaku' of Kada no

Azumamaro, was suppressed by the shogunal government.[48] We must fill these details in from other sources.

In the same evening hour, the Court ritualist places the *shinza*, or divine bed, in the middle of the inner room of each of the two lodges. It is almost the only one of the inner furnishings mentioned specifically in the *Engi-shiki* (49; *1269*). It was formerly prepared by the Komoribe (Preparations Office).[49] The *shinza* is a great couch made of piled *tatami* mats like the ancient throne. At the head is a triangular pillow, the *sakamakura*. Over the uppermost tatami and the pillow are spread eight layers of reed matting, the *yaedatami*. Over all of this is the *ofusuma*, or coverlet of pure white raw silk. At the head is folded a simple unlined garment of white silk, the *onhitoe*. To the east of the pillow is a box of willow containing a folded cloth of white silk, the *uchiharai-nuno*. According to Holtom, its usage is forgotten: it may be a primitive garment, or for warding off insects, or for cleaning, or for magical purposes. On the same shelf is a fan of white wood and a comb of white wood, wrapped in paper. At the foot of the bed is an uncovered willow box containing a pair of slippers of purple with a flower design in white.[50] None of the above items are actually used or touched during the ceremony as it has been performed in historical times.

To the east of the *shinza* and its accoutrements is the place of ritual action. Here were placed at the beginning of the ritual two rush mats about 3 *shaku* square. One, put on a low table, is called the *kami no sugomo* or *kami no kegomo*, the 'food-mat of the *kami*'. It is where the food offerings of the deity are arranged by the emperor. Just to the north of it is the other, the *onsugomo* or *misugomo*, where the emperor's food was spread. The emperor sits behind it on a raised *tatami*. These two are placed at an angle bringing them in line with the Grand Shrine of Ise.

On either side of the foot of the *shinza* is placed an eight-legged

---

[48] Kada wrote four pieces on the *Daijō-sai*: 'Daijō-e gishiki gushaku', 'Daijō-e zushiki', 'Daijō-e bemmō', and 'Daijō-e bemmō gokyūtemmi'. The second and third are books of illustrations. All are published in *Kada no Azumamaro zenshū*, x. The first is a full account of the ritual. These represent the first complete description, with an interpretation of it as revealing the divine nature of the land of Japan and a philological exegesis of the important terms; they have been the basis of all subsequent study. They are based on the *Daijō-sai* of Gembun 3 (1738) and were published that year and the next. Kada did not witness the rite himself but depended on the accounts given him by participants and by the partial previous rituals, but his telling is regarded as quite accurate. The books were suppressed by the shogunal government, and the few surviving copies of the original now command a great price as rare books. They were republished in Meiji 14 (1881). The last of the four was written by Kada partly in self-defence.

[49] Yamada, *Gosokui-rei Daijō-sai tairei tsūgi*, p. 137.

[50] Holtom, pp. 121–2 (*96*).

table and on each table is a basket. Table and basket are tied with *sakaki* branches. These are for the 'divine garments' whose making we have mentioned: the one on the west for the 'smooth cloth' (*nigitae*), on the right for the 'rough cloth' (*aratae*). Within each chamber are also two lamps, one of white wood and one of black.

The preparation of a few of these items is indirectly alluded to in the *Engi-shiki* text. We have seen that a quantity of *tatami* mats are made. Moreover, as we have seen, the rough and smooth cloth offered by the Ministry of Official Shinto and the Imbe, and tables ornamented with cloth (*yū*) and *sakaki* branches are mentioned, in one place as by the *shinza* itself (49; *1269*). Placing the *saka-makura*, or pillow, on the *tatami* (bed) is referred to in connection with the building (42; *1259*).

But the other items, the fan, comb, slippers, clothes, and the like, are not mentioned, perhaps because they are seen as possessions of the deity and not, like the cloth, offerings of man to him.

Holtom discusses the similarity of the Yuki and Suki ornaments to the emblems of royalty of various southeast Asian nations.[51] No doubt there is significance in the resemblance. But there seems also to be a very ancient tradition in Japan itself of setting apart the place of residence of the *kami* as a lodge with such appointments. The best example is the very ancient Sumiyoshi shrine of Osaka. The principal building of each of the main shrines is a house containing a couch of *tatami*, a pillow, and a small table remarkably similar to those of the *Daijō-sai*. Moreover Sumiyoshi has a tradition of periodical rebuilding, as at Ise.[52]

To return to the *Daijō-sai* rite, at 8 p.m., after the above preparations have been made, the emperor approaches the Purification House (Kairyū-den). After leaving the Palace where he had taken his first purificatory bath, he had proceeded to an intermediary hall called the Tongū, where he had met the empress and the crown prince. The text says: '[T]he first warning [is] given of the Imperial approach to the Kairyū-den. The Bureau of Palace Caretakers proffers the august hot water.' (50; *1270*).

In the Purification House the emperor takes another bath in hot water. The 'warning' means not trumpets but the reverential saying of 'O-o-o', by which the sovereign and *kami* were greeted. The bath was taken in the inner room of the Purification House. The emperor pours the hot water over himself out of a square tub

---

[51] This and the above description is from Holtom, pp. 122–6 (*96, 98*).

[52] The Izumo Shrine also contains an inner room set apart for the *kami* within a large house-like edifice, and as well a ritual rebuilding tradition.

of archaic construction called the *onyu no fune*, 'hot-water boat'.[53]

After the bath the emperor puts on a robe of pure white silk which he wears throughout the rest of the ceremony, including his entry into the Yuki and Suki lodges. This garment is called the *hagoromo*, or 'robe of feathers', though the *Engi-shiki* calls it only *saifuku*, 'festival robe'. The use of the term '*hagoromo*' is most interesting, though, for as we have seen it turns up in Japanese folklore and literature as the garment of *tennyo*, heavenly maidens in the service of the moon *kami*. Let us recall the most famous of these stories, that of the *hagoromo* of Miho, cited in Chapter II. A fisherman named Hakuryo put to shore on the strand of Miho and found a *hagoromo* hanging on a pine tree. He was about to carry it off when a beautiful *tennyo* appeared and implored him for it, saying it was hers and without it she could not fly back home to the moon where she was one of the attendants of the lunar deity. Hakuryo finally returned it to her, but not until he had made her promise to show him one of the dances unknown to mortals. Draped in the feather-robe, she did this dance, then caught in the breeze she soared up to the moon.[54] The *hagoromo* then again suggests the heavenly, if not lunar, descent and function of the emperor in this rite. The text reads:

> Then the ceremonial garments are assumed [by His Majesty] and he enters the Daijō-gū. As for the route thither, the Ministry of Treasury beforehand lays a double width of unlined ordinary cloth on the route. The Bureau of Housekeeping prepares leaf-matting, and also lays it on top of the cloth runner where the august footfall will tread —rolling it out before and rolling it up after. (Two persons, Vice-Minister of the Imperial Household or above, spread it, and two persons, Secretaries of the Bureau of Housekeeping or above, roll it

---

[53] Sasatani derives the name Kairyū-den for the emperor's Purification House from its characters, which mean 'Recurring Flow Hall', and thus identifies the water used in the imperial ablutions with the eternal waters brought from the Other World (*Kamigami no sekai*, p. 64).

[54] The term *hagoromo* occurs in the *Hokuzanshō*, p. 422, and in the *Gōkeshidai* (*Kojitsu sōsho*, XVII, p. 420) for this *Daijō-sai* garment. Many variants of the myth about it are found. In Tamba, it was said that the man who tried to steal it was the father of Toyouke of Ise (Origuchi, 'Daijō-sai no hongi', p. 225). The putting on of the *hagoromo*, Origuchi says, is distinctly related to the bath in hot water before. The hot water, like that of hot springs, is sacred life-giving water from the Other World, *tokoyo*. But the moon-maiden wearing the robe becomes human when she takes it off to bathe in the spring or the sea, and hence is then in the power of the man who robs her of it. When she puts it back on she is again divine and able to fly to the moon. Thus by analogy the emperor, when he bathes, restores his human life, and when he puts on the *hagoromo* becomes the deity. Moreover, the *miko* who then attend him, Origuchi wrote, are like the *tennyo*, or moon-maidens ('Daijō-sai no hongi', p. 225). See also his 'Ama no hagoromo' in 'Mizu no onna', *Minzoku*, II, No. 6 and III, No. 2 (September 1927, January 1928), published in *Origuchi Shinobu zenshū*, II, pp. 102-3. The version of the story here presented was told me by Prof. Ono Sokyō.

up.) No one shall dare to step on it. On the return the same procedure is followed. As for the route in the Palace and through the
garden, 8 layers of ordinary cloth 8 widths wide are laid. One Great
Minister or Great or Middle Counselor and one Nakatomi and one
Imbe (Nakatomi on the left and Imbe on right), then Sacred Maidens
and Sarume on left and right proceed in line. (The Great Minister
stands in the center, the Nakatomi and Imbe lead the lines to left
and right on the street outside the gates.) The Sovereign deigns to
come forth; two of the Caretakers carry the lights and worshipfully
approach, one Court noble who is carriage attendant carries the
royal sedge umbrella; one Kobe of *sukune* rank and one Kasatori of
atae rank together carry the cords of the umbrella and push themselves forward on their knees as they perform their duty (the same
is done on the return).   (50-1; *1270-1*)

Thus we see that the emperor goes from the Purification House
to the Daijō Palace proper in the pure white silk garments (also
holding a *shaku* or baton) on a carpet which is rolled up behind
him as it is unrolled before him. No one else is allowed to step
on it (at one time the *kampaku*, a kind of dictator, had this privilege) nor may his feet, which are bare, step off it to touch the
ground. The procession is said to re-enact the descent of the Imperial Grandchild; it is indeed as though the sacred sovereign
were travelling alone on a beam of light. The prime minister and
male and female hierophants follow to the Daijō Palace gate,
where they stand aside as he enters alone, save for two serving
maidens. As he walks, a sedge hat, actually an umbrella in size, is
held over his head, with two servants holding the rope cords dang-
ling from it on either side. At night, with only the light of the
lanterns and torches, one can imagine the impressiveness of this
scene. Holtom compares the taboo against the sovereign touching
the ground with the practice of Polynesian sacred kings, and the
umbrella with the south Asian symbol of royalty.[55]

> As the progress is made to the august *yuki* communion hall, the
> group of officials under particular taboo each take their seats therein
> (the group of officials under general taboo may not enter the Kairyū-
> den enclosure or into the Daijō-gu). When that is done two persons
> each of the Tomo and Saeki Uji open the south gates of the Daijō-gū.
> The Outer Palace Guards open the south gate of the Chōdō-in.
> Officials of the Imperial Household Ministry lead 12 persons of the
> Kuzu of Yoshino Province and 12 Nara flute players (all wearing
> tunics of blue-printed cloth). They enter from the east side gate of
> the Chōdō-in, and on reaching their places they play an ancient air.
> The governor of the *yuki* province leads the singers and enters

---

[55] Holtom, p. 130 (*104–5*).

through the same gate; on reaching their places they sing an ancient air. One Tomo of *sukune* rank and one Saeki of *sukune* rank each lead 15 Narrators (wearing blue-printed tunics). They enter from the east and west side gates, and on reaching their places they recite ancient legends.[55]   (51; *1271*)

This intriguing note means that folk songs and dances native to the area are given by the artists of Yoshino, famous in early imperial history, Nara, and the Yuki province (always 'general taboo' province in the pre-Meiji period). This has traditionally been compared with the greeting of the Emperor Ōjin by the natives of Yoshino with sake and songs of the region, repeated at the *Daijō-sai* and New Year's because of the joy it gave the emperor. But Miura says the songs tended to be like those of the *Man'yōshū*, regional only in form, or even newly composed.[57] The Narrators gave ancient ballads, perhaps like those included in the *Kojiki*, thus linking the present reign, now consummated, with the past and present of the nation.

The Heir Apparent enters from the southeast side gate. The Imperial Princes enter through the west gate; Great Ministers and down to 5th Rank courtiers enter through the south gate. All take seats under the awning. Those of 6th Rank and below remain behind the Kishō and Shushiki buildings. They stand in line in order of rank. When the host of officials first make their entrance the Hayato raise their voices. When everyone is standing in place they cease. They proceed to a point in front of the shields. They clap their hands; they sing and they dance. Those of 5th Rank and above rise together and go to the posting-board in the middle courtyard. They kneel and clap their hands four times. Each time there are eight claps (in sacred language this is known as *yahirade*). The Heir Apparent first claps hands and then steps back, then those of 5th Rank and above clap their hands. Those 6th Rank and below clap hands in concert and repeat it in the same way (but those under particular taboos do not enter this procession).   (51; *1272*)

Presumably a Harvest Festival *norito* was said at this point before the clapping, following the modern usage. Next is more detail

---

[56] Certain songs of the Yuki and Suki provinces are attributed to the *Daijō-sai* of the Heian and medieval periods, but it is not clear whether they were those used here or at the banquets. They will be discussed later. The *Hokuzanshō* states here that the *kataribe* of the seven provinces listed above recited, and adds that the Hayato sang, clapped, danced, and gave their dog cry (p. 423). According to the *Kojiki* the Hayato, from Kyushu, were descended from Hiko-ho-ho-demi's elder brother, Hoderi-no-mikoto. The latter promised to guard this imperial heir and performed a dance which enacted a drowning episode in the myth. According to Origuchi, by hearing the songs of the various provinces here the emperor received their spirits. More doubtfully, he equates *kuni-furi* with *mitama-furi* ('Daijō-sai no hongi', p. 213).

[57] Miura, p. 175. For the Ōjin story, see Aston, *Nihongi*, ii, p. 264.

on the ranks, and the presenting of a book with the names of the officials and their families. Then:

> When this is completed, the *yuki* feast is presented (it is presented at the beginning of the hour of the boar [10 p.m.] and retired at the fourth). The order of succession (in presentation) is that in the very front are the chefs of the Office of the Sovereign's Table, 1 Court chieftain (who carries the fire-kindling set) and 2 *uneme* of *ason* rank from the Office of *Uneme* (forming left and right vanguards), next a chief diviner (wearing the bark-cloth headdress and sleeve-ties and carrying a bamboo rod), next 1 water-carrier of *muraji* rank from the Office of Water (who carries the ritual elongated basin), then 1 water-carrier (who carries the ritual water-pitcher), then 10 *uneme* (1 carries the box of brushes, 1 the box of towels, 1 the food-mats for the *kami*, another the food-mats for the Sovereign, 1 the box of august leaf-dishes, 1 the box of cooked rice, 1 the fresh seafood, 1 the dried foods, 1 the chopstick box, and another the box of fruits). Next comes a Takahashi of *ason* rank of the Sovereign's Table Office (who carries the abalone sauce pickle), 1 Azumi of *sukune* rank (who carries the seaweed sauce pickle), 5 chefs (1 carries the vessel of hot abalone soup, 1 the vessel of hot seaweed soup; 2 carry the offering-table with pots of soup; but the one who guards the shelves does not enter the procession), 4 sake brewers (2 carry on their shoulders the offering-table for sake and 2 carry the tables for dark and for light sake). All are in prescribed order and stand for the presentation. As soon as it is over everything is taken away in like manner.
>
> (51-2; *1272*)

The abalone and seaweed are carried on *tsuki* (a word, for whatever it is worth, homonymous with the word for 'moon'), round flat tables mounted on a single high pedestal. After this impressive procession of the offerings into the outer room of the Yuki lodge, the emperor's act of worship is performed. The *Engi-shiki* text again gives no information concerning it. What happens, however, is that next the emperor, to the accompaniment of Sacred Music (*kagura-uta*), passes from the outer to the inner chamber of the Yuki lodge. The prince, the prime minister, and the *miyaji* take places in the other chamber together with three female ritual-ists (*mikannagi*).

Within, the emperor seats himself on his raised *tatami* to the east of the *shinza*, facing southeast, toward Ise and toward the table where the foot-mat of the *kami* will be placed. Then two of the female ritualists, designated the *haizen* and the *shindori*, enter with utensils for the hand-cleansing ceremony. The *haizen* pours three times from the *tashiraka* vessel onto the emperor's hands, the *shindori* catching the water in the Shrimp-Handled Vessel. The emperor then dries his hands on the towel. The hand-washing utensils are withdrawn before the food offerings are brought in.[58]

Next, the two maidens bring in the two rush mats, the *kami no sugomo* and the *onsugomo*. The former is placed on the low table, the latter, which is much smaller, directly in front of where the emperor is seated. Then the *haizen* and *shindori* maidens bring in the food and utensils one box at a time. It is carried in the square, lidless, oak-leaf boxes which the two maidens hand to the emperor. The emperor first places eight of the oak-leaf plates on the food-mat of the *kami* and one on the emperor's food-mat in front of him. The boxes brought in contain each nine balls or pieces of each item of food. The emperor, using the chopsticks, places one on each of the eight plates for the *kami*.

Whether the remaining piece is placed on the emperor's food-mat, or is left in the box, seems to be unclear. The former would seem natural, but it is not stated in any published document, and there are two opinions on the matter.

After the food has been thus distributed, the black and white sake is brought in. The emperor pours it over the food into each of the oak-leaf plates. The emperor then makes a gesture of inviting the *kami* to feast.

The emperor, out of deference, does not move to eat while the *kami* are presumed to be dining. But thereafter taking the chopsticks he goes through the motions of raising three bites of rice and three bites of millet—one would imagine from the oak-leaf plate on the emperor's food-mat—to his lips. He does not actually eat it. Then he takes the sake, and goes through the motions of drinking, without actually drinking, three times of the white sake, and three times of the black. Finally he drinks actually once of each kind of sake.[59]

Then the utensils and food are withdrawn. The food which had been offered in the sacred halls is never actually eaten, but is later buried. The napkin and toothpick are not used by the emperor,

---

[58] The first connected presentation of this action is in Kada's work cited above. However, the *Dai-dairi-zu koshō*, op. cit. p.248, includes a citation from the record of the *Daijō-sai* of Enkei 2 (1308) which mentions the titles of the two handmaidens, *haizen* (or *baizen*) and *shindori*, and the bringing in of the Shrimp-Handled Vessel (*ebi no hatafune*) and the food-mat. The spreading of the mats is also mentioned in the *Gōkeshidai*, p. 420.

[59] The offerings and their arrangement in the outer room is illustrated in Miura, pp. 178–9. My description is dependent largely on the explanations of Prof. Tanaka. If the above is correct, Holtom's account of this part of the rite in his *The Japanese Enthronement Ceremonies*, while useful for giving the Western reader its general flavor, is incorrect or misleading in several particulars. For example, the emperor's food is not brought in after the *kami*'s, but is part of the same; the oak-leaf boxes are lidless, so the *haizen* does not uncover them; the emperor does not actually consume any of the rice or millet, and takes only two sips of sake.

being intended for the *kami*. After a closing hand-washing ceremony, the emperor withdraws to the Purification House.

The same rite is next performed in the Suki lodge. The text
says:

> At the hour of the rat [12 midnight], *Jingi-kan* officials lead the
> chefs of the Sovereign's Table Office and move to the *suki* Food Hall
> to cook the sacred food-offerings for the *kami*. The Sovereign returns
> to the Kairyū-den. (This ceremony is the same as the first one.) The
> august hot water is proffered. That done, the august garments are
> changed and [the Sovereign] progresses to the *suki* Food Hall. The
> ceremonial for this is the same as for the *yuki*. Again, the Kuzu
> perform an ancient air, and the clapping of hands by Heir Apparent
> and those below and the other procedures are all the same as in the
> *yuki* ceremonies. At the first moment of the tiger hour [4 a.m.] the
> *suki* august feast is presented. The procession and recession are as
> before. (For the affair see the *Gishiki*.)
>
> On the dragon day in the first quarter of the hare hour [6 a.m.] the
> return to the Kairyū-den is made. (This ceremony is the same as the
> first one.) The august garments are changed and [the Sovereign]
> returns to the Palace. The warning to clear the road and the military
> guard are the same as for ordinary ceremonies.   (52; *1273*)

VII   THE CONCLUDING ACTION

THE NEXT stages are the immediate dismantling of the Yuki lodge
and Suki lodge, and celebration with banquet and sacred dancing.
The text says:

> When the festival affairs are finished the host of officials severally
> withdraw. The members of Tomo and Saeki Uji close the gates. At
> the second quarter hour the Nakatomi and Imbe of the *Jingi-kan*
> lead the Sacred Maidens in the festival of propitiation of the build-
> ings of the Daijō-gū. Symbolic offerings for this are the same as at
> the first ceremony. This completed, the people of the two provinces
> are ordered to break the ground and then retire; after which the
> area of the propitiation ceremony is leveled; then they ceremonially
> pacify that ground. . . . The august garments, quilts, tunics, narrow
> *tatami,* seats, and the things for offerings at the Kairyū-den and
> august hot water are bestowed on the Imbe and various articles
> which have had contact with fire are bestowed on the chief diviners.
> The remainder of multiple articles and the various buildings are all
> bestowed on the Nakatomi.   (52-3; *1273*)

There is next entertainment and celebration of the presence of
the *kami*. As we shall see, this element must be considered an integral part of Shinto worship.

At the 4th quarter-hour the officials of the *Jingi-kan* according to precedent worship in the Jijū-den. Again, the various articles of the portable storehouses of *yuki* and *suki* provinces are lined up in the garden of the Buraku-in. The officials in charge will have already cleansed the Buraku-in before this. Both *yuki* and *suki* provinces provide and hang august curtains in the palaces (the *yuki* on the east and the *suki* on the west). The arrangement for the host of officials inner and outer is the same as for ordinary ceremonial. (53; *1274*)

The Buraku-in was a large pavilion located outside the Palace Enclosure to the northwest. It was a gravelled, rectangular open court with halls on the long sides and a stage at one end where the emperor and empress sat and where the Yuki and Suki displays were set up. The positioning signs bearing the names of the various offices, one for each rank and office to indicate its place in the formal assemblies, were erected by the Bureau of Rankings (*shikibu*).

This may be as good a place as any to discuss another very interesting item, not mentioned in the *Engi-shiki* text but worthy of note. This is the *shirushi no yama*, mountain displays. According to the *Shoku-Nihon-kōki*, vol. 2, at the *Daijō-sai* of the Emperor Nimmyō in A.D. 833, two of these three-dimensional models of symbolic mountains were set up in the Buraku-in, one submitted by the Yuki province and one by the Suki. The symbolism of the Nimmyō examples, rather fully described in the above text, while thoroughly Chinese in form was yet also not unrelated to ancient Japanese Harvest Festival themes, indicating a possible congruence. Each of the two models centered around a single mountain. The Yuki mountain was capped by a great tree, in whose upper branches were the sun and moon. In its middle branches flew a phœnix. Under the tree was a wizard and an animal. The Suki exhibit similarly had a mountain and a tree, but no sun and moon. However, there was a phœnix flying over the tree, and under the tree a crane, a deer, and a wizard with a servant offering him food.[60] Behind the two mountains were clouds in the five colors. Despite the fact that the *shirushi no yama* both in concept and particular symbolism is a Nara-period import from China and thus has no profound connection with the *Daijō-sai* as an ancient Japanese institution, but rather is an aspect of the more superficial pageantry of Heian Japan, one is struck by the reminders of the *tsuki* (moon) tree of the *Kojiki* myth (Yūryaku section), the renewal

---

[60] Text in Miyagi, I, p. 151. The *shirushi no yama* is illustrated and discussed in Miura, pp. 166–9. *Shirushi no yama* may be seen at the Wakamiya Hachiman Shrine in Kyoto.

symbols such as the phœnix, and the offering of food. Of course this proves little more than the universality of such cosmic symbols.

The *shirushi no yama* were perhaps not set up in the Buraku-in after the rite at other *Daijō-sai* than the Nimmyō, but throughout the Heian period they were carried on carts from the North Field—the first location of the grain and personnel of the two provinces—in the procession of these to the Daijō Palace about two weeks before the rite, as a part of the public spectacle which all such things became in the Heian period. They would then have been part of the display of the two provinces, probably in the Gai-in building, for these two busy weeks. The carts with the display were pulled by human beings, as were the *mikoshi* palanquins.[61]

To return to the *Engi-shiki* text:

> In the 2nd quarter-hour of the dragon [8:30 a.m.], the Imperial carriage approaches the Buraku-in and the Sovereign progresses to the *yuki* curtain. The disposition of the various guards is as for ordinary ceremonies. The Heir Apparent enters from the gate on the northeast side. (From Imperial Princes on down, their highnesses wait until ranks have been conferred and then enter.) Those of 5th Rank and above enter through the south gate and each goes to the posting-board. Those of 6th Rank and below make their entrance in double file. They stand in their places and the *Jingi-kan* Nakatomi bear the *sakaki* branches and carry batons. They enter through the south gate and go to the posting-board. They kneel and recite the congratulatory words to the deities of heaven. The Imbe now enter and present the items of divine regalia: the sacred mirror and the sacred sword. When that is done they withdraw. (If rainy or wet, they may present them while standing.) (53; *1274*)

The 'baton', or *shaku*, is the Shinto ritual wand, made of wood, flat, about six inches long, carried by priests and, traditionally, officials on ceremonial occasions. We have previously discussed the *yogoto* and the presentation of the regalia done at this point.[62] 'Next one Controller of 5th Rank or higher again goes to the posting-board, he kneels and announces to the Throne the gifts presented by both provinces and the list of *tametsu* offerings.' (53-4, *1274*)

---

[61] Fujiki Kunihiko, in his *Heian jidai no kizoku no seikatsu*, writes that on the day of the banquet and *yogoto*, the two provinces put their *shirushi no yama*, or *shimeyama*, before the Daijō Palace. He says that the origin is in the *dashi*, or portable mountains, of the festival (p. 204). Origuchi confirms this, saying that like the *dashi* of the ordinary shrine they represent the places where the *kami* descended from the High Plain of Heaven to Earth. 'Shimeyama', in *Origuchi Shinobu zenshū*, II, pp. 246–8.

[62] This is one of the three times when the *yogoto* was said: it was recited at the *Daijō-sai*, the Accession (*sokui-rei*), and the New Year (originally the spring festival, before the New Year was established by continental influence; see discussion by Origuchi, 'Daijō-sai no hongi', p. 207. According to Fujiki, p. 204, white and black sake was taken after the *yogoto* —interesting symbolically.

These are the *kugo*, dry offerings, and *tametsu-mono*, food and sake offerings, presented to the emperor by the entire Yuki and Suki provinces. Here only the list (*shikimoku*) of these items is presented. They are listed elsewhere in the *Engi-shiki* (48; *1268*); see also the earlier appointment of a *tametsu-sakanami* (food-gift sake woman) in the province and the note on the preparation of the *tame* sake (34, *1248*; 35, *1250* and 40, *1256-7*). These are, of course, distinct from the produce of the divine fields used for the nocturnal offerings. We see that the *tame* goods were brought into the Ministry of Official Shinto enclosure first, then offered in the Daijō Palace on the night of the ceremony, then moved to the Buraku-in, at least in token, to be presented to the emperor.

> The Heir Apparent first claps his hands, then withdraws. Then those of 5th Rank and higher all clap their hands. Those of 6th Rank and below clap their hands in concert. The whole is like the previous ceremony. Then they withdraw and go out. (Officers of Ceremonial take the posting-board and go out.) Officers of the Imperial Household lead the staffs of Offices of Palace Tables and of Imperial Sake to go and inspect tray-tables and flat dishes which were made ready in the garden. That done, they are led away. At this hour the Great Ministers who are attending the palace summon those of 5th Rank and above (first they call the *toneri*, then the Lesser Counselors, as in the case of ordinary ceremonies). Then together with them they enter and take places in the two halls—Ken'yō and Jōkan. Those of 6th Rank and below make their entrance. They arrive and enter the Kantoku and Meigi halls. That completed, the separate tribute goods from the *yuki* province are brought in.
>
> (54; *1274*)

These four halls are those along the two sides of the Buraku-in, the Kantoku and Ken'yō on the east, the Meigi and Jōkan on the west.

> In the first quarter-hour of the snake [10 a.m.], persons of the *yuki* province offer the august meal and serve the banquet to those of 5th Rank and above. (*Yuki* province personnel serve it to nobles under particular taboo and the Office of Palace Tables serves those under general taboo.) This is done in the same way as ceremonial for palace banquets. The *tametsu* foodstuffs from the two provinces are distributed by the Controllers to the host of officials. The *yuki* province persons offer at the proper time the delicacies of fresh seafood. Then the governor of the province leads out the singers, who render a provincial air. When they finish, the morning food offering is presented. In the 2nd quarter-hour of the goat [2:30 p.m.], His Majesty removes to the august *suki* curtain. The Heir Apparent and those under him go to their *suki* seats. The separate tribute offerings are

brought in. At the appropriate time the delicacies of fresh seafood are offered. The august feast is offered. The performing of provincial airs and so forth is all the same as for the previous ceremony. When it is finished, emoluments are bestowed on the *yuki* province personnel. On the day of the snake, in the 2nd quarter-hour of the dragon [8:30 a.m.], the Imperial Progress is made to the *yuki* curtain. In the 3rd quarter-hour [9 a.m.] the august feast is offered. Next, the *Yamato-mai* is performed. All those of 5th Rank and above are invited, and a banquet is bestowed. Then those of 6th Rank and below make their entrance. Popular music and dance is performed. All is the same as on the dragon day. In the 2nd quarter-hour of the goat [2:30 p.m.], the Imperial Progress is made to the *suki* curtain. August food is offered and after that *Ta-mai* is danced. The various details are the same as in the previous ceremony. When it is finished, emoluments are bestowed on the *suki* province personnel.   (54; *1275*)

Thus we see that on the two days following the completion of the nocturnal rite, the dragon and snake days, banquets are presented by the two elect provinces respectively. In the high and sacred festivity of these days, the difference between two kinds of banquet which follow the Japanese festival, the *naorai* and the *gesai*, is evident. The former is food and drink taken in the continuing 'sacred time' of the festival, with a sense of the solemn joy of the continuing presence of the *kami*. *Gesai*, 'breaking abstinence', or better, 'breaking sacrality', is the freer, almost orgiastic eating and drinking and dancing of release which is the route of return to normality. The two are not always clearly distinguished in ordinary shrine festivals, but the *Daijō-sai* presents a classic example of the two.

During the two days of *naorai*, when the Yuki and Suki provinces present their *tametsu-mono*, or food-gift offerings, dances are presented which express the immanent divine presence. The *Yamato-mai*, or dance of Yamato, mostly posturing and bows and singing of old songs by soldiers, interpreted through a heavy male rhythm the immemorial activity of the divine spirit in the emperor and people of Yamato. The *Ta-mai* ('rice-field dance'), by maidens, presented the continual work of the gods in the terrestrial cycle, enacting as it undoubtedly did the planting, transplanting, and

---

[63] Honda Yasuji, in his recent work on Sacred Dance has published a number of songs attributed to the Yuki and Suki provinces at the *Daijō-sai* (pp. 1152–69). They represent a document of uncertain date in the Palace Library entitled 'Daijō-e Yuki-Suki eika'. Many of these also appear in the *Kokinshū* of 922. They are very brief *waka*. Each is attributed to a certain reign, beginning with the Nimmyō *Daijō-sai* (833) and ending with that of Sanjō (1011). They include odes, rice-pounding songs, and other types, but are all obviously composed and not genuine folk-songs. It is interesting that most of them contain a reference to mountains—a mountain in the province whose strength is compared to the emperor's—or to some other natural feature, a river or fountain.

harvesting of grain. Both are essentially eternal, non-historical concepts, compatible with the festal return to the immediacy of the Divine Age.

The activities of the next day, the horse day, on the other hand, exhibit a controlled return to the ordinary. First the stages are taken down, a clear sign of 'breaking' the sacred situation. At the banquet, ranks are bestowed, as if in anticipation of the restitution of the secular order; these ranks, based on Chinese Court usage, in Japan are always seen as something apart from the sacred, theocratic world of pure Shinto, which in its ritual heart fell back always on the family or charismatic priesthoods of the archaic world: Chinese titles were necessary for 'modern' government, but rested lightly on the world of the *kami*.

The text reads:

> On the day of the horse in the first quarter-hour of the hare [6 a.m.], the curtains of each province are taken away. The officials in charge set up the usual august curtains. At the 2nd quarter-hour of the dragon [8 a.m.] the Imperial Progress is made to these curtains. Nobles of 5th Rank and above as well as those of 6th Rank and below are invited. They all make their entrance as on the preceding day. In the 4th quarter-hour [9:30 a.m.] Court Rank is conferred on the governors of the two provinces and titled families. (The number of persons for rank conferral is according to disposition of Imperial Command.) At the 2nd quarter-hour of the snake [10:30 a.m.], the officials in charge present the august food offering. (As utensils for this and the various sacred articles, utilize as convenient those provided by both provinces for august food offerings on the preceding day.) The *Kume-mai* and *Kishi-mai* are performed.   (55; *1275-6*)

Concerning these dances, the *Kume-mai* dance was presented by the Kume clan. It is said to have originated when the Emperor

---

[64] The Jōgan Ritual stated that eight persons did the *Yamato-mai*, but the *Yōhyōki* (*c.* 940), *Gōkeshidai, Hokuzanshō*, etc. make it ten dancers, plus ten singers, two *koto* players, and one flutist. For the *Yamato-mai, udoneri* (*uchi no toneri*) were employed, according to the latter documents (*Kojiruien, Bungaku-bu*, p. 431). The Jōgan Ritual also says that *gagaku*, the Chinese Court dance, followed these two indigenous dances, as it were to balance them, but the *Engi-shiki* merely speaks of 'customary entertainment'. The *Ta-mai*, the Jōgan Ritual says, was performed by eighteen persons of the Suki province. (See Honda, op. cit. p. 255, for a helpful outline of the Jōgan music and dance usages.) The *Yamato-mai* became exclusively male only under continental *gagaku* influence. How it was done in the Heian period (or before) is not too well understood, but by the Edo period it had become a very formal matter of the dancers facing each other in two lines and bowing, wearing archaic court dress, and singing 'Yamato songs'. However, shrine dances also called *Yamato-mai* are preserved which contain definite *furi-shizume* and *torimono* elements. Honda describes one at the Kanda shrine in which the dancers wear swords and carry *sakaki* while wearing a headpiece full of chrysanthemums (op. cit. p. 845). Reminiscent of the *Chinkon-sai*, Nishitsunoi and Kurabayashi relate that at the Kasuga and Nachi-Kumano *Yamato-mai*, one dancer holds a *todakara*, or box of ten treasures, which he shakes or sways during the performance. At Nachi it is done by adults, at Kasuga by children. Nishitsunoi and Kurabayashi, 'Yamato-mai kō', pp. 77–87.

Jimmu ordered Michi Ōmi to perform a song. There are four male dancers in red wearing swords and shoes, plus three instrumentalists and singers. The dance has a militant air. The *Kishi-mai* dance also sings of arms, being a celebration of the victory and triumphal return of the Empress Jingū from Korea. It is presented by the Abe clan, and is said to have been brought from Naniwa (modern Osaka and a place associated with Jingū) to the capital after it was performed there for the Emperor Shōmu in Tempyō 6 (734) while he was visiting in the port city.[65]

These two dances, significantly, are not so much expressions of direct divine presence and action, like the *Yamato-mai* and *Ta-mai*, but are said to derive from events in the careers of two more earthly —if still archetypal—sovereigns, Jimmu and Jingū, and hence are transitional gestures toward the historical world. (It is not relevant in this connection, of course, that these two may actually be more or less fictional.)

Next follows:

> At the first quarter-hour of the monkey [4 p.m.], the grand chorus sings, and the *Gosechi* dances are performed. In the 3rd quarter-hour [5 p.m.] the depuration dance is presented. Kanhatori women perform first (number limited to four persons). Next the Nakatomi and Imbe of the *Jingi-kan* as well as chamberlains under particular taboo, and down to guards, enter divided into left and right columns. They bestow oak leaves on each of the members of the Imperial Sake Office. Thereupon they receive sake and drink it. When that is done, they don headdresses and perform the dances.[65]   (55; *1276*)

The *Gosechi* dance is a bit problematic. Its intrinsic meaning is not clear, but it is associated with Temmu, bringing us to a still

---

[65] According to the Jōgan Ritual, the *Kume-mai* was performed by twenty persons of the Ōtomo and Saeki clans, who as we have seen were also gatekeepers of the Daijō Palace. Its relation to Jimmu is mentioned by Kada no Azumamaro, op. cit. p. 101. The Jōgan Ritual also mentions that twenty of the Abe family did the *Kishi-mai*. The family relations are confirmed by the *Hokuzanshō* (p. 419). But the *Seikyūki* has different numbers: six for the *Ta-mai*, 26 for the *Kume-mai*, 30 for the *Kishi-mai* (p. 152). Perhaps this includes musicians as well. The Jōgan Ritual also has 'Yoshino no Kuzu' songs with flute music from Yoshino, reminiscent of the Ōjin story, on the 'horse' day before the Kume and Kishi dances, a custom not mentioned in the *Engi-shiki*. In the Jōgan Ritual they also appeared on the 'hare' day before the Yuki and Suki songs and the *kataribe* recitals. The Yoshino no Kuzu were mountain people. On the 'hare' day, twelve of them performed in Jōgan times, followed by twenty city people (from Nara). None of this appears in the *Engi-shiki*.

[66] In the Jōgan Ritual, the *Gosechi*, like the *Yamato-mai* of the 'snake' day, is followed by *gagaku* performed by the Jibu office. The concluding dances are all also stated to be *Yamato-mai*, suggesting that originally this was—as it still is in shrines—a quite general term. The order is: *Gosechi, gagaku, gesai Yamato-mai* by four weaving maidens, a *gesai* song by the Ministry of Official Shinto and *gagaku* officials, *Yamato-mai* by all palace officials. See chart in Honda, op. cit. p. 255, for an outline of this and the above.

more recent and solidly historical point.[67] This dance is sometimes associated with the *Yamato-mai*, but in the Saigū and elsewhere was always performed after the *Yamato-mai* and in the Gesai Hall.

After this an explicitly *gesai* ('breaking sacrality') dance is performed by all the ranks in turn, as though 'unwinding'. A single large oak leaf was given to each person. He dipped it into the sake, drank out of it, then fastened it around his head with a piece of vine so that it stood upright like an Indian feather, and began to dance. These vine headpieces, as at the Ise Divine Fields festival, are often associated with the frenzied and even orgiastic descending action of the festival. Here, clearly, the *Daijō-sai* rapidly moves from solemnity to uproarious play, and thence to normality.

After this, there are only 'housekeeping' details:

> In the 2nd quarter-hour of the cock [6:30 p.m.], the Heir Apparent and all nobles down through the 5th Rank are given emoluments, each being different. Moreover, on the host of officials of 6th Rank and below, and on the personnel from both provinces down to the outrunners, are bestowed emoluments (the chief and assistant chief of the *Jingi-kan* and on down to vice-chieftains of sacred districts each receive one horse also). The 4th-class officials of the *yuki* and *suki* provinces and on down to the prefects and 4th-class officials of the districts all carry batons and are recipients of Court Rank by Imperial Command, by extraordinary disposition. (The host of officials from 6th Rank down receive emoluments; on 4th-class officials and below of both provinces rank is conferred; it may be done on the day of the goat. See the *Gishiki* for the affair.) On this day the chamberlains and below under particular taboo advance to the Imperial Household Ministry and carry out depuration. The singing and dancing is as usual. To chefs, cooks, and brewers, and to personnel of both provinces, sake and food are given. When that is done, they doff their ceremonial robes and return to the usual.

---

[67] The female *Gosechi* dance is also a Court dance, done by four women, although it is traditionally said to have originated when Temmu played the *koto* (a kind of harp) at the Yoshino palace at dusk and the heavenly maidens danced there. The name means 'five parts' and may refer to five-fold sleeves worn or to five songs sung. It was also a dance for the most solemn religious occasions, being performed before the emperor at the *Niiname-sai* and the *Daijō-sai*. According to the *Seijiyō*, while Temmu played the heavenly maidens appeared; they were so lovely, the text says it is as though they were from 'noble T'ang'. Temmu is reported to have said, 'The maidens, the maidens, they are so beautiful, with rare jewels folded around their wrists, the maidens are beautiful' (cited in *Kōbunko*, v, p. 30; see the entire article here on the *Gosechi-mai*). This poem also appears in the *Nenjūgyōji hishō* and, in a variant, in the *Man'yōshū*. The jewels around the wrists suggest shamanistic paraphernalia, but, oddly, they are not used in the Palace *Gosechi* itself. The dance consists of four of the maidens circling around the fifth, who stands in the center of the circle, this role being traded off among them in the course of the dance. At the ordinary Harvest Festival only four dancers participated, but five at the *Daijō-sai*. Three were daughters of Court nobles, the other of a provincial governor; in the *Daijō-sai*, they were all daughters of the governors of the Yuki and Suki provinces. See Fujiki, p. 192. Also see the article in *Cultural Nippon*, VII, No. 3, pp. 97–106, entitled 'Gosechi-no-mai or "Five Notes Dance"', by P. D. Perkins and Fujii Keiichi.

At all times, when the celebration is finished the various structures
in the sacred area of the north moor are destroyed.   (55-6; *1276*)
At all times, when the *Daijō* Festival is over, two persons, *negi* and
diviner, are dispatched to the two sacred provinces to worship the
eight *kami* of august food.   Then they carry out depuration.   The
following day they burn the sacred area.   Offerings to the *kami* are
to be supplied by the two provinces respectively. [At all times,] on
the last day of the month the host of officials in the capital gather
for the purification ceremony. This is done the same as purification
at the two times of year.   (56; *1277*)

This concludes the text of the *Daijō-sai*, save for a short additional note listing offerings used for the Palace Blessing and other
building-pacifying rites of the *Daijō-sai*. The long text as a whole
has a remarkable unity. We have just seen how, on the two or
three days after the nocturnal New Food Festival, while the buildings of the rite itself are dismantled, and vanish as though they
had been but ephemeral glimpses into another world, rich feasts
are held. In this way they are like the earliest form of the agricultural shrine, the *yashiro* (temporary house) of the harvest deities.

But after the sovereign and his Court return to the more sub-
stantial Heian Palace, as a kind of afterglow, banqueting rites of
solemn joy are held. We have seen how these first manifest and
celebrate the present *kami*, then break the sacred time of the rite.
Even though the Heian Court banquet on its secular side owes
much to the Chinese Court banquet, and even if the most ancient
Harvest Festival may not have so sharply differentiated the sacred
communion and the festal meal, the fact of the integrally Shinto
concepts of feasting and dancing in and with the *kami* presence,
and then formally breaking the sacred atmosphere, should not be
obscured. In essence, the banquet procedures are thoroughly part
of the *Daijō-sai* and anciently Shinto, and in fact illustrate important Shinto concepts excellently.

CHAPTER V

Conclusions

THE *Daijō-sai* integrates history and the agricultural or natural cycle, as do all kingship rituals. From one point of view the *Daijō-sai* rites are perpetuations of the mythical, archaic orientation into an age shaped by history. This is in fact definitely intended. Yet it is too simple to say that the Heian rites are merely, in Professor Brandon's phrase, 'ritual perpetuation of the past'. First, the 'past' is not just one thing: even the archaic, 'prehistoric' past has seen changes and discoveries which are reflected in rites. In the *Daijō-sai*, the discovery of agriculture may be reflected in the difference between its 'new grain' succession rites and the 'new fire' succession rites of Izumo also hinted at in the mythology. The *Chinkon-sai* too may well reflect an earlier period than the first-fruits. The *Kojiki* and other such documents obviously show that the ancient Japanese thought of the past memorialized in the old religion as a time of long temporal sequence. Discoveries and prototypal actions are placed into narrative.

In other words, to perpetuate ritually the past is not necessarily to perpetuate a wholly atemporal orientation; it may also be, as Professor Brandon would certainly recognize, to perpetuate the ritual repetition of another history into the flow of the present ongoing history. We have seen ways in which the Heian ritual perpetuates a pure 'eternal return' view of time, and ways in which it ritually repeats or crystallizes segments of earlier histories. The separation of the *Daijō-sai* from the *Niiname*, for example, is certainly the result of an increased recognition of history, as distinct from the annual cycle. History lies behind the roles of the special groups of reciters and dances. On the other hand, the first-fruits idea itself suggests an 'eternal return' view of time.

But the fusion of symbols pointing to historical and to eternal time is not merely confusion; it is also insight. Kingship, as we have seen, wants to reconcile these two experiences of time; liturgical institutions in general tend to be conservative, that is, to unify the experience of the numinous Holy with the sense of grandeur and power which historical man inclines to feel before his past and those symbols which preserve the presence of the past. That is, he assimilates to the past that same splendor worthy of ritual perpetuation which archaic man attributed to the mythical time of cosmogonic origin. This is especially true of that which recalls an idealized, heroic time within history, or the memory of the archaic theocratic world before awareness of history broke upon man to bring disconcerting awareness of irreversible change.

Thus in rite the numinous quality of the past of 'ages upon ages undying' and that of the wholly transcendent may not be well distinguished. They may converge so intricately that one becomes the bearer of the other for religious man in history. (Through this process, after a sufficiently adequate experience of history, religion and nationalism or progressivism may exchange value.)

Therefore so long as the rite retains openness both to the transcendent and the past, both values may be operating in reinforcement of each other. The *Daijō-sai* was an attempt to preserve in historical times something of the power of the theocratic Court. But for this to have meaning sufficient to justify the seriousness with which its preparation and taboos were taken, it must also be supposed that the emperor was believed to stand before the transcendent deities on the sacred night. It was not merely a historical pageant.

In fact, the creation of new forms is, in a real sense, an affirmation that the passage of historical time has not destroyed the transcendent. The *Daijō-sai* is from this point of view a striking rite of the defiance of historical change and temporal decay. If the Yuki and Suki-den preserve the past, it is not through the atmosphere of ancient and fading buildings which boast the actual wood worked by archaic hands. Rather it is through making ever new and fresh what was also new and fresh in another time also aware of the transcendent. It is intended to show that the numinous transcendent glory is not, for historical man, locked into the past as into a tunnel, but that both the glory and the past are as one in being ever with him, and ever capable of total renewal.

If these problems centering around the ambiguities of time, history, and society are those dealt with by kingship everywhere, it is of interest to compare the *Daijō-sai* with other kingship rites. Despite the qualifications concerning Hocart's work advanced in the first chapter, it may be of use here to present his table of the elements commonly found in coronation ceremonies. I add comments concerning the place of that element in the Japanese rite.

The general outline of elements of the coronation ceremony,

a conflation of all rites he studied, reads as follows:

A   The theory is that King 1) dies; 2) is reborn; 3) as a god. This seems to be implied by the *hagoromo* symbolism in the Japanese rite.

B   By way of preparation he fasts and practices other austerities. Yes; the emperor and his entire Court practice preliminary purificatory practices.

C   1) Persons not admissible to the sacrifice, such as strangers, sinners, women, and children are kept away, and not allowed to know anything; 2) an armed guard prevents prying eyes. In Japan the *Daijō* enclosure certainly keeps out all non-participants, and it was guarded by traditional groups such as the Ōtomo, Mononobe, etc.

D   A kind of sabbath is observed; the people are silent and lie quiet as at a death. In Japan it was and is clearly a reverent time, but it is not certain how widely taboos on noise and so forth were observed.

E   The king must fight a ritual combat 1) by arms or 2) by ceremonies and 3) come out victorious. This is implied by the Japanese myths of testing clearly associated with the *Daijō-sai*, but ritual combat is not explicitly given place in the historical ritual.

F   The king is admonished to rule justly and 2) promises to do so. This is approached in the *yogoto*, and again in the *sokui-rei*, but an extreme sense of imperial legitimacy and sacrality would prevent too positive an admonitory note toward him.

G   He received communion in one or two kinds. Yes.

H   The people indulge at one point in obscenities or buffoonery. While still rather decorous, this is hinted at in the descending action of the banquets.

I   The king is invested with special garments. Yes.

J   He is baptized with water. Yes; we may note that this, or rather bathing to the same end, is very important in the *Daijō-sai*. The *yogoto* material relates it both to the most ancient Japanese religion, and to kingly rites in India, Egypt, Fiji, and elsewhere.

K   He is anointed with oil. No; in Japan water is sufficient.

L   A human victim is killed. No; though the mythology points to the time of Harvest Festival as a precarious time when death by the gods was possible.

M   The people rejoice with noise and acclamation. Yes; note the last lines of the *yogoto*.

N   A feast is given. Yes.

O   The king is crowned. No; no special headdress designates the emperor, although a comb, which has sacred significance, is among the items in the two lodges; note also the sedge umbrella in the procession.

P   He puts on shoes. Note that a pair of slippers are also among the regalia in the two lodges.

Q   He receives other regalia such as a sword, sceptre, ring, etc. Yes.

R   He sits on a throne. Not literally, doubtless because chairs were uncommon in ancient Japan, but we may note the symbolic presence of the sacred couch in the two lodges, and the sovereign's special place in the banquets.

s   He takes three ceremonial steps in imitation of the rising sun. This point is too restrictively based on Indian usage, but we may observe that the Japanese emperor does make the solemn progress to the lodges and back.

T   At the conclusion of the ceremonies he goes the round of his dominions and receives the homage of the vassals. No; but through the Yuki and Suki provinces they yield it at the banquets.

U   He receives a new name. Yes; the era title.

V   The Queen is consecrated with the King. No; following Chinese practice she had no special pre-modern role. But there is evidence this may have been done in ancient times, if the Jimmu account in the *Nihon-shoki* stating the first emperor made his wife empress at about the same time he proclaimed the empire is to be credited.

w   Vassals or officials are honored either at the coronation ceremony, or in the course of the king's tour. Yes.

x   Those who take part in the rites are dressed up as gods, sometimes with masks. No; they wear Court dress, except that the *kazura* is shamanistic. But clearly something of the divine descent is re-enacted.

Y   This disguise may be that of animals, thus identifying the wearer with some kind of beast. We may note the peculiar dog-bark of the Hayato guards from Kyushu, and their mythical background.

z   A king may be consecrated several times, going up each time one step in the scale of kingship. No.[1]

When we consider that Hocart was obviously unaware of the Japanese *Daijō-sai* ritual, we may rightly feel that the degree of correspondence is impressive. Perhaps no other one rite in the world fits markedly better into this synthetic schema. Probably this is due to the fact that in Japan several cultures within Hocart's ambit, from India to Polynesia, melted together.

Yet we must observe points of distinctiveness too. The *Daijō-sai* is the only major *accession* rite which is definitely and unambiguously tied to the Harvest Festival. This gives it obviously a deep grounding in the natural cycle, but also a grounding in history, since agriculture was relatively recent in Japan. Yet this harvest relation also indicates a degree of defiance of history. Coronation in Europe is set into the Mass, with a comparable climax in communion. But the European rite is more decidedly historical in orientation, since it is set free from integration into the seasonal cycle, even if spring was preferred. Hocart does not mention the veneration of royal ancestral spirits, although that is very common. But this element, although ancestrism certainly is important in historical Japan, does not appear explicitly in the *Daijō-sai*. An-

---

[1] Hocart, *Kingship*, op. cit. pp. 70–1.

other feature, omitted by Hocart but represented in Japan, is the building of new houses for the ritual—but this is less common for coronations than it is for the Harvest Festival. The duplication of rites seems to be paralleled only in Egypt. Finally, we may remark the extreme passivity of the principal person, the emperor, in the Japanese rite; he does not outwardly perform any combative action, nor even speak.

We may close by noting that the *Daijō-sai* is a miniaturization of the genius of the Shinto religion. Perhaps a greater focus on the *Daijō-sai* would dispel some of the misconceptions of that faith which still obtain in much Western writing, for it is surprisingly little considered. Yet to discuss Shinto without the *Daijō-sai* and all it implies is almost like discussing, for example, the meaning of Judaism and leaving out the Passover. Too often Shinto is spoken of one-sidedly as 'nature worship', or as a rather airy sort of 'national spirit', or a modern nationalistic ideology, or as just a 'folk superstition'. It has indeed appeared in all these guises, but the *Daijō-sai* taken as pivotal sacrament and touchstone of interpretation indicates a balanced view of the place of each of these characterizations.

The *Daijō-sai* exemplifies a Shinto related to both nature and history. The accession ritual is rooted in the chronological mythology as a model of history. At the same time, it vividly reveals the archetypal Shinto myth of the marriage of heaven and earth, which is also fundamental to the cultus of most shrines.

The *Daijō-sai* also shows that the imperial idea, of which so much has been made, is properly set into a sacramental, agricultural, and archaic setting.

Moreover, the *Daijō-sai* indicates the importance and role of the *ujigami*, or clan *kami*, concept in Shinto. We see what amounts to an *ujigami* rite of the Imperial Family. The retainer clans stand in ritual feudal relationship to the sovereign line after the model of their mythological ancestors accompanying the Imperial Grandson at the time of the descent.

The interaction of Great and Little Tradition in Shinto can be observed in the *Daijō-sai*—here are rites which parallel those of rustic harvest and New Year's enacted in the midst of the Court, and made much of by scholastic commentators.

Professor Hori's *hitogami*, the counterpart of the *ujigami*, is represented in the person of the emperor himself as 'mysterious visitor' to the Harvest Deities. Here is capsulized the mystery of man as child of earth and heaven.

The role of the pure child, reflected here in the *sakatsuko*, is also not unimportant to the roots of Shinto. It links it to its shamanistic origins, as does the *Chinkon-sai*. In the latter we also see suggested a Shinto concept of the soul, and its estrangement and pacification, better expressed than in most of the more metaphysical discussion.

It is not inappropriate that the study of a rite should seem the most adequate way to intuit the essence of Shinto. Every religion has in some form all the diverse means by which religion expresses itself: rite, doctrine, myth, social group, spiritual practice, eminent figures, sacred writings. But each faith seems to offer one of these categories as the fact which expresses most directly its heart. In the case of Islam one begins and ends by studying a book, in the study of Confucianism one thinks of philosophical ethics, in reflection on Japanese Buddhism one is drawn irresistibly to the handful of great charismatic figures who have summed up its epochs. While this approach, unless carefully balanced, may lead also to blind-spots, at the same time it gives us in each case a means of access to the particularity of each experience of the sacred. In Shinto, the largely non-verbal language of rite and festival best bespeaks its experience. The heart of this heart of Shinto is the *Daijō-sai*.

The Ministry of Official Shinto
and the Eight Gods

THE *Jingi-kan,* or Ministry of Official Shinto, was the office established by the Taihō Code to take charge of Court Shinto affairs.
These duties included responsibility for the seasonal rites presented in the Code (or rather its dependent documents), the Grand
Shrine of Ise, and general supervision of the shrines throughout
the land. Unlike the other bureaus of the new constitution, the
Jingi-kan had no real precedent in the Chinese codes, and was
given a position vaguely superior to all other bureaus, directly
under the throne.

Thus the *Jingi-kan* held a place at once new and a concession
to conservatism. The bureaucratic externality and some of the
rituals were ostensibly new. But the very fact that a role of this
scope was given to Shinto indicates the success of the Temmu
reaction; it was not intended that the native tradition be wholly
submerged to the foreign. Moreover, when we note that the Ministry of Official Shinto was dominated by the Nakatomi and Imbe
clans, immemorially a priesthood close to the Throne, we can
easily imagine that continuity was as well enforced as novelty.

Thus when the Ministry of Official Shinto, although continuing
ancient precedents, was officially inaugurated by the Taihō Code,
the revision seems to have corresponded to a partial change in the
official understanding of the intent of Shinto worship in the Palace.
As the very names of the priestly families Imbe and Nakatomi
represent, previous archaic Court religious activities had been
largely in abstinence and offering in the service of sovereign and
state. Certainly the employment of such devices did not suddenly
disappear, but the main concept of the role of official rites was
modified. Although previous rites also probably were seasonal and
agricultural, as well as related to sovereignty, at about this time
they were connected with Confucian and Taoist ideology concerning the adjustment by rite of the proper seasonal balances of the
five elements and *yin* and *yang*. The notion of the official recognition and worship of the deities of Heaven and Earth by the

sovereign as vicar of Heaven on Earth became prominent, again following the Chinese model, and the Ministry of Official Shinto was the agency through which this worship was offered. All of this, of course, required that worship in the Court assume an atmosphere of gravity and decorum, and hence the emphasis on liturgical elements.

An excellent example may be seen in the evolution of the *norito*, or prayer. In the opinion of such scholars as Origuchi Shinobu and Kaneko Takeo, the prayer, while holding much the same place in the structure of worship, was originally a message *from* the deity rather than prayer *to* the deity, and was delivered by a priestess (*miko* or *mikannagi*) or priest (*kannushi*) who went into trance.[1] (However, as we have seen, one may question whether this was always the case in regular worship in the archaic period.) But, as Yamada Yoshio has demonstrated in some detail,[2] *norito* are words said to the gods ostensibly by the emperor, though delivered in his name by the Ministry of Official Shinto, and hence have a structure very similar to the imperial edicts (*semmyō*), the often moralistic words from the throne which, in the tradition of the Shōtoku Constitution, flourished into the Nara period. It was in the Nara period that the form reached its greatest distinctiveness and prominence. Imperial edicts were delivered with considerable ceremony, and are recorded in the *Shoku-nihongi*.[3]

Under the concept of government as rite (*matsurigoto*), which has been a continual ideal in Japan, civil rule and worship are seen as one thing. When the emperor addresses the gods of the realm, he sends a rescript, as to a provincial official, by means of an emissary from the proper bureau. In much the same way, the edicts of the *Shoku-nihongi* were delivered in his name, and the listeners made submissive response. The assignment of Court Rank to the shrines and deities by the Throne suggests the same atmosphere. However, we must also allow Yamada to remind us that this apparent condescension toward the *kami* by the Throne was actually a way of honoring them, and did not imply that the deities were regarded as no more than servile minions.[4] An examination of the edicts and *norito* will show that the content, if not the form,

[1] *Origuchi Shinobu zenshū*, I, p. 105. Kaneko, *Engi-shiki norito-kō*, p. 495.
[2] Yamada, *Norito semmyō*, pp. 1–6.
[3] *Shoku-nihongi*, in *Kokushi taikei*, II. The imperial edicts alone are found in *Shinten*, pp. 913–70. For partial translations see Sansom, 'The Imperial Edicts of the Shoku Nihongi (700–790)'; and J. B. Snellen, 'Shoku Nihongi: Chronicles of Japan, Continued, A.D. 697–791 (Books I–VI)'.
[4] Yamada, op. cit. p. 6.

is quite different. The *kami* are addressed with great deference regarding their antecedents and present glory, the offerings are spread with thought to their honor and pleasure by the 'sovereign grandchild', and above all the *norito* rarely, if ever, command or request boons from the *kami* beyond general blessing and protection. The strong dominant note is one of exalted adoration—'to fulfil the praises'; even in the *Toshigoi*, or spring offering prayer, the desire for a fair harvest is stated with a certain indirectness.

To continue, it is proper then to speak of the function of the Ministry of Official Shinto as one of representing the sovereign emperor in his presentation of offering and praise to his divine ancestors and 'the gods of Heaven and Earth' for the sake of preserving the harmonious functioning of Heaven and Earth and the averting of disaster. The phrase 'gods of Heaven and Earth' is Chinese, though, as has been suggested, the idea has some Japanese background too. The function of representing the emperor in worship implied, then, the delivery of messages and offerings much more than the receiving of them.

The officials of the Bureau of Official Shinto included a chief minister (*kami*), inevitably a Nakatomi, who was responsible for the proper performance of Shinto ceremonies and for keeping a register of all Shinto priests and shrine serfs (*kambe*). He thus had charge of all the traditional religious ceremonies connected with the accession, the Harvest Festival, the placating of spirits, oracles, divination, and so on.[5] The chief minister took the place of the sovereign when the latter was prevented by illness from taking his place in the ceremonies.[6] The important posts in the Ministry of Official Shinto were hereditary in the Nakatomi and Imbe families, and from the eleventh century on the chief minister was a Shirakawa, a branch of the Nakatomi of princely rank with the title Ō (prince). One sometimes reads of the 'Four Families' of the Ministry of Official Shinto, referring to its four important surnames: Nakatomi, Imbe, Urabe, and Ō (Shirakawa). The first three controlled the Ministry of Official Shinto during the *Engi-shiki* period, and together with the shrine serfs are frequently mentioned in our text. The house of the Urabe (which does not appear until the Taihō documents) later took the name Yoshida when they gained effective supremacy in Shinto affairs after the fourteenth century. The chief officiator (*saishu*) at Ise was a Fujinami, a branch of the Nakatomi.

---

[5] Sansom, 'Early Japanese Law and Administration', p. 67.
[6] Aston, *Shinto: The Way of the Gods*, p. 20.

Below the chief minister was the vice-minister, or *taifu*; the junior vice-minister, or *shōfu*; the secretary, or *taijō*; the assistant secretary, or *shōjō*; the recorder, or *taishi*; the assistant recorder, or *shōshi*. There were thirty shrine serfs (*kambe*), of a more fortunate hereditary class than the serfs on shrine fields, attached to the office. There were twenty Urabe, thirty servants, and two watchmen. Because these persons often have diverse roles in the liturgies, it is important to distinguish them.[7] We must also remember the four *ranks* of Ministry of Official Shinto personnel, termed *kami*, *suke*, *jō*, and *sakan*.

The Ministry of Official Shinto performed its palace rites in an enclosure 370 feet (*shaku*) north and south and 350 feet east and west, called the Sacred or Western Hall (Sai-in or Sei-in). It was located in the southeast corner of the Imperial Palace enclosure (*dai-dairi*). The Western Hall had gates on the north, east, and south walls. Against the west wall were the shrines of the Eight Gods (*hasshin*), the eight *kami* protecting the Palace. They were worshipped by the Ministry of Official Shinto, and their honor was especially the responsibility of the priestesses (*mikannagi*) who were in some way attached to the Ministry of Official Shinto. Like all the Court priestesses, they were daughters of the Nakatomi. The Western Hall was paved with white gravel and open to the sky. But within it were four shelters called 'offices' (*chō*), one on each of the four sides. In the center, and also in the southeast corner, were shelters for offerings. A treasury for valuable imperial offerings permanently kept before the *kami* was in the northeast.

It will be noted that the Western Hall, although the scene of some of the most solemn rites of the nation, was not a shrine at all architecturally. It did not center around a particular sacred center. Rather, it was simply an open-air enclosure, like the most ancient places of Shinto worship. The Grand Shrines of Ise also preserve the idea of such an enclosure, unlike most shrines, but also have central buildings (*shōden*). The small shrines of the Eight Gods, in a row against the wall, are more like the auxiliary altars of more conventional shrines.[8]

However, these Eight Gods are the most interesting aspect of the Western Hall. These *kami* are not all named in the *Kojiki* and

[7] The section of the *Ryō no gige* listing the Ministry of Official Shinto personnel and outlining their functions is found in *Shinten*, pp. 975–9.

[8] At the Munakata Shrine in northern Kyushu near Fukuoka such a *shiki*, a rectangular space of white gravel with a small altar in the center, is still preserved on high ground near the sea and is used for ceremonies several times a year. The Munakata shrine is a treasury of survivals of very ancient Shinto and would repay a careful study.

Nihon-shoki, but a list is found in at least three ancient sources. In the *Kogoshūi* we read: 'Then [after Jimmu had subdued the eastern lands], in strict obedience to the ordinance of the two ancestral Heavenly Gods [Takami-musubi and Amaterasu], a holy site with sacred trees and stones was erected in the Imperial Court and in consequence the following divinities were worshipped there.' The list follows.[9] In the *Engi-shiki*, these deities in the Western Hall are listed at the head of the shrine register, as being enshrined in the chief shrine within the Palace. Later the list is given in the *norito* for the *Toshigoi* (also in the *Tsukinami norito*, which is identical with the former for the most part) under the words, 'Before the mighty *kami* to whom the great Sacred Maidens offer words of praise, we humbly speak.' The Eight Gods are also listed in the *Chinkon-sai* (Soul Pacification rite) ritual in the *Engi-shiki*. They had three places of worship within the Palace: in the Western Hall, in the Middle Palace (of the empress), and in the Eastern Palace (of the crown prince).

The list is as follows:

1 Kami-musubi-no-kami ('Divine Creator God'). One of the three creator gods of the official myth.

2 Takami-musubi-no-kami ('High Creator God'). A creator and high god with a much more flourishing mythology than any of these other '*musubi*' deities, hence doubtless the original. One feels that he is as well the original sovereign god of the Yamato tradition.

3 Tamatsume-musubi-no-kami ('Spirit Woman Creator God'). Also called Tamaru-musubi-no-kami. Not found in the official mythology. Said by Katō in his notes on the *Kogoshūi* to be a 'divine spirit who takes charge of a person's soul and prevents it from going astray, leaving its body behind'. Hence, he says, the *Mitama-shizume no matsuri*, or *Chinkon-sai* rite.[10] However, I personally know of no evidence that this *kami* had any special relation to the *Chinkon-sai*, or 'Soul Pacification rite' of the Palace.

4 Iku-musubi-no-kami ('Life Creator God'). Not in the *Kojiki* or *Nihon-shoki*.

5 Taru-musubi-no-kami ('Increase Creator God). Not in the *Kojiki* or *Nihon-shoki*.

6 Ōmiya-no-me-kami ('Great Palace Lady Goddess'). This female deity is also not found in the *Kojiki* or *Nihon-shoki*, although according to the *Kogoshūi* she was appointed to serve before Amaterasu, and Satow states that she is a personification of successive female attendants in the Palace.[11] She has something of a cultus of her own, having shrines throughout the Palace and the Saigū, spe-

[9] Katō and Hoshino, p. 34.
[10] ibid. p. 68.
[11] Satow, 'Ancient Japanese Rituals, No. 1', p. 126.

cial mention in the *norito* (especially the *Ōtono-hogai* prayer, where she is represented as the divine co-ordinator of all the work of the Palace), and a festival day with Kotoshironushi on the second of the eleventh month. She seems to have a special relation to the Imbe.

7   Miketsu-no-kami ('Food Goddess'). Found in the *Kojiki* in the Chūai reign section, as a shrine deity in the *Izumo fudoki*, and as the deity of several shrines in the *Engi-shiki*. However, Miketsu, or Ōmiketsu, is also generally believed to be identical with Toyouke, the food-deity of the Outer Shrine at Ise.

8   Kotoshironushi-no-kami ('Thing-implement-master God'). The son of Ōkuninushi, who advised his father to surrender his claim to the land of the Imperial Grandson. He would thus be a representative of the 'vanquished' Izumo tradition within the Palace. But Koto-shironushi also delivered the oracle to Jingū which encouraged her to go to Korea, and another on the return trip advising her to 'worship me in the land of Nakata'.[12] This suggests he may have a non-Izumo tradition as well.

Thus the first five of the Eight Gods seem to be transcendent creator gods, the last three earthly deities with a fairly strong mythological and cultic tradition. One imagines that all of the first group, except Takami-musubi, are contrived '*musubi*'[13] deities deriving from about the same time and the same schools of thought which compiled the official *Kojiki/Nihon-shoki* mythology.

Later writers such as Motoori, thinking it strange that Amaterasu herself, the imperial ancestress, was not worshipped in the Palace sanctuary, speculated that these titles were all epithets of the solar goddess.[14] Others developed elaborate schemes of descent integrating them all into the official mythology. For us it is interesting that 1) apparently the 'new' gods coincided with the century of building 'new' palaces of a more permanent sort, first at Nara, then at Kyoto; and 2) that the kind of studied conservatism and Shinto renewal represented by the Temmu period apparently produced an exfoliation of cosmological speculation reflected in a peculiarly abstract kind of myth and cosmic cultus for which the single virile high god of the past was not sufficient. A similar stage may be detected in other cultures—one thinks of the Theban theo-

---

[12] Aston, *Nihongi*, I, p. 237.

[13] The word *musubi* is commonly used in the names of 'high gods' in the Yamato tradition. I have pointed out in a previous chapter that the word has philological connections with words meaning 'to tie' and 'to give birth'. It can no doubt be fairly translated 'Creator'. Shibata Minoru has recently stated that the term indicates ancestral rather than agricultural potency—that in fact the 'musubi' deities may derive from pre-agricultural concepts, insofar as such a statement can be made at this point (*Chūsei shomin shinkō no kenkyū*, p. 39).

[14] Satow, p. 125.

logy of Egypt. The absence of Amaterasu is not hard to understand in terms of the thinking of the day: *kami* were still regarded as generally firmly rooted in one place of worship, however great; Amaterasu had been moved out of the Palace in the days of Sujin and was now established at Ise, therefore she could not be worshipped, except by 'distant worship', in the Palace. If this were not the case, it would not be necessary to send the Saigū princess and imperial offerings to the Grand Shrine. Mythological universality did not affect this cultic reality. The mythological integration was really an integration of the gods of many shrines or clans. Minor inconsistencies, such as the presence of Palace *kami* in the Saigū at Ise, must not obscure the general pattern.

It is interesting to compare this list of eight gods with the list of eight gods set up at the sacred fields in the *Daijō-sai* rite. These *kami* are clearly less 'abstract' than those of the Palace. The temptation to believe this is an older set, on the grounds of their more 'earthy' character and the general conservative nature of the *Daijō-sai*, is very strong. Perhaps this is the oldest set of imperial deities we have.

One is immediately reminded of the Eight Gods of the Ministry of Official Shinto chapel in the Palace which we have just discussed. Here also eight *kami* are lined up at a place of worship which has close connection with imperial sovereignty, and one cannot doubt but that this number has some significance, perhaps related to the metaphorical use of eight in the *Kojiki* and *Nihon-shoki*. But the two lists are not at all identical. The Ministry of Official Shinto list replaces four of the agricultural deities in the *Daijō-sai* list with *musubi* ('creator') *kami*. All of these *musubi kami* presumably share the transcendental sky father qualities of Takami-musubi and Kami-musubi in the mythology. It can be said that the Ministry of Official Shinto list is balanced in favor of this element, with the *Daijō-sai* list, which contains only Takami-musubi with the rest apparently earth *kami*, being opposite. But while the other *musubi kami* look rather contrived, the additional seven *Daijō-sai kami*, while almost as obscure, seem to have some cultic basis.

The list begins however with an agricultural *kami* who is not obscure, at least within the world of the *Engi-shiki*. He is Mitoshi, the male harvest deity who finds some prominence in the *Toshigoi* service and a myth in the *Kogoshūi*. His worship must have roots at the Mitoshi shrine in Katsuragi, where the mountains meet the Yamato plain. He is an offspring of Ōkuninushi in the *Kojiki*.

The second is Takami-musubi, the 'High Creator' or 'High Unifier' of the mythology. He is clearly the original 'high god' of the Yamato-imperial tradition, who only after some altercation was generally replaced in the sovereignty function by Amaterasu, but who never quite lost pre-eminence in the prayers and altars of the Palace itself. He is not a heavenly *kami* who descends to earth, although he may send down descending *kami*, but corresponds in heaven to the sovereignty of the emperor on earth, and protects his terrestrial Court. In our documents his name is spelled with the character usually read *tama*, 'spirit', but here read *musubi*. As we have noted elsewhere, this word is obviously cognate to *musubu*, 'to tie', and to *umu*, 'to give birth'.

The third *Daijō-sai kami*, Niwatakatsuhi, appears only here in the *Engi-shiki* and in one place in the *Kojiki*, where he is named as a *kami* engendered by Ōtoshi. The name, perhaps 'Fire (or Sun) of Garden Heights', suggests highness, however, and perhaps the deity is a mountain-descending agricultural *kami* like others of Ōkuninushi's progeny. Kotoshironushi is also a son of the latter and prominent among the 'Izumo group'. Mitoshi is also a son of Ōkuninushi, but not so clearly connected with Izumo.

We have discussed the next three above, in connection with the Ministry of Official Shinto group. Ōmiketsu is a food deity parallel to Toyouke (in the Jōgan Ritual, the name is written with the character *kura*, 'granary', as if it were Mikura-no-kami); Ōmiya-no-me is the female palace spirit, perhaps a counterpart to Takami-musubi, terrestrial as he is celestial but on the model of the queen-priestess rather than agricultural; Kotoshironushi, son of Ōkuni-nushi and connected with the capitulation of that line to the Imperial Grandson. The last two, Asuwa-no-kami and Hahiki-no-kami, present a special problem. In the official mythology, they are children of Ōtoshi born of the same wife as Niwatakatsuhi, and thus grandchildren of Susano-o. In the *Engi-shiki norito*, they appear as deities of the land where the Palace stood, along with others equally obscure. It has been suggested that they were at one time *kami* of the ground on which rice-storehouses were built, hence invoked for its protection. By extension they were similarly related to the Palace, and naturally to the cultus of the sacred fields with its storehouses.

It is difficult to ascertain any principle by which these eight names were selected, unless it be just to represent the spectrum of types of *kami* reverenced in Yamato in perhaps the Temmu period. All the types are there: the male sky father; two kinds of female earth *kami*, agricultural and sovereignty-shamanistic; two kinds of male progeny of sky and earth, the hero and the localized place-guardian. What is conspicuously missing, of course, is the unique type represented by Amaterasu, and *kami* of the Ise and maritime groups generally. This list must be older than the national prominence of names made familiar by the *Kojiki* mythology, for though it is rather an odd list, it yet seems to be somehow intended as representative of the nation as well as of just the Palace cultus.

It includes a sovereignty *kami*, Takami-musubi, as well as those who could be considered mere local land deities. If Mitoshi is especially a *kami* of Katsuragi, and Kotoshironushi of Miho in Izumo, a wide geographical distribution is indicated. Despite this, it has also been suggested that these *kami* represent serving *kami* of the emperor, guardians and preparers of food, and hence the exclusion of clan and imperial ancestral *kami* from the list. In any case, they are not *ujigami* of retainer families, but a band which has a special relation to sovereignty, the Court, food-production, and place independent of clan connection. From this distance in time, we can say little more to unravel their mystery.

BIBLIOGRAPHY

JAPANESE-LANGUAGE SOURCES

(Published in Tokyo, unless otherwise stated.)

Fujiki Kunihiko 藤木邦彦. *Heian jidai no kizoku no seikatsu* 平安時代の 貴族の生活 (The life of the Heian nobility). Shibundō 至文堂, 1960.

Honda Yasuji 本田安次. *Kagura* 神楽 (Sacred dance). Mokujisha 木耳社, 1966.

Hori Ichirō 堀 一郎. *Wagakuni minkan shinkō-shi no kenkyū* 我が国民 間信仰史の研究 (Studies in the history of Japanese folk beliefs). 2 vols. Sōgensha 創元社, 1953 and 1955.

Inō Hidenori 伊能頴則, *Daijō-saigi tsūran* 大嘗祭儀通覧 (Survey of the *Daijō-sai* rituals). Joransha 如蘭社, 1913.

Jingū Shichō 神宮司庁. *Shintō gobusho* 神道五部書. Ise, Jingū Shichō, 1958.

————, ed. *Kojiruien, Jingi-bu* 古事類苑神祇部 (Encyclopedia of an-cient matters, Official Shinto part). Kyoto, Kojiruien Kankōkai, 1927–8.

Kada no Azumamaro zenshū 荷田春満全集 (Collected works of Kada no Azumamaro). 10 vols. Rikugō Shoin 六合書院, 1944.

Kaneko Takeo 金子武雄. *Engi-shiki norito-kō* 延喜式祝詞講 (Lectures on the *Engi-shiki* prayers). Musashino Shoin 武蔵野書院, 1951.

Kishimoto Yoshio 岸本芹雄. *Shintō no rekishi* 神道の歴史 (History of Shinto). Sagami Shobō 相模書房, 1956.

Kobayashi Yukio 小林行雄. *Sōshoku kofun* 装飾古墳 (The decorated tombs of ancient Japan). Heibonsha 平凡社, 1964.

Kōbunko 廣文庫 (Treasury of ancient literature). Kōbunko Kankōkai, 1917.

Kojitsu sōsho 故實叢書 (Library of antiquities). Vols. I–XXVIII, Yoshi-kawa Kōbunkan 吉川弘文館 1899–1906. Second series, vols. I–XLI, Yoshikawa Kōbunkan, 1928–33. Third series, vols. I–XXXVII, Meiji Tosho Shuppan Kabushiki Kaisha 明治図書出版株式会社, 1951–7.

Kokushi taikei 國史大系 (National history materials). First series, 58 vols., 1929–43. Second series (largely reprints with different divisions of volumes in same editions), 1951–66. Yoshikawa Kōbunkan.

Kurabayashi Masatsugu 倉林正次. *Kyōen no kenkyū, girei-hen* 饗宴の研 究・儀礼編 (Study of Court banquets, ritual volume). Taihei In-satsusha 太平印刷社, 1965.

Miura Hiroyuki 三浦周行. *Sokui-rei to Daijō-sai* 即位禮と大嘗祭 (The accession ceremony and the *Daijō-sai*). Kyoto, Kyōto-fu Kyōikukai 京都府教育會, 1914.

Miyagi Eishō 宮城栄昌. *Engi-shiki no kenkyū* 延喜式の研究 (Study of the *Engi-shiki*). 2 vols. Taishūkan Shoten 大修館書店, 1955.

Nakamura Toshikatsu 中村敏勝. 'Yamato seiken no saishi kōzō' 倭政権の祭祀構造 (The ritual foundation of Yamato political authority), *Kokugakuin zasshi*, LXIV, no. 4 (April 1963).

Naoki Kōjirō 直木孝次郎. *Nihon kodai kokka no kōzō* 日本古代国家の構造 (Structure of the ancient Japanese state). Aoki Shoten 青木書店, 1958.

Nishida Nagao 西田長男. *Shintō-shi no kenkyū* 神道史の研究 (Study of Shinto history). Yūzankaku 雄山閣, 1933.

Nishitsunoi Masayoshi 西角井正慶. *Kodai saishi to bungaku* 古代祭祀と文学 (Ancient ritual and literature). Chūō Kōronsha 中央公論社, 1966.

_____ and Kurabayashi Masatsugu 倉林正次. 'Yamato-mai kō' 倭舞考 (Thoughts on the Yamato dance), *Kokugakuin zasshi*, LXIV, nos. 2–3 (February-March 1963).

Ōbayashi Taryō 大林太良. *Nihon shinwa no kigen* 日本神話の起源 (Origins of Japanese myth). Kadokawa Shoten 角川書店, 1965.

Ōkura Seishin Bunka Kenkyūjo 大倉精神文化研究所. *Shinten* 神典 (Sacred writings). Yokohama, 1936.

Ōnishi Gen'ichi 大西源一. *Daijingū shiyō* 大神宮史要 (Historical materials on the Grand Shrine). Heibonsha, 1960.

_____. *Sangū no konjaku* 参宮の今昔 (Pilgrimage to the Grand Shrine, past and present). Ise, Jingū Shichō, 1956.

Ono Sokyō 小野祖教. '*Nihon shinwa to Niiname no matsuri*' 日本神話と新嘗の祭 (Japanese myth and the Harvest Festival), *Shintōgaku*, no. 8 (August 1956).

Origuchi Shinobu zenshū 折口信夫全集 (Collected works of Origuchi Shinobu). Chūō Kōronsha, 1954–9.

Sasatani Ryōzō 笹谷良蔵. *Kamigami no sekai* 神々の世界 (The world of the gods). Azuma Shuppan 東出版, 1966.

Shibata Minoru 柴田実. *Chūsei shomin shinkō no kenkyū* 中世庶民信仰の研究 (Study of the faith of medieval common people). Kadokawa Shoten, 1966.

Takamure Itsue 高群逸枝. *Bokeisei no kenkyū* 母系制の研究 (Study of matrilinealism). Risōsha 理想社, 1966.

Tanaka Hatsuo 田中初夫. *Senso Daijō-sai no kenkyū* 践祚大嘗祭の研究 (Study of the accession *Daijō-sai*). vol. I. Privately pub., 1959.

Tsuda Sōkichi zenshū 津田左右吉全集 (Collected works of Tsuda Sōkichi). 28 vols., and 5 supplementary vols. Iwanami Shoten 岩波書店, 1963–6.

Tsugita Uruu 次田潤. *Norito shinkō* 祝詞新講 (New lectures on the *norito*). Meiji Shoin 明治書院, 1927, 1942.

Uemura Seiji 植村清二. *Jimmu Tennō* 神武天皇 (The Emperor Jimmu). Shibundō, 1957.

Umeda Yoshihiko 梅田義彦. *Jingi seido-shi no kiso-teki kenkyū* 神祇制度史の基礎的研究 (Basic study of the history of the Official Shinto system). Yoshikawa Kōbunkan, 1964.

Yamada Yoshio 山田孝雄. *Gosokui Daijō-sai tairei tsūgi* 御即位大嘗祭大禮通義 (Ritual commentary on the accession ceremony and *Daijō-sai*). Hōbunkan 寶文館, 1928.

_____. *Norito semmyō* 祝詞宣命 (The ritual prayers and imperial edicts). Mombushō 文部省. 1940.

Yamamoto Nobuki 山本信哉. 'Toshigoi to Daijō-sai to no kankei' 祈年と大祭との關係 (The relation between the *Daijō-sai* and the *Toshigoi*), *Kokugakuin zasshi*, XX, no. 10 (October 1915).

WESTERN-LANGUAGE SOURCES

Aston, W. G. *Nihongi*. 2 vols. in 1, London, George Allen and Unwin, 1956.

——. *Shinto: The Way of the Gods*. London, Longmans, Green, and Co., 1905.

Bock, Felicia G. *Engi-shiki*: *Procedures of the Engi Era*, Books VI–X. Tokyo, Sophia University, 1972.

Bownas, Geoffrey. *Japanese Rainmaking and Other Folk Practices*. London, George Allen and Unwin, 1963.

Brandon, S. G. F. *History, Time and Deity*. New York, Barnes and Noble, 1965.

Chavannes, Edouard. *Le T'ai Chan*. Paris, Leroux, 1910.

De Bary, William T., ed. *Sources of Chinese Tradition*. (Text edition: New York, 1966, Columbia University Press).

Dorson, Richard M. *Studies in Japanese Folklore*. Bloomington, Indiana, University of Indiana Press, 1963.

Eliade, Mircea. *Patterns in Comparative Religion*. New York, Sheed and Ward, 1958.

——. *Shamanism*: *Archaic Techniques of Ecstasy*. New York, Pantheon, 1964.

Engnell, Ivan. *Studies in Divine Kingship in the Ancient Near East*. Uppsala, Almqvist and Wiksells, 1943.

Frankfort, Henri. *Kingship and the Gods*. Chicago, University of Chicago Press, 1948.

Frazer, Sir James. *Lectures on the Early History of Kingship*. London, Macmillan and Co., 1905.

Gonda, J. *Ancient Indian Kingship from the Religious Point of View*. Reprinted from *Numen*, III and IV, with Addenda and Index. Leiden, E. J. Brill, 1966.

Harding, M. Esther. *Woman's Mysteries*. New York, Pantheon, 1955.

Harva, Uno. *Les représentations religieuses des peuples altaïques*. Paris, Gallimard, 1959.

Hocart, A. M. *Kingship*. London, Oxford University Press, 1927.

Hodous, Lewis. *Folkways in China*. London, A. Probsthain, 1929.

Holtom, Daniel C. *The Japanese Enthronement Ceremonies*. Tokyo, Kyo Bun Kwan, 1928. Second edition, Sophia University, 1972.

Hooke, S. H., ed. *The Labyrinth*. London, Macmillan Co., 1935.

——, ed. *Myth and Ritual*. London, Oxford University Press, 1933.

——, ed. *Myth, Ritual, and Kingship*. Oxford, Clarendon Press, 1958.

Hori, Ichiro. 'Hitotsu-mono: A Human Symbol of the Shinto Kami', in J. M. Kitagawa and Charles H. Long, eds., *Myths and Symbols: Studies in Honor of Mircea Eliade*. Chicago, University of Chicago Press, 1969, pp. 291–308.

——. 'Rites of Purification and Orgy in Japanese Folk Religion', *Proceedings* of the XIth International Congress of the International Association for the History of Religions; Vol. II, *Guilt or Pollution and Rites of Purification*. Leiden, E. J. Brill, 1968, pp. 192–3 (abstract).

Jobes, Gertrude and James. *Outer Space*. New York and London, Scarecrow Press, 1964.

Katō, Genchi and Hoshino, Hikoshirō, trans. and annotators. *The Kogoshūi: Gleanings from Ancient Stories*. Tokyo, Meiji Japan Society, 1926.

Kindaichi, Kyōsuke. *Ainu Life and Legends*. Tokyo, Japanese Government, 1941.

Kitagawa, Joseph M. 'The Prehistoric Background of Japanese Religion', *History of Religions*, I, no. 1 (Winter 1963).

——. *Religion in Japanese History*. New York, Columbia University Press, 1966.

Kōno, Shōzō and Sakai, Atsuharu, 'The Hitachi Fudoki', *Cultural Nippon*, vol. 8, no. 2 (June 1940).

Langer, Suzanne. *Philosophy in a New Key*. New York, Mentor, 1953.

Lebra, William P. *Okinawan Religion*. Honolulu, University of Hawaii Press, 1966.

Legge, J. *The Chinese Classics*. 5 vols. Hong Kong, University of Hong Kong Press, 1960.

——. *The Li Ki*. 2 vols. New York, University Books, 1967.

Lévi-Strauss, Claude. *The Savage Mind*. Chicago, University of Chicago Press, 1966.

Middleton, J. and Tait, D., eds. *Tribes Without Rulers*. London, Routledge and Paul, 1958.

Nippon Gakujutsu Shinkōkai. *The Manyōshū*. Tokyo, Iwanami Shoten, 1940.

Philippi, Donald L. *Norito: A New Translation of the Ancient Japanese Ritual Prayers*. Tokyo, Kokugakuin University Press, 1959.

Pierson, D. L. *The Manyōshū*. 21 vols. Leiden, E. J. Brill, 1929–64.

Ponsonby-Fane, R.A.B. *The Imperial House of Japan*. Kyoto, Ponsonby Memorial Society, 1959.

——. *Studies in Shinto and Shrines*. Kyoto, Ponsonby Memorial Society, 1954.

Quain, B. *Fijian Village*. Chicago, University of Chicago Press, 1948.

Sacral Kingship/La Regalità Sacra. Leiden, E. J. Brill, 1959.

Sansom, Sir George B. 'Early Japanese Law and Administration', *Transactions of the Asiatic Society of Japan*, Second Series, IX (December 1932); XI (December 1934).

——. *A History of Japan to 1334*. Stanford, Stanford University Press, 1938.

——. 'The Imperial Edicts of the Shoku Nihongi (700–780)', *Transactions of the Asiatic Society of Japan,* Second Series, I (1924).

Satow, Sir Ernest. 'Ancient Japanese Rituals, No. 1,' *Transactions of the Asiatic Society of Japan, Reprints* (December 1927).

Schwartz, W. L. 'The Great Shrine of Idzumo', *Transactions of the Asiatic Society of Japan,* XLI, Part II (October 1913).

Smith, D. H. 'Divine Kingship in Ancient China', *Numen,* IV (1957).

Smith, Robert T. and Beardsley, Richard K. *Japanese Culture: Its Development and Characteristics.* Chicago, Aldine, 1962.

Snellen, J. B. 'Shoku Nihongi: Chronicles of Japan, Continued, A.D. 697–791 (Books I–VI)', *Transactions of the Asiatic Society of Japan,* Second Series, XI (1934); XIV (1937).

Soothill, William E. *The Hall of Light.* London, Lutterworth, 1951.

Tanaka, Kashihi. *A Comparison of the T'zu Ling and the Jingi-ryō.* Unpublished thesis. Claremont, 1966.

Wang Yû-ch'üan, 'An Outline of the Central Government of the Former Han Dynasty', *Harvard Journal of Asiatic Studies,* vol. 12, nos. 1–2 (June 1949).

Watson, Burton. *Records of the Grand Historian of China.* 2 vols. New York, Columbia University Press, 1961.

Williamson, Robert W. *Religion and Social Organization in Central Polynesia.* Cambridge, The University Press, 1937.

INDEX